FROM JEHOVAH TO JAZZ

"MY COUNTRY, 'TIS OF THEE"

FROM JEHOVAH TO JAZZ

MUSIC IN AMERICA FROM PSALMODY TO THE PRESENT DAY

By

HELEN L. KAUFMANN

Illustrations by
ALAJALOV

DODD, MEAD & COMPANY
NEW YORK   1937

PRINTED IN THE UNITED STATES OF AMERICA
BY THE VAIL-BALLOU PRESS, INC., BINGHAMTON, N. Y.

ACKNOWLEDGMENTS

Every book, it seems, must have an author, and every author the assistance of a large number of co-authors whose names never appear on the title page, although they have contributed largely.

To previous writers on the subject of American music whose researches have guided me in preparing this volume, my warmest thanks are due. To kindly composers who granted interviews and discussed with me their own and other works, I am both grateful and apologetic, the latter because lack of space prevented the inclusion of so many of their interesting comments. The staff of the Music Division of the New York Public Library have been co-operative in every way. Robert I. Center, to whom I first broached the idea of the book, has been on hand ever since to urge it to completion. In the final revision of the manuscript, Arthur Loesser, friend and critic, has made invaluable editorial suggestions.

To them all, and to the countless others whose encouragement has caused this book to be, I take this opportunity of expressing my sincere appreciation and deep gratitude, and the hope that they will find no cause to blush for the net result of their and my combined efforts on behalf of *From Jehovah to Jazz*.

HELEN L. KAUFMANN

September, 1937

FOREWORD

American music is today in its adolescence, a youth possessed of challenging possibilities and compounded of engaging attributes. It has proceeded from a pious infancy of song inspired by Jehovah to a lusty but uncertain adolescence conditioned to jazz and dissonance.

Before its birth, there came to this virgin country, then populated only by redskins, an invasion of men from across the sea, bringing civilization with them. A not inconsiderable part of that civilization was in their music. Children who grew up in the New World had their pick of tunes from half a dozen different countries, ranging from the Spaniards in Mexico, the French on the Canadian border and in New Orleans, the Dutch in New Amsterdam, the English Cavaliers in Virginia and their Puritan cousins in New England, to the Swedes in Delaware and the Germans in Pennsylvania.

Polyglot as these musical beginnings were, they had one common bond. The fear of God, hand in hand with His worship, pervaded them. The most, almost the only, important musical expression of early days took place in the churches. Secular music then was surreptitious—in New England so repressed as to be practically nonexistent. The period until 1720 was a primitive time, an early childhood during which the settlers were too busy fighting nature and the Indians, and praising God in their own way, to give ear to music as an art. The native Indian song and dance, which is geographically, if not technically, the only true American music, was

vii

held in small regard until recent ethnological researches called attention to it.

The years from 1720 until about 1800 were marked by noticeable growth. Musicians slung their instruments in the bundles they carried on their shoulders when they came to seek their fortune in the new country. Music publishing houses came into being, manufacturers of musical instruments set up shop. A thriving music trade was in the making. Psalmody remained a power in the land throughout these formative years. The first public concert, in 1731, roused the protests of God-fearing citizens against the repetition of such performances as "tending to discourage industry and frugality, and greatly increase impiety." Certainly William Billings, James Lyon, and Francis Hopkinson, the first recognized native composers, all of whom were born before 1800, devoted their talents largely to the church. New York, Philadelphia, Charleston, and New Orleans led the way toward opera and instrumental music, while New England's brow was still contracted in a frown upon these blandishments of the Devil. The expression of national consciousness in music received a fillip with the Revolutionary War, which inspired patriotic ditties, many borrowed, some few original.

In 1800, the uncertainty of the growing art of American music as between the native and imported product began to grow acute. There had been performances of *The Beggar's Opera* and some few others, all imported. But not until Garcia brought the *Barber of Seville* and other Italian works to New York in 1825 was the issue really raised. Then William Fry and George Bristow, American composers who had written grand operas of their own, made protest against the foreign invasion. It continued, but at least they had gone on record with an American declaration of operatic independence. American folk songs and sentimental ballads, culminating in Stephen Foster's work, led to the minstrel show, a characteristically American entertainment beloved from coast to coast, wherein spirituals, plantation and folk melodies of the negroes supplemented and inspired the buck and wing and songs of Mr. Interlocutor and his End-men. Cowboys in the West, mountaineers in Virginia, sailors, miners, stevedores, tramps and convicts all contributed their bit to the folk-song saga of America. The Civil War added patriotic songs and more sentiment.

Meanwhile, the Revolution of 1848 in Europe sent hundreds of European musicians, especially Germans, to carry the cultural tradition of a tired old world to a fresh young one. The ties of respect, almost subservience, to European tradition were strengthened, while the assertion of native talent became less assured. American composers went abroad to study; European teachers came here. Many of the former learned to speak in echo of the rolling sonorities of their European masters. International music festivals, free interchange of music publications and of printed music helped to break down what remained of national barriers.

Most of the so-called serious music of America—its opera and oratorio, symphony and sonata, instrumental music and art song—may be traced to European influence. On the other hand, folk song, negro ragtime and blues culminating in jazz are indigenous. Jazz is said in Europe to be the distinctive contribution of America to music, an assertion resented with some justice in serious musical circles here, for the syncopated melody with improvisational accompaniment, to which the term jazz is generally applied, has long been regarded askance as the cheap and vulgar outlet of the uncultured. The gulf between serious music and jazz has been, and still is in some quarters, as irreconcilable as that between Hitler and Einstein. Yet composers in the larger forms today do not hesitate to employ jazz, as they have both Negro and Indian melody, as one means of expressing a certain aspect of their country in music. Assuredly not America's final, most emphatic or lasting word, it may be set down as a manifestation of native musical personality which is individual and arresting.

There is one great advantage in writing about an adolescent. It is not necessary to approach the subject with uncovered head, muffled voice, or other abracadabra required in the presence of the great. It is permissible to laugh occasionally, especially when the lad is in danger of taking himself too seriously. There is so much that is thrilling and adventurous in the growth of American music, and so much that is amusing, too, that it has seemed best not to dwell unduly upon dry facts, or to overload with historical details when they dull the edge of the story. If a favorite composer's name is omitted, or a particular work not fully analyzed and discussed; if certain aspects of American music, related but not strictly pertinent, do not appear, the reader is urged to bear his disappointment as philosophically as possible until another volume can be written. This is a book to be read, not studied; a cheery bird's-eye view, not an historical treatise or critical essay (adolescents can't bear criticism); a book written, not by a musicologist, but by a music-lover who has delved into the subject for the pure joy of it.

To other music-lovers the world over, particularly to the gigantic parents' association interested in the psychology and development of the adolescent stripling, American music, this book is affectionately dedicated.

"Blessed are the music-makers, for they shall uplift
and unite the earth."

WILLIAM ARMS FISHER

CONTENTS

CHAPTER I

ONE LITTLE PSALM BOOK AND HOW IT GREW

IT was fortunate for our American music that there were Pilgrim mothers as well as Pilgrim fathers, for they it was who probably brought Jehovah to these shores. Surely, when the order went forth for an exodus from Holland, it was the mothers who thought of the necessity of packing their household goods, petticoats, kerchiefs, and whatnots. And among the whatnots—perhaps thrust hastily into the bosom, perhaps laid reverently in the travel chest among the folds of the Sunday best—were a few English psalm books.

From all accounts, the first act of the Pilgrims upon landing at Plymouth Rock in 1620 was to kneel and raise their voices in thanksgiving to the God who had guided them safely across the stormy seas to this rugged, yet welcome, haven of refuge. Did they rummage for Henry Ainsworth's *Psalter* on this oc-

1

casion, that they might praise the Lord with all due decorum from the printed page? Or did they relax so far as to jubilate spontaneously in their own words? History records merely that they bent the knee and sang a prayer, establishing a psalm-singing precedent which was maintained in Massachusetts for many years to come.

Some ten years later the Puritans, landing in Salem, enacted a similar scene, only with a different English psalm book to inspire them to prayer—*The Booke of Psalms;* "Collected into English Metre by Thomas Sternhold, John Hopkins and Others Conferred with the Hebrew; with apt notes to sing them withall. Set forth and allowed to be sung in all Churches of the People Together, before and after Morning and Evening Prayer. As also before and after Sermon, and moreover in Private Houses for their godly Solace and Comfort, laying apart all ungodly Songs and Ballads, which tend only to the Nourishment of Vice and Corrupting of Youth." From this title it may be seen that English preachers had liberally seasoned their sermons, not only with the pepper of probable damnation, but with the psalter of a somber faith in possible salvation. The soil of Massachusetts was freely besprinkled with the same seasoning. So potent was it that it almost killed the herbs and simples growing in that same soil, which were destined also to flavor the brew of American music. Although psalmody could not wholly shut the door to other song, it dominated the musical life of the country right up to the Revolution, and while it lost ground during those fighting days, later it bobbed up serenely. And, in the form of hymn, oratorio, chorale, and cantata, with evangelical and camp-meeting songs as a popular supplement, the praise of Jehovah continues to resound.

But let us raise the Puritans and Pilgrims from their uncomfortable kneeling position on the rocks and transport them to their churches. When we read about the New England Sundays, we are impressed with the staying powers of these early settlers. At nine o'clock, all were summoned to church by a blast on a conch shell or trumpet, or a roll of drums, or perhaps the simple display of a flag—bells came later. Sitting rigid through an interminable sermon in an unheated church, they must have derived a certain solace from the interpolations of song and the grateful exercise of removing hats during the singing. The deacon would rise from his seat, facing the congregation. Rapping with his knuckles on a brass candlestick, or a curtain rod, he would set the key according to the resulting tone. Then he would "strike up" the tune which, in his opinion, fitted the psalm for the day. It was the custom to take these from the book in rotation, without relation to the subject of the sermon. The deacon would sing one line at a time, which was repeated after him with great fervor by the congregation. He would then proceed to the next line, and so on until the end. Having been selected for his lung power, he made up in volume what he lacked in pitch. This practice was known as "deaconing" or "lining out," and what with the exhibition complexes of the deacons, and the ambitions of their fellow members to become deacons likewise, it proved one of the most difficult practices to change. It played some strange tricks, especially when the arbitrary breaking up of the psalm led to apparent contradiction. A sailor who strolled into a church in Connecticut one Sunday, thinking perhaps to purify his spirit by joining in the service, arrived just as they were "lining out" the day's psalm. The clerk gave out the line, "The Lord will come, and He will not," the congregation burst into song, and the sailor stared, wondering if he could believe his ears. But when he heard the next line, "Hold your peace, but speak aloud," he left the church, convinced that he had wandered by mistake into a company of lunatics.

Having sung unquestioningly from their English books for many years, the congregations must have experienced a certain relief when the *Bay Psalm Book,* the first book of any kind to be printed in the New World, was published in 1640. True, tunes, being relatively unimportant, were omitted, and only the words of the psalms were printed in a form supposedly suitable for singing. For example, the Twenty-third Psalm in their version was rendered:

"The Lord to mee a shepheard is,
want therefore shall not I,
He in the folds of tender grasse,
doth cause mee downe to lie.
To waters calm mee gently leads
Restore my soul doth hee:
he doth in paths of righteousness
for His name's sake lead mee.
Yea, though in valley of death's shade
I walk, none ill I'll feare:
Because thou art with mee, thy rod
and staff my comfort are.
Fore mee a table thou hast spread,
in presence of my foes:
thou dost anoint my head with oyle,
my cup it over-flowes.
Goodnes and mercy surely shall
all my dayes follow mee:
and in the Lord's house I shall dwelle
as long as dayes shall be."

When they sang, "Beside the waters of Babilon," it went like this:

> "The rivers on of Babilon
> There when wee did sit down,
> Yea, even then we mourned when
> We re'membered Sion."

As these words could be sung to any one of five tunes, the elders were not constrained to the reading of notes.

Time went on, the same five tunes were pressed into service twice a day for family worship, and three times on Sundays, and the monotony must have produced a certain indifference as to the necessity for any tune at all. *Old Hundred, York, Hackney, Windsor,* and *Martyrs,* the doughty five which bear a strong family resemblance to each other, cracked under the strain of so much repetition. They suffered most on those occasions when several congregations would meet together for a joint session of song and prayer, for even these few tunes, supposedly known to all, were not sung alike by any two congregations, or even two members of the same congregation. What with the beating of time with heads, hands, and feet, and the general disagreement as to pitch and volume, the Lord must sometimes have felt that the Tower of Babel had become an accomplished fact during those years from 1620 to 1750. This is according to the accounts of many commentators, although the *Bay Psalm Book,* in mentioning that its verses fall into six different meters, adds: "the first whereof may be sung in very neere forty tunes as they are collected out of our chief musicians by Thomas Ravenscroft."

The people were not barbarians. They had brought the love and knowledge of music with them, but there was no time nor incentive to use what they knew. Many who had been taught that a true Christian should make melody only in his heart opposed any form of church music. Others—even those who had sung or played an instrument back home—stuffed cotton in the ear which listened to music, until they were ready to remove it.

A tentative essay at giving them notes to sing from was an edition of the *Bay Psalm Book* issued in 1647. It offered crude staffs printed from wood blocks, a full line at a time, without measure divisions to guide the singers, who assuredly needed guidance! But the church elders opposed singing from the *Bay Psalm Book* on the ground that it was not divinely inspired; that even if it were, their parishioners could not afford it; that with the proper deacon they needed no book, and so on. Its use was not generally sanctioned until some years after its publication.

If there was opposition, first to singing at all, then to singing from a new book, there must have been considerable disturbance when an attempt was made to introduce instruments into the church service. The knuckles and the brass candlestick were supplanted fairly painlessly by the pitch pipe. But some time late in the seventeen hundreds, a sacrilegious foreigner who sang in the choir of a New England church smuggled his cello into the choir loft. Some describe it as a bass viol, which makes even deeper the mystery of his introducing it undetected. He played a very soft obligato to the singing, which improved it immensely. Yet, though the elders could not but admit that the sound was most agreeable, they felt it their Christian duty to "faithfully admonish" him for his breach of rules. He humbly countered with the statement that indeed it was not a fiddle, but an instrument he had caused specially to be made for the church, called a Godly Viol. Much relieved, they then permitted its use, although some murmured that they had been saddled with a fiddle "as big as a hog's trough," and that "Satan came also amongst them" along with the fiddle, and derisively dubbed the church a "catgut church." However, the flute, unobtrusive and inexpensive, slipped in shortly after the cello; the oboe, clarinet, and bassoon followed.

Instruments in church did not prove an unmixed blessing. They had a way of squeaking at unexpected moments during the sermon, and they were never properly in tune, thanks to the extremes of heat and cold in the poorly ventilated churches. When the introduction of an organ was suggested as a partial solution, however, it took a long time to make the elders see its possibilities. Brattle Square Church, in Boston, showed its progressive spirit by unanimously voting in 1699 that "ye psalms in public worship be sung without reading line by line." Nevertheless, when, in 1713, Thomas Brattle bequeathed an organ to the church of his name, it was piously refused. The Queen's Chapel, which accepted the gift, was obliged to leave it packed and standing disconsolately in the porch of the church for seven months, until the opposition to its installation died down. As late as 1790, when the Brattle Square Church finally ordered an organ from London, one of the pillars of the church passionately pleaded to be permitted to pay for it, and offered to make a handsome donation to charity besides, if only the devilish instrument could be dumped into Boston Harbor.

The battle of the instruments is but one round in the long conflict between standpatters and innovators. In 1700, the Reverend Walter Roxbury complained that psalm singing had become "a mere disorderly noise, left to the mercy of every unskilful throat to chop and alter." In 1792, we find some lines written, "rather out of temper," on one of the pews of Salem Church, as follows,

> "Could poor King David but for once
> To Salem Church repair,
> And hear his Psalms thus warbled out,
> Good Lord, how he would swear!"

Yet, between these two pronouncements, a number of tune books were published and a really earnest attempt at improvement was made. In 1712, the Reverend John Tufts issued *A Very Plain and Easy Introduction to the Whole Art of Singing Psalm Tunes,* wherein he offered thirty-seven tunes for three-part singing. None of them was original, and the book is charmingly naïve, the names of the notes instead of notes being written on the corresponding lines of the staff.

The book issued a few years later by the Reverend Thomas Walter and entitled *Grounds and Rules of Music Explained, or an Introduction to the Art of Singing by Note* contained a list of earnest instructions for "tuning the voice." It contained, too, the first music written with lines to mark off the measures, although the music itself was still British, the words versions of the Psalms of David.

The question raised by the *Bay Psalm Book* as to the religious permissibility of church singing from notes was not answered in the gentle pronouncements of the Reverends Tufts and Walter. One troubled writer in the *New England Chronicle* in 1723 thus unburdened himself: "Truly, I have a great jealousy that, if once we begin to sing by note, the next thing will be to pray by rule; and then comes Popery."

Some of the ministers, however, had borne as much as they

could of the "squeaking and grumbling" denounced in the *Bay Psalm Book*. One of them, the Reverend Thomas Symmes, having heard all the arguments for and against, thrashed out the subject of singing by note, "the new way," in a *Dialogue on Singing*, the principal points of which show, by their very earnestness, how close the question lay to all hearts.

The Reverend Thomas wrote: "Now, it being my purpose to encourage Singing Meetings in the Town in the long winter evenings, I tho't it prudent to make another essay, introductory to my setting forth such a Laudable Practice, that if it be possible, I might ease the minds of all amongst us, that remain dissatisfy'd on this score." He goes on with the seven objections to the "new way": "(1) That it is a New Way, an unknown Tongue. (2) That it is not so melodious as the Usual Way. (3) That there are so many Tunes, we shall never have done Learning. (4) That the practice of it gives Disturbance; Roils and Exasperates Men's Spirits; grieves sundry good People and causes them to behave themselves indecently and disorderly. (5) That it is Quakerish and Popish, and introductive of Instrumental Musick. (6) That the Names given to the Notes are Baudy, yea Blasphemous. (7) That it is a Needless way, since their good Fathers that were strangers to it are got to Heaven without it." In addition, "(1) It is said to be a Contrivance to get Money. (2) They spend too much time about Learning, they tarry out a-nights disorderly, and Family Religion is neglected by the means. (3) They're a company of Young Upstarts that fall in with this Way and set it forward, and some of them are Lewd and Loose Persons." All these objections the Reverend himself answered with the utmost piety and good sense, concluding with an injunction not to be absent from Prayers, to sing at your work when you can do it decently, to learn to Sing as well as ever you can, "that we may at length meet together, and Bear our part in Singing the Song of all Creatures."

Still the controversy went on. Other song books swelled the libraries of those who elected to sing by note. A collection issued in England by Williams and T'ansur was reprinted and issued here. James Lyon's *Urania,* published in 1761, was held in high esteem because half a dozen of the forty tunes it contained were original with him. Besides, he interspersed his plain choral melodies with those of "a light fuguing character," which must have taken considerable courage at that time. Josiah Flagg's book followed in 1764, the first to be printed on American paper, if that is a distinction. And the stage was set for William Billings.

It was only with the advent of Billings and his *New England Psalm Singer,* a collection of psalms issued in 1770, that American music reared its head. Under Billings it did more than rear—it roared. He was a blustering, shouting, vital little man, with a withered arm and a lame leg. Neither physical disability, Puritan ancestry, New England upbringing, nor ministerial disapproval could quench his fire. Were he alive today, he would be writing hot jazz, if not bringing it into the very church. What he did was almost as blasphemous in his day. The "fuguing tunes" which he blithely introduced into the service disregarded all rules of harmony. And why not, since Billings did not know the rules? A tanner in his youth, he had amused himself chalking tunes on the walls while he waited for the mill to grind his bark. He had allowed himself three weeks' training in music, then immediately started to teach and compose. After he had given up tanning, he turned out tunes with the same lavishness with which he took his snuff, which, contrary to the custom of pinching it delicately between thumb and forefinger, he snuffed lustily from the palm of the hand.

With no crippling modesty, he described his own *New England Psalm Singer* as follows: "It has more than twenty times the power of the old slow tunes; each part straining for mastery and victory, the audience entertained and delighted; their minds surprisingly agitated and extremely fluctuated, sometimes declaring for one part, sometimes for another." In 1778 appeared *The Singing Master's Assistant*, or *Billings' Best*, then came *Music in Miniature, The Psalm Singer's Amusement, Suffolk Harmony*, and *Continental Harmony*. In the course of a life of fifty-three years (1746–1800), this untaught composer established the principle of perpetual motion in composition. Like Haydn, he might have replied to the question as to why his church music was so cheerful: "I cannot make it otherwise; I write according to the thoughts I feel. When I think on God, my heart is so full of joy that the notes dance and leap, as it were, from my pen; and since God has given me a cheerful heart, it will be pardoned me that I serve Him with a cheerful and devout spirit."

To Billings' healthy common sense is due much of the credit for finally abolishing deaconing. There was the same wearisome opposition to change in this institution as had been raised to reading by note. The "Old Hundreds" set themselves against the "Fuguing Singers" with the usual result, a wordy feud.

Billings and his song books weighed heavily on the side of the "Fuguing Singers." So, too, did the Stoughton Singing Society, which he founded, taught, and led, schooling them thoroughly in his own songs. Singing schools had been started in very simple form in 1717. By the time Billings came along, some of the advanced churches had choirs recruited from these schools. The members of the Stoughton Singing Society drew the singing members of the congregation around them to form a choir, do away with deaconing, and sing *Billings' Best*. Billings wrote, with a shrewd twinkle of the one eye which was not blind: "As all now have books, and all can read, 'tis insulting to have the lines read in this way [deaconing], for it is practically saying, 'We men of letters, You ignorant creatures.' "

The Connecticut Valley passed valiantly through the Dark Ages of Discord. The "Battle of the Books" between psalms and "hymns of human composure" was resolved in favor of the latter, thanks largely to Jonathan Edwards and his revival meetings. *The Northampton Collection of Sacred Harmony*, 1797, edited by Elias Mann, was a landmark. This collection reflects the best taste of its time, including pieces by Billings, Timothy Swan, Holyoke, and Oliver Holden, one of the most learned and lovable reformers of whom we have record. Moreover, it printed poetry on its title page. This was the distinguishing mark of a hymn book as opposed to a psalm book, Scriptures and nothing else being permissible as introduction to the latter. This collection quoted the rhymed instructions for finding *mi* in different keys, as offered by Billings' *Continental Harmony:*

> "By flats the mi is driven round
> Till forced on B to stand its ground.
> By sharps the mi's led through the keys
> Till brought home to its native place."

After the Revolution, there was a justifiable reaction in the churches against the floridity of *Billings' Best* and his imitators' worst. Still, he was not only a picturesque, but a creative figure who gave a valiant boost to the manner of singing, even when the matter he provided left much to be desired. After his death, the choruses of Handel, the anthems of Dr. Arne, Dr. Blow, and Henry Purcell, the writings of Mozart and Haydn came gradually to be heard. The comparison with the crudity of American music proved odious even to the most faithful followers of the Billings fugue, which promptly fell into disrepute. A speech made by Professor Hubbard of Dartmouth before the Middlesex Society in 1807 left the American composer not a leg to stand on. He said, in part: "Almost every pedant, after learning the eight notes, has commenced author. With a genius sterile as the desert of Arabia, he has attempted to rival the great masters of music. On the leaden wings of dulness he has attempted to soar into those regions of science never penetrated by real genius. From such distempered imaginations no regular productions can be expected. The unhappy writers, after torturing every note in the octave, have fallen into oblivion, and have generally outlived their insignificant works." Francis Brown, in a similar speech, pronounced American music of the time as "calculated rather to produce levity than to kindle devotion." Cowed, the American composer yielded to the European and slunk into a corner to write baby tunes for the church, with only the simplest and most fool-proof harmonizations. An American with European training rescued him from his plight.

His deliverer appeared in the person of Lowell Mason (1792–1872), one of three teachers who set the feet of church music firmly on the way they have since trod. With his contemporaries Nathaniel Gould and Thomas Hastings, Lowell Mason gave to choirs songs worth singing, and instruction in singing them. Coincident with his advent, psalmody in New

England took a decided turn for the better. He administered a series of transfusions, first of foreign blood, then of American red corpuscles.

When the Handel and Haydn Society of Boston was formed, in 1815, "for the improving of the style of performing sacred music and of introducing into more general use the works of Handel and Haydn and other eminent composers," Lowell Mason was a charter member. He became a partner with the Society in the publication of the *Boston Handel and Haydn Society Collection of Church Music,* harmonized for three or four voices, figured bass, organ, and piano. Beginning with this collection, published in 1822, which he selected, edited, and harmonized, he left a formidable array of compilations and original tunes. The influence he exerted upon his time may be deduced from this recommendation in Webb and Mason's glee book, *The Moralist:* "See that the songs of your families are pure in sentiment and truthful in musical taste, avoid 'negro melodies and comic songs,' for mostly their tendency is to corrupt, both musically and morally."

New England colonies were not alone in stressing the worship of Jehovah. The Quakers were to music in Pennsylvania what the Puritans were in New England, and went a step further in disapproving of any music whatsoever. At the yearly meeting in 1716, in Philadelphia, the members were earnestly admonished against "going to, or being in any way concerned with games, plays, lotteries, music and dancing." That they persisted in this attitude is evidenced by an entry in the *Journal of Thomas Wentworth Higginson* more than a hundred and fifty years later. He wrote: "The best recent occurrence in this scene! Mrs. Dame's house full of Quakers; a prayer meeting in the evening. Suddenly, strange, discordant, inexplicable sounds come up. What are they—animal, vegetable, or mineral? Investigation shows that it is the Quakers—for the first time in their lives—singing a *Hymn!* Till lately, you know, they have all utterly forsworn music, though a few radical Quakers in Worcester used to own musical boxes. Now, as Mary says, 'when their religion is two hundred and fifty years old, it suddenly occurs to them that it is a religious duty to squawk.'"

However, a nucleus of better church music in Pennsylvania was a German group, led by Johann Kelpius, who settled near Philadelphia in 1694; the members not only had fine voices, but musical instruments and a knowledge of music. They were not averse to being farmed out for musical chores, and cheerfully lent themselves to such events as the dedication of a new church or the breaking in of a new organ. That instrument they welcomed as warmly as the Bostonians rejected it. Certainly their leader, Kelpius, and his successor, Falckner, set a tempo several degrees faster than that of New England.

In the Ephrata Cloister, also in Pennsylvania, Conrad Beissel led a group of mystics in the singing of choral music in as many as seven parts, when there was no part singing elsewhere in the colonies. These celibate mystics wrote all their music by hand, with illuminated letters resembling those in the medieval manuscripts. Where they learned these things was a mystery. They were like the reincarnation of medieval churchmen of the Old World, seeking salvation in the seclusion of the new—a strange anomaly. Beissel gave them plenty of seclusion, and a complete system of harmony with it. In his *Apology for Sacred Song,* a dialogue in justification of singing, he asked: "Did the early Christians sing at table?" and replied earnestly: "Yes. In place of disgraceful laughter and unnecessary conversation at the table, they, with wife, children and guests, intoned hymns of praise and thanksgiving."

Disgraceful laughter was not a part of the church services of the Moravians who settled in Bethlehem, Pennsylvania, either. Yet religious belief, of which they had a fair share, was not permitted to handicap them in the business of singing well. Remembering the old folks at home, these settlers transplanted singing of high quality, and instruments, too, to their new dwelling place. One of their pastors is even said to have imposed a fine on a member of his flock for missing a beat in the day's hymn.

Thus, except for the Quakers, the people of Pennsylvania were permitted to worship with a certain amount of tunefulness and variety. It is not surprising that Philadelphia should have had the honor of sheltering Hopkinson and Lyon, two of the three composers always lovingly grouped together as the first American music writers. Billings of Boston, the vulgarian, did not limit himself to composing music for the church, although he made it his main preoccupation. James Lyon was the only one of the three who might be called a church-music specialist.

Hopkinson, born in Philadelphia in 1737, was that rarity, an effective amateur. With a distinguished talent for writing songs and ballads, he combined considerable ability as an organist. He performed on that instrument in his church, taught psalms to Sunday-school classes, and is said to have compiled a *Collection of Psalm Tunes with a Few Anthems, Some of Them Entirely New* for the use of the United Churches of Christ Church and St. Peter's Church in Philadelphia. His life was that of a man of wealth and culture; his interests were wide and varied, his religious sincerity unimpeachable. His name suggests the eggshell-china teacups, tinkling harpsichords, and beautiful spindly mahogany furniture of the homes of the most aristocratic scions of England in Philadelphia, far removed from the rugged log cabins of the New England settlers. But his talent was sufficiently robust to enable him to escape from the rarefied atmosphere of perpetual religious writing into the realm of secular song, and to become our first song writer. As such, he is a significant figure in the musical pageant, although his songs do not wake the echoes in our homes, nor shake the rafters of our night clubs. If his fame rested entirely upon his psalms, its proportions would be considerably less.

Hopkinson's contemporary, James Lyon, also an amateur, labored as a minister in a poverty-stricken settlement in northern Maine, where he apparently palliated the rigors of his labors by praising the Lord in song. Unfortunately, these works of his later days have been lost, and he is known for an early work, brought out shortly after his ordination at the College of Philadelphia. *Urania,* his collection of Psalm-Tunes, Anthems, and Hymns, went into three editions, and a fourth appeared in New England, where its weight was brought to bear heavily on the side of those who believed in singing by note. At least six of the tunes were original with Lyon, and his simple directions for singing them, while not calculated to turn out Carusos, were more complete and well grounded than those of Tufts and Walter. *God Save the King,* known as *Whitefield's Tune,* is found here, as well as about thirty-four other tunes by English writers. It took courage for Lyon to include his own offerings among the sacrosanct, but his courage was rewarded, his tunes accepted.

If Jehovah dominated, he did not monopolize all that there

was of music in America up to 1800. In New York, as well as New Orleans, Charleston, and other colonies of the South, there was a deplorable tendency to kick up frivolous heels on weekdays, however decorous the churchgoing spirit on Sunday. The sun of life and laughter was not to be clouded completely or indefinitely by the prohibitions of church elders, but it peeped out with greater daring outside the boundaries of New England. There was a discreet hint of derision in the cheers directed at the contestants in the great Church-world War, especially after another war, the American Revolution, set people to thinking for themselves and freed them from many English fetishes, including their devotion to the Church of England. The steady infiltration of laughter-loving French, Spanish, and Italians, and music-loving Germans, also helped to break the stranglehold of the church. But it was a gradual process, and certainly the impelling force in all the music of our first Americans—white, red, and black—was the worship of Jehovah.

CHAPTER II

INDIAN WAR AND OTHER WHOOPS

THE musical stage of the New World was set with a magnificent copper-colored backdrop when the first actors from across the sea trod its boards. Against that tawny curtain, illumined by the flickering light of Indian council fires or the flare of Indian war torches, the gray, spare figures of the psalmodists, and of the gayer Cavaliers, are silhouetted in the softening perspective of time. The whites never paid the despised "savages" the compliment of taking their music even as seriously as they took their own. Their indifference persisted for so many years that it is a wonder we have any record of primitive Indian songs and their singers. It is the integrity of the Indian race, and the faithfulness with which they themselves preserved its traditions by handing them down from father to son, that enables us to reconstruct that early music with any accuracy.

The whoops of Indian warriors have gone echoing down through history, drowning out the still small voices of Indian squaws singing lullabies and of storytellers, poets, and medicine men, equally expressive if not as noisy. Not until a German student decided to write his doctor's thesis on the subject of the music of the North American Indian did the United States Government tardily set its ethnological department to figuring out the musical habits of its earliest inhabitants. The thesis of Dr. Theodore Baker, the German who made the initial study, was published in 1880, and is still the point of departure for other researches on the subject.

One thing which the Indians had in common with the whites who came to overrun them was the worship of God. Wakonda, the Great Spirit, they revered continuously, in song and dance. Not for them the ceremonial blanket of weekly prayer to cover up the spiritual nudity of the weekday. Their Great Spirit they had always with them. According to their belief, He abode in everything, from a moccasin or a blade of grass to a magnificent sunset. In their legend of the Creation, the Great Spirit sang the world into life, an indication of their attitude toward both Song and the Great Spirit. Thus, the Indian sang his prayers, not to a remote supernatural being, but to a very near and dear one. When Natalie Curtis wrote: "The Red Man's song records the teachings of his wise men, the great deeds of his heroes, the counsel of his seers, the worship of his god," she might have added, "especially the worship of his god."

The Indians had their own method of voice production. Although their songs were based, for the most part, on the five-tone, or pentatonic scale, they made use of many in-between notes set extremely close together, not found even in our diatonic gamut. A quivering, quavering effect ensued, which the white man's voice simply cannot duplicate. Nor can it be recorded in written notes. In addition to the quaver, they had a way of bringing rhythmical pressure to bear when singing a long note, somewhat as a violinist presses his bow hard on the string in regular rhythm in order to produce a sustained tone. Apparently, they were acutely sensitive to infinitesimal differences in pitch, judging from results of a test given to a young modern Indian, who recognized an interval of an eighteenth of a tone, whereas most whites are rather proud if they know a quarter tone when they hear it. Most of the ancient songs began on a high note, and came down for as much as two or three octaves. Sometimes the descent was unbroken, sometimes there was a temporary rise in the middle, before the ultimate decline and fall. There is an impression that all Indian songs are sad plaints, in a minor key. They sound that way, but in this case, sounds are deceptive. They have as many major as minor intervals, and the impression of sadness probably comes from the lack of melodic variety. Rests are few and far between—perhaps the need for them was held to be an unmanly weakness. The melodies were usually short, the simple expression of a single idea, and were repeated again and again to the accompaniment of drum and rattle. The Indians knew no harmony, but sang in unison, usually with a strong-voiced leader to set the pace. When a few hundred of them sang in their peculiar quavering tones, it must have sounded more like a weird harmony than strict unison.

There were some sixty varieties of language and custom among as many widely scattered tribes in the days of early settlement, with practically no communication between them. The warlike Navajos lived side by side with the peaceful agricultural Hopis, but each tribe sang in its own dialect, and in the fashion approved by the leaders of the tribe and their fathers before them. Today, the sixty tribes have quintupled, but still—triumph of individualism!—each of the three hundred clings to the song and story of its forefathers. So it is only with the utmost caution that we venture any generalizations about "Indian" music, past or present. The Indians themselves were never considerate enough to meet for a powwow on its rules and characteristics.

Even the quality of the tone varied from tribe to tribe. Some sang with lips tightly pressed together, in shrill nasal tones. The Pueblo opened his mouth wide and sent out a full, clear cry from powerful lungs, a cry quite unlike the shrill coyote howl of the Plains warrior. Navajos and Apaches chanted sacred songs in a low nasal swing, proclaiming their game songs, however, in solid lusty fashion. The voice of the Pueblo women has been compared with an oboe, mellow, nasal, and penetrating; the Hopi women crooned in veiled, slurred outline, while the women of the Rio Grande and the Zuñi Pueblo uttered high, flutelike sounds. All these tribes can be heard today by visitors on their reservations, and though they have had to make many changes in their way of living, they cling so closely to tradition in respect to the use of the voice that a student can determine a singer's tribe after hearing his song.

The Indians furnished accompaniments with drum and rattle and notched sticks, producing rhythms so complicated that they baffled, and continue to baffle, the white listener. In their scheme, it was not necessary for accompaniment to stay with the song, so long as it stayed with itself. Thus the big drum would pound out at a pace much slower than the voice, catch up and keep it company for a while, then, growing impatient, increase its speed and leave the voice behind. In fact, the drum was as dear to the Indian as wife or child, and he had drums of all sizes. At least one went with him on every expedition, to speed his song to the Great Spirit by percussion. A white visitor to a modern Indian village tells of a friendly visit from neighbors while she lay ill. They came to sing her back to health, but she could distinguish no song for the noise of the drums, and not until they paid another visit, leaving their drums at home, could she perceive the melody in their incantations.

The Indian was most poetical when he raised his voice in solitude, after long fasts and vigils. It was the custom in many tribes for a boy, when he reached the age of twelve or thirteen, to repair alone to a mountaintop, high enough to reach up and touch the stars in his fancy, and to remain there, fasting and solitary, for three days and nights. A vision was almost guaranteed under such conditions, and when it came it was promptly made into a song. In some tribes, the song was a secret to be divulged to no human being, a treasure to be guarded as his open sesame to manhood and to the Great Spirit. In others, it was proudly carried back to be shared with other members of the tribe as a token of the favor of the Great Spirit. These were known as "dream-songs," and were cherished as tenderly as any psalm, on the same ground—that they were divinely inspired. They gave no evidence of being "composed" consciously, as did some of the later ones.

Of primitive love songs there is not much evidence. The old-time Indian made his plea indirectly—to a charm, begging it to procure him his beautiful beloved. The direct appeal was the product of a later and more sophisticated age. However, some writers mention the romantic wail of the flute played at sundown or sunrise outside of the maiden's tepee by her suitor concealed in the shrubbery. If she favored his suit, she showed some sign of her favor, such as throwing her moccasin through the opening, and he issued forth from hiding. If his solo bored her, however, she let him play away until his breath or his patience was exhausted, and he withdrew from the scene.

The Indians had no way of writing down words and tunes, but they did have song pictures, which gave them plenty of leeway in the matter of words. Frances Densmore took down these songs made by a medicine woman, who said the words simply came to her:

> "In the great night my heart will go out,
> Toward me the darkness comes rattling,
> In the great night my heart will go out."

and again:

> "How shall I begin my songs
> In the blue night that is settling?"

and another:

> "I have made you,
> The red evening I give you."

The tunes they learned by heart and sang always the same, even to the key. They must have had something approaching absolute pitch. But each singer could interpret the picture symbols to suit himself, so there were numerous sets of words sung to the same tunes. They would barter songs for ponies, both within the tribe and with other tribes, the owner of the song teaching it painstakingly to the purchaser before riding off on the purchase price. When one medicine man bought a song from another, he bought the curative, or the curse-ative herb that went with it, in that way adding simultaneously to his medical and vocal repertoire.

Although the Indian's most poetic songs were those of solitude, they were not his only contribution, for ceremonials of all kinds were dear to his heart, and each called for its special song. The harvest rites, in which a whole village participated, invoked in song the spirit of everything connected with the harvest—the grains of corn as they were planted in the ground, the rain clouds overhead and the sun shining behind them, the birds and beasts of the field.

The same was true when the braves went out to hunt. There would be a snowshoe dance at the first snowfall; or, before a bear hunt, a big evening jamboree around the campfire, with invocations to the arrowheads to be used, and to the spirits of bears about to be slain. The young men, masked in bearskins, would caper about the fire, following the actions of the medicine man, similarly enfolded. Their attempt to conciliate the bear into being killed without objection on his part was rather touching. However, they did not trust entirely to their ceremonial "dilly-dilly-dilly-dilly, Come and be killed," but looked to it that their arrowheads were sharp and straight, their young men wise in the technique of the chase, and took with them their medicine man and his drum to continue the ceremonial.

The medicine man was the star actor in most of their ceremonials, but particularly, of course, in the healing of the sick. In the medicine lodge, which was church and hospital combined, the droning of his voice, now high, now low, in nasal singsong, would continue for days on end. Masked, he would issue forth at intervals from the lodge, always singing. Sometimes with colored sand which he had blessed, sometimes with herbs, sometimes with a lash to flagellate the evil spirit and drive it forth, he interceded with the Great Spirit to restore the patient to health. His songs and incantations lasted so long, and were so continuous, that the patient was bound either to die or recover.

No ceremonial was complete without its dance, with steps vastly more complicated than the waltz or fox trot. The sun dance, one of the oldest and most popular of their repertoire, was prohibited by the United States Government in 1882, after centuries of practice, because of the brutal physical suffering which attached to it. It was a three days' endurance test, though the Indians called it a dance. Certain warriors who had vowed a sacrifice to the Great Spirit presented themselves after a three days' fast, during which they were constantly singing or being sung to. There was a specially built lodge, and a large gallery of "fans" to witness their trial. A cut was made in the flesh above each dancer's breast, leather thongs were drawn through the cuts, and were flung across horizontal bars overhead. So they were pulled upwards, straining toward the sun. And so, to sacrificial rattle and drumbeat, they would dance, blood streaming from their wounds, eyes uplifted in prayer to the blazing orb, while the priests sang on and on. Finally, they would faint from exhaustion, and, in falling, would tear the flesh from the thongs, winning release and spiritual purification simultaneously.

The scalp dance, in celebration of a victory, was hardly less grim. Held at night after the return from the warpath, it went on, sometimes for fifteen successive nights if the victory had been worth its salt. The gentle squaws of the tribe would stand in the center of a circle, holding up the scalps which had been taken, while the men, brandishing their weapons, yelping and barking like animals, leaped and jumped about them. In the darkness, lit only by the firelight, the dancers' glaring eyeballs and snapping teeth in their copper-colored faces, the drumming and shouting and howling noises, the savage rhythm of it all, must have made a diabolical picture.

The snake dance, by which the Hopi Indians invited rain, afforded another opportunity to test the mettle, this time with rattlesnakes. Held between the teeth, while the dancers, in threes, advanced and retreated endlessly to the sound of song and drum, the rattlesnakes were finally deposited in a heap on the ground, left there while more figures were enacted, then picked up again with the teeth, and the whole dance was repeated. The actors held their rhythm, what is more, although it is difficult to conceive of more rhythm-disturbing circumstances.

The Indians were such inveterate storytellers that they probably wore threadbare the phrase "once upon a time." Stories were passed down from father to son as nonchalantly as the pipe was handed from lip to lip. The tales of the old men around the campfires at evening were comfortable family affairs, probably of far more educational value, musically speaking, than anybody present suspected. These are the songs which collectors treasure today. They have been taken down on gramophone records, so that no whit of their Indian character is lost in the attempt to transcribe them on paper. And they are dated according to whether the teller heard them from a father or a grandfather. The guile of investigators in drawing out the singers is a story in itself, for the old men were great sticklers for fitness and would not dream of singing a hunting song if they were not setting out to hunt, or a love song when they had passed the age of romance.

Indian music has been classified in three time-groups. There are the earliest songs, relayed to this generation from preceding ones by word of mouth, undoubtedly authentic, and preserved with a tenderness never credited to the red man—his original contribution. There is a second group, repeated by Indians who have heard them sung, although they have not received them wrapped in cellophane, as it were, a precious heritage from a revered ancestor—these are fairly trustworthy, although not ex cathedra utterances like the first. Finally, the songs of the present, more secular in character, show the "civilizing" influence of the white man's music, and are not to be considered as intrinsically Indian.

But the more we hear of the Indian's music, the more we rejoice that the difficulty of writing it down, and the preoccupation of early settlers with other matters, caused it to remain untouched. To be sure, Falckner, pastor of the Wissahickon hermits' church in Pennsylvania, mentioned in a letter to England that "music would not only attract and civilize the wild Indians, but it would do much good in spreading the Gospel truth among the sects." Perhaps the modern Indian's habit of singing the Doxology as the finale to any event of importance in his life is a relic of the efforts to "attract and civilize" him. He may sing all the traditional melodies for an Indian marriage at his wedding, but he concludes with a rousing *Old Hundred*. This is probably not so much the triumph of the white man's song as the tacit affirmation that Jehovah and the Great Spirit are one and the same.

For American composers who have made use of Indian songs, the reader is referred to the Appendix.[1] * The list, while not complete, is sufficiently imposing considering that it is less than forty years since this material has been used to any extent. Some composers handle it very simply, supplying only the most unobtrusive harmonic background to actual song themes. Others produce a more sophisticated effect by embroidering and amplifying, while still others make no attempt to reproduce anything but the spirit, and create their own themes to that end.

It is generally difficult for a layman to recognize Indian themes in a composition unless they are pointed out, or presented "as is." When the composer's creative sense gets the better of him, and he elaborates too freely, the words of the modern Indian chief Haomori seem wholly true: "The Great Mystery caused this land to be. . . . It was meant by the Great Mystery that the Indians should give it to all people. But there are two roads, the White Man's and the Indian's. Neither has ever known the other."

* The inquiring reader who refers to the Appendix when he sees a small numeral beside a word will find supplementary information under the same numeral there.

CHAPTER III

BLACK AMERICANS, THEIR SPIRITUALS AND FOLK SONGS

TWENTY black men and women were herded between the decks of a Dutch-African trading vessel in 1619, to be carried into slavery in America. The trader into whose hold this human windfall descended casually put down a few glass beads in exchange. Little did he suspect that this simple transaction made him, in a sense, the father of American music. Never was fatherhood achieved with fewer pangs of apprehension, nor maintained with less consciousness of its responsibilities. The trader did not even search his cargo for concealed weapons, nor, if he had, would he have found any. These slaves had something of immense value to smuggle in, but they were more proficient than the Americans who try to beat Uncle Sam's Customs duties today. For, like poor old Uncle Tom of cabin fame, they realized, mutely, that the white man "might get their bodies, Massa, but he couldn't get their souls." So they cunningly concealed their treasure in that inner sanctum, where they might bring it in unchallenged. Their gift was a combination of melody, harmony, and rhythm in a poignantly appealing form which, from being individual with them, has come to exert a most powerful influence upon the strange hybrid product which we call American music.

They left behind them jungles throbbing with rhythm. The air of Africa vibrated with it; it beat daily into their ears, into their very being. Men sitting astride hollowed-out logs, rata-planning on skins stretched across both ends of the log, made the drum do everything but talk. It was the Western Union of the jungle, and figured, besides, at every occasion of any importance. To its beat, men and women, drugged with rhythm, wriggled lithe naked bodies in the dance. Songs, usually on the five-note scale, starting at the top and coasting down, with pipes and marimba to supplement the melody of the voice, carried on the rhythmic orgy. How the Africans originally stumbled upon the beat which we call syncopated is their secret. Perhaps some drummer, trying to outdrum his rival from the neighboring tribe, accented the offbeat instead of the first beat of the measure. And conceivably, being savages, and not civilized, they did not pillory the innovator for his temerity, but applauded his ingenuity. This is surmise. It is known that this rhythm probably came from Africa, as a part of the musical background of the slaves, and that it arrived in the New World a year before the Pilgrim Fathers happened on Plymouth Rock. We have a ribald inclination to speculate upon what might have happened to psalmody if these syncopators had caught it young and transfused it with their snappy rhythms.

But the slaves were landed in Virginia, not in New England, and so they were not immediately exposed to psalmody in its most acute form, nor psalmody to them. They were distributed among the incipient plantations, while the slave ship went back to Africa for a refill. It was a pity they had to be so scattered, for besides their own special rhythm, they also brought with them a quick response to the beauties of harmony. In Africa, they had sung in unison. Introduced to harmony by their white masters, they beat the latter at that game almost overnight. Although for harmony two are company, and even three are not a crowd, it is truly a case of the more the merrier. All young negroes might be divided into quartettes, somewhat as the rest of the world is divided into committees. Any four, collected in one spot, could be trusted to burst into spontaneous song, in very pleasing harmony, which, seemingly, "jes' grew."

If there is one thing in negro music more appealing than another, it is the way it "jes' grew" and continues to grow. There were the blacks, in a brand-new country. They who had killed their own meat in the hunting grounds of Africa were allotted rations of corn and drippings. Having worshiped their own Deity in voodoo rites, which, bloody and obscene as they appear to us, to them represented a tribute to the only supernatural being they knew, they were suddenly introduced to Christianity with its strange doctrine of love and forbearance. Family and tribal life had been sacred; in the New World they were brutally torn from husband or wife, parent or child, as the auctioneer's hammer decreed. The broiling sun of the cottonfields, the miasma of the rice swamps, and the overseer's lash were the lot of the less fortunate. Even the house servants, or field hands with indulgent masters, had the sword of Damocles in the form of possible sale perpetually hanging over their heads.

Yet they sang! And the songs which "jes' grew" out of slavery were full of hope. Sorrow songs they have been called: sorrow songs, in a sense, they were. A member of their own race, Burghardt Du Bois, writes of them: "These songs are the music of an unhappy people, of the children of disappointment." However, they are not the laments of a people without hope. Even a song with the mournful refrain

"Po' me, po' me,
Trouble will bury me down"

reminds listeners in the next breath that "The Lord is on the giving hand," and that "The more I pray, the better I feel." And although, in order to be double-distilled melancholy as popularly conceived, it should be in the minor mode, the melody of *Po' me,* chanted in the key of F major, is by no means cheerless in character. Another sorrow song has the refrain

"And before I'd be a slave,
I'd be buried in my grave,
And go home to my Lord
And be saved."

But let it be noted that the negro *can* go home to his Lord, surely a comfort to him in his hours of despondency.

The glimmer of hope flickering through his plaints became an incandescent ray when the spirit of the Lord entered the singer and sent a religious song bubbling to his lips. These were the spirituals, the classics of negro song, as fresh and appealing in their simple faith today as when they first sprang into being. Though the days of slavery are past spirituals are still being created in much the same spontaneous fashion.

When the negroes took up Jehovah, they did so with whole-hearted abandon. Faith became their all. Those who had not got religion went after it with all the fervor of the get-rich-quick man with a million in view. The hope of a hereafter better than the here sustained them, and inspired them to make up songs about putting on "dem golden slippers" and crossing "Deep River" to get to "de Promised Land." A religious negro refused to sing any but such songs, even at his work. The unconverted would go wandering through the swamps at night, praying aloud that they would "find dat t'ing," and hysterical was the rejoicing when they returned, haggard and weary, proclaiming that they were saved. Some would sit on the mourners' bench in church, week after week, waiting for the prayers of preacher and flock to bring them through religion. In the slave cabins of an evening, groups would gather to invite the holy spirit and when the master was known to disapprove of such gatherings, an inverted soup pot propped on sticks in the middle of the floor was the magic instrument which kept the sound of their voices from escaping into the night. Very early in their history they started to hold Sunday meetings, like their white masters. In such mangers spirituals were, and still are, born.

The spiritual was sung "settin' down," to the swaying of bodies and waving of heads, almost always in two-four or four-four time. Probably they were all clapped or "stomped" to start with, and then later calmed down. The instruments used to supplement the voices were such as they could lay hands on. Drums, of course, when they could get them, otherwise they shook a rattle, or drew a stick across the jawbone of some animal, or plucked quills, to establish the indispensable rhythm. Later the plunk of a banjo was heard in the land. They robbed the rattlesnake of some of its terror by utilizing it as a music-maker, its skin making an ideal banjo head, and its rattles an aid to the guitar. In the day of Thomas Jefferson, who described the negro's "banjar," it took five strings to produce the proper plunkety-plunk; today, four are generally considered sufficient. These instruments hark back to Africa. For the scrape of the fiddle which was his idea of the summit of sweetness, the negro had the whites to thank.

Into his spirituals the black man poured his childlike faith in de Lawd and fear of de Debble; his trust that in the blood of the Lamb he would be washed clean of transgressions; his groping for a light in the darkness; his resignation to his lot. A slave who had seen his wife and children sold away from him bowed his head in grief beside the auction block. He started to croon to himself "Nobody knows de trouble I've seen, Nobody knows but Jesus." His fellow slaves took up the plaint, repeating the first line, and ending with a "Glory Hallelujah!" to strike the note of hope. Which of them knew when his own turn would come to sing it for the same reason? From one plantation, it spread to the next. The tune may have been an old African one, or a hymn tune he had heard. At any rate, he changed its character in the singing, and gave it the pathos of a whole people. This is one time where the pathos is heightened by the stress on the weak syllable, particularly in the phrase "Nobody knows." Other stanzas were added as the song passed from mouth to mouth, but the tune, meanwhile, thanks to the imitative faculty of its singers, remained pretty much as it had started. They took liberties with rhythms, they interjected and interpolated and quavered strangely and freely, but they stuck to their tune.

One old negro, describing the birth of a spiritual, said: "We'd all be at Prayers' House on de Lawd's day; de white preacher he'd be hired ter 'splain de word; de Lawd would come a' shinin' thoo dem pages and revibe dis old nigger's heart; and I'd jump up dar and den, an' holler an' shout an' sing an' pray, an' dey would all cotch de words, an' I'd sing it some old shout song or war song I'd heard 'em sing fum Africky, an' dey'd all take up de tune an' keep 'long at it, an' each time dey sing it dey keep a'addin' mo' an' mo' verses to it, an' den dar it would jes' natchelly be a sperichel."

"Some good sperichels are start jes' out o' curiosity. I bin a'raise a sing myself once," was the reply of another to the question: "How are spirituals composed?"

Perhaps because groups instead of individuals could claim authorship of their being, the spirituals are as variegated in mood as the many-colored ribbons on Topsy's pigtails. The throaty sob of the negro voice is needed to do adequate justice to songs of such poignant pathos as *Were You There When They Crucified My Lord, Sometimes I Feel Like a Motherless Child, I'm Troubled in My Mind, The Blood Came Twinklin' Down,* and the more personal plaint, *I Lay Dis Body Down.* Tears coursed down the cheeks of Taylor Gordon as he sang them from the concert stage. When the stanzas were "lined out" in church, in sonorous syllables with the unreproducible quaver, and the refrain taken up full blast in harmony by the congregation, "the walls come tumblin' down," however adamant their resistance, like the walls of Jericho in the dramatic spiritual, *Joshua Fit de Battle of Jericho.* The words of *I Lay*

Dis Body Down, even without the music, convey the pathos of these songs:

> "I know moon-rise, I know star-rise,
> I lay dis body down,
> I walk in de moon-light, I walk in de star-light,
> To lay dis body down.
> I lay in de grave, an' stretch out my arms,
> I lay dis body down.
> I go to de judgment in de evening of de day
> When I lay dis body down.
> An' my soul an' yo' soul will meet in de day
> When I lay dis body down."

When "Death laid his cold, icy hand" on a member of a community, all the others rallied around to speed the parting soul and console the bereaved family. In the room with the dying, or the one adjoining, sat a group intoning, in mournful monotone, a continuous succession of spirituals. Newcomers drifted in and out, joining in song while they remained. Many a poor sinner, thus adjured that "de gospel train am leavin'," hurried into eternity on the wings of lugubrious song rather than tarry to be reproached for his delay. Fervent were the personal messages to Jesus, or to departed friends, sung into fast-closing or already closed ears. Mourners broke down and wept, although friends assured them that "dese bones gwineter rise again," and *Roll, Jordan, Roll* promised safe transport to the Promised Land.

But the spirituals were not all pathos. There was intense religious fervor in such songs as *Way Up on de Mountain, Lord,* and *Steal Away to Jesus,* the latter one of the most popular songs of slavery days. Joyous vigor marks *All God's Chil-*

lun Got Wings, and *Gimme Dat Ol'-Time Religion.* As for drama, the negro is almost invariably an excellent actor even when he is a "bad actor." *Daniel in de Lions' Den* would have enjoyed the dramatic fervor with which his escape was celebrated in song, while *Little David, Play on Yo' Harp* would have drawn songs from a much less willing composer than that prolific psalmodist. *Go Down, Moses* is among the best known for the sheer power and beauty of words and music.[2]

The "shouts," which were a variant of the spiritual proper, were in quite another mood; they might be called spirituals improper. While they did not, in so many words, jazz up the spiritual, they brought clapping hands and stamping feet as well as swaying heads and shoulders to the bodily performance. They were sometimes called "running sperichels" to distinguish them from the more sedate "settin' sperichels." In South Carolina and some of the states farthest south, both the song and its accompanying dance were known as shouts; in Virginia, the name was applied to the dance only. This undignified younger sister of the spiritual is probably a primitive African dance partly converted to Christianity, but not wholly convinced. On Sunday or "praise nights," the plantation hands assembled in one of the cabins. After long-winded prayer and hymn singing, the benches would be pushed back. Those in the mood started to shuffle around the floor in a circle, with a peculiar hitching step, singing a spiritual, while the others stood by to sing and clap the rhythm. With their feet they set a marching tempo, while their hands beat at a faster pace, somewhat like the big and little drums of Africa. The thud of the dancers' feet went on, hour after hour, far into the night, while their hysteria and that of the onlookers mounted feverishly. Women fainted and fell to the floor, men rushed out into the night, but the ranks closed up and the ring remained unbroken. The song, meanwhile, was no longer the spiritual with which they had started, but a chant which grew more and more barbaric as the dance mounted in frenzy. The end was complete exhaustion.

Even after a perfectly legitimate church assembly, the spirit might move some member of the congregation to start a "shout." It was the only form of dancing permitted in some religious communities, but there it was carefully watched. A song like *Rock, Daniel, Rock, I Tell You, Rock* might tempt a frivolous young sister, forgetful for the moment that she was a repentant sinner, to dance more vigorously than discreetly. An older sister would be quick to rebuke her with:

> "Watch out, Sister, how you walk on de cross!
> Yer foot might slip, an' yer soul got los'!"

But in spite of such essays at policing, the "shouts" were too wild and unrestrained to meet with the sanction of either the whites or the better-educated negro ministers, and today are practiced little, and then only in secret.

It seems strange that, outside of their native Southern habitat, nobody knew or cared much about the spirituals until after the Civil War. While this was brewing, some sentimental collectors purported to find in spirituals the negro's expression of his yearning for freedom. Anti-slavery propaganda was easily made of this aspect of them, with complete disregard of the fact that the whites sang with equal fervor of their hope of deliverance. Men of both races were as one in crying to heaven for help, the difference being that the white man called his cry a hymn, the negro his a spiritual.

It was no religious urge, but so mundane a factor as the need for money, which impelled an intrepid little group of colored singers, after the Civil War, to experiment in offering programs of spirituals to white audiences. They came from Fisk University in Tennessee, an institution established in 1866 to give freedmen the opportunity for a college education. Their leader, Dr. White, sacrificed his own last dollar to launch their concert tour, which at the outset presented all the difficulties of any pioneering project, further complicated by race prejudice. Feeling ran so high after the war that they never knew when they would be facing an audience who shouted insultingly, "Why couldn't those God-damned niggers stay where they belonged?" nor could they be sure, from one town to the next, whether the local hotel manager would receive them, and whether their concert receipts would permit them to pay even their current expenses. The tour of these Jubilee Singers made history. Not only did they raise more than seven times the twenty thousand dollars they required, but they were the first to carry spirituals to the Northerners who had never heard of them. At the giant Gilmore Music Festival in Boston in 1872, the audience rose in a body, twenty thousand strong, waving handkerchiefs, clapping and stamping, and crying "Jubilee forever!" The Jubilee Singers were the first to introduce spirituals to England, Scotland, and Ireland; to Holland, Switzerland, and Germany. Crowned heads beat time to their rhythm with as much enthusiasm as the unwashed poll of the lowliest subject. Wherever the singers went, they were hailed as ambassadors of true American folk song. Franz Abt, in Germany, declared, "We could not take even our German peasantry and reach, in generations of culture, such results in art, conduct, and character, as appear in these freed slaves."

Quartettes from Hampton and Tuskegee followed the lucra-

tive example of their Fisk brethren, and went out to coax dollars for the education of their people from those who had been
their exploiters. In the course of time, spirituals have taken a
place on the concert programs of such soloists as Roland
Hayes, Paul Robeson, Taylor Gordon, and choirs like the
highly trained Hall Johnson group. The sophistication of the
concert hall sits less gracefully upon their dark brows than
the simplicity of their own environment, yet so sincere is the
quality inherent in them that it comes through with poignant
appeal, whatever the surroundings.

The voice of the white man is too much like his skin. It has
not the color to render spirituals, for it lacks the cadences, the
throaty catch and insidious rhythm. But he tries to sing them
anyway, for he cannot resist the temptation of their con-
tagious melodies. This is made easier for him by the books of
spirituals collected and harmonized by James Weldon Johnson
and his brother Rosamond, and by the many arrangements of
such devoted artists as Nathaniel Dett, Harry Thacker Burleigh, Lawrence Brown, Carl Diton, and others.

Ever since becoming spiritual-conscious, musicologists have
been trying to put the spiritual in its place. Just how much did
the negro actually bring with him from Africa? they ask. Did
he make up his own words and music, or only the words, or
only the music? Did he imitate the French, English, and Spanish songs he heard his white masters sing? And even admitting
that he did actually beat the whites in creating a song of his
own, is it true American folk song? There is no categorical reply. Here is a body of song which satisfies the requirements of
folk song as enunciated by authorities, that "it should come
into existence without the influence of conscious art, as a
spontaneous utterance filled with the characteristic expression

of the feelings of a people," that it "compose itself." It was composed under conditions supposedly ideal for the production of true folk song, arising from the clash of an unsophisticated, unspoiled, naturally musical people with the adverse conditions of slavery. It is warm, melodious, rhythmical, harmonically satisfying and individual. Why not, then, take the gifts the gods provide, without asking too insistently whether the godly skin is black or white? This is the music which makes an American in a foreign land see stars and stripes. It carries him back, first to ole Virginny, then to all America.

The spiritual, though the most aristocratic, was not the sole negro music. Louisiana and Florida not only escaped the rigors of English morality in their daily lives, but succeeded in fostering, in their local music, a pleasantly pagan spirit. Possibly the jungles of Florida suggested those of Africa to this transplanted race and, by the power of suggestion, kept alive savage instincts which elsewhere would have weakened. Without a doubt, the songs of their French and Spanish masters, drifting out through closed green shutters or from the depths of gardens drenched in moonlight, stimulated other emotions than those which evoke a pious Amen. Hence the Creole songs, as the songs of these slaves of Creole masters are called, are primarily of love, with words in a soft French patois. Those of Louisiana are mellifluously dubbed mellows, short for melodies, and take in the musical street cries of fish vendors and flower sellers, as well as their love life in and out of the home. Often accompanied by a poke in the ribs or a joke, their tunes are frequently cribbed from the Spanish or French, and overlaid with negro rhythms. *Suzanne, Suzanne, Jolie Femme* is in praise of a lady of simple tastes, a paragon who is content to dine on gumbo filé, most economical of dishes, while her sisters are being fed Burgundy wine and other delicacies by their white masters. In *Musieu Bainjo,* the negroes poked fun at the dandy in their midst, jeering:

> "See that mulatto playing the banjo,
> Isn't he insolent?
> Hat on one side, O M'sieu Bainjo!
> Cane in right hand, O M'sieu Bainjo!
> Boots that say Crink crank, O M'sieu Bainjo!
> See that mulatto playing de banjo,
> Isn't he insolent?"

Another satirical song, *Michié Préval,* was used for political lampoons on the one hand, and for a nursery song on the other. Children took their baths to it, with a joyous flop into the tub at the refrain in the chorus, "Dansez, Calinda, bou-*djoum,* bou-*djoum."*

But Creole negro music truly put its bawdiest foot foremost in the dance. The sensuous *Habanera* originated in Spain, but when married to African rhythm its own mother would have blushed to acknowledge either the music or the accompanying dance. The *Bamboula,* so called because it was originally danced to drumming on a bamboo log, so captivated the composer, Louis Moreau Gottschalk, that in 1850 he transcribed it for piano, and made other of these melodies the basis of his compositions. *The Counjaille, Belé, Babouille,* and *Calinda* were dances which might not have passed the censor, but which, in addition to their own wild beauty, had the merit of preserving tunes which otherwise might have been lost.

These negroes had their spirituals, too—not all their time was spent in love-making and dancing. But the music in which they celebrated those two important acts of life is their most characteristic, an arrow significantly pointing the way to certain later developments in negro music.

The negro has never been noted for his talent for hard work. He has been the despair of many a brisk efficiency engineer trying to extract foot-pounds of energy from him in the production of goods. But in the production of songs, even while at work, he has never given cause for complaint. For he sings constantly, and is encouraged to do so by any employer far-seeing enough to recognize, in his response to rhythmic stimulus, a method of getting work out of him. A white man stopped to listen to the song of the negro leader of a working gang in South Carolina. "Law, Captain, I'se not a-singin', I'se jes' a-hollerin' to he'p me wid my wuk," said the object of observation with a toothsome grin, and went on digging. But as he tossed out each shovelful of earth, he brought a line of his song to an end with a grunt. The other men of the gang timed their shoveling to his voice, supplying it with a rhythmically clinking accompaniment which was doubtless more truly music to the foreman's ears than the song itself. While the monotonous work of excavation went on, hour after hour, he kept his beat slow and steady. When a big stone had to be broken out, with rapid, powerful strokes, he changed to a humorous song, to which the men, singing louder and striking faster, worked harder without knowing it. He began by singing of John Henry, the steel driver who died with his boots on and hammer in his hand. The tale of John Henry's life and death in innumerable stanzas has brought many a digging job to a happy conclusion.

Stagolee was another hero whose exploits in ballad form kept the ball of work rolling, although he, like *Bad Man Lazarus, Steamboat Bill,* and *Casey Jones,* robbed, burned, killed, and finally dangled from a rope's end. Good or bad, men of action appealed to the lackadaisical negro, a true attraction of opposites. He was willing to sing about their doings by the hour, and even to work to the song. He sang with relish of his animal friends also. Bre'r Tarrypin and Bre'r Rabbit, who appear in the *Uncle Remus* tales of Joel Chandler Harris, were celebrated in many a negro working song.

Those who grew up on the plantations dwell lovingly on their memories of black mammies singing at the washtubs while the aroma of yellow soap mingled with their song, of the rhythmic thud of the iron pressing out frilly underthings to song, of the chug of the butter paddle while the churner sang:

> "Come, butter, come,
> De King and de Queen
> Is er-standin' at de gate,
> Er-waitin' for some butter
> An' a cake.
> Oh, come, butter, come."

From the cotton fields rose the plaintively sweet voices of the field hands, singing one of the many versions of the boll-weevil song. In the streets of the towns, shoes were blacked to a merry reel tune. Stevedores on the river front sang as they loaded bales, while in their few hours of ease, after work, they "patted de Juba" with zest, slapping knee and hip to the gay refrain, "Juba here and Juba there."

Many a foot of rail was laid to *Wukkin' on de Railroad*. In fact, the bosses hired "singin' liners" who did no work but to set the pace in song for their mates. The tune and rhythm are much more valuable than the random phrases fitted to them by perspiring singers. Yet even the words, by their very haphazardness, create a vivid picture. A gang digging in the hot sun optimistically assured one another that:

> "O next winter gonna be so cold, so cold,
> O next winter gonna be so cold, so cold,
> O next winter gonna be so cold, so cold,
> Fire can't warm you, be so cold."

In a wheedling song, the workers implored their white boss, "Don't let your watch run down, Captain." Once in a while they let self-pity assert itself, especially if they were on the lonesome road, as they put it, in search of work. Then they would sing:

> "I can't keep from cryin',
> Look down dat lonesome road an' cry,
> You made me weep, you made me moan,
> Woke up in de mornin', couldn't keep from cryin',
> I got de blues and can't keep from cryin'."

Even the dreaded chain gang produced its songs. *Water-Boy,* a favorite concert number, was originally a cry of anguish from parched convict throats. On Sundays, when they were herded into cages like animals, given neither work nor play, their voices, at least, could go free. After a few spirituals they might swing into the ballad of *Frankie and Johnny,* of which there are about three hundred versions, or a slave song like:

> "My Old Mistis promised me
> When she died she'd set me free,
> But now old Mistis dead an' gone,
> An' left ol' Sambo hoein' corn."

Ol' Rattler, the bloodhound who tracked down escaped convicts, and Black Betty, the whip with which they were "whammed," crept into their Sundays, as well as working days.

Records of their workaday songs are fragmentary and unsatisfactory, since they were too shy to sing when anybody was around with paper and pencil to take them down. Like children, they dreaded the ridicule or criticism which had sometimes followed too free a revelation of themselves to the whites. Many an enthusiastic would-be collector of their songs has had his leg pulled. There is the tale of a professor out for a folk-song killing, who stationed himself with his notebook on a wall near a colored road gang, and waited patiently for several hours. They were working to a sort of chant, of which he had great difficulty in deciphering the words. It was some time before he finally made out the following, and a rude shock it was:

> "White man settin' on de wall,
> White man settin' on de wall,
> White man settin' on de wall,
> All day long.
> Wastin' his time,
> Wastin' his time,
> Wastin' his time,
> All day long."

Negro song being a group product, this discussion cannot be concluded with a list of outstanding composers. An itinerant musician known as "Singin'" Johnson, mentioned by James Weldon Johnson, is said to have had a phenomenal memory, which enabled him to exchange songs for board and lodging wherever he cared to lay his head. He circulated among colored communities for twenty years or so after the Civil War, adding new stanzas to the already existing repertoire, and occasionally perhaps a new tune. But he started his wanderings long after negro song was an established power. Fusing into unity many contributory elements, it yet, in some mysterious fashion, permitted of the separate existence of each. We are reminded of the comedian who was jocularly demonstrating, by radio, the bleaching powers of some fictitious ointment. He applied it to the skin of a coal-black negro, and with many exclamations noted how the subject's skin grew rapidly whiter, until, to loud applause, the negro dropped his dialect and announced, "I bane a Swede." Never does negro music thus lose the color of its skin, not even for a moment, not even in fun.

When Dvořák used a spiritual as the theme of the first movement of his *New World Symphony*, in 1893, he was hailed as a foreigner with more sense than the Americans whom he celebrated in song. By the use of syncopation without stint, and a plentiful sprinkling of flat sevenths in the minor key, and by the almost bodily reproduction of the spiritual, *Swing Low, Sweet Chariot*, he gave it the negro character. When he followed it with the *American Quartette*, based on songs heard from his colored pupils in the New York conservatory where he was teaching at the time, there were those who were ready to tear their hair with envy when they perceived how effectively these themes could be employed.

Before Dvořák, George Chadwick of Boston had used negro material in his *Second Symphony*, but it did not "catch on" as did Dvořák's. There were, however, plenty of other composers, black and white, following Dvořák, who played joyously with the black beauty of negro song.[3] Not all of them have mined diamonds from the coal. Much depended upon their setting of the jewel, which easily comes to resemble paste if not properly handled. Merely affixing harmonies to a spiritual, or orchestrating its melody, merely borrowing a theme, or using negro dialect, barbershop chord, or syncopation are not sufficient to carry over the essential spirit. In the days of slavery, the negro imposed his individuality upon certain music, much of which he took from the white men. They, in receiving it back, have further enriched it, emotionally and intellectually, and have used it to create the genuine expression of the life and character of their own times in their own country.

Later on, after blues, minstrels, and ragtime have had their say, jazz will appear, in the twofold form of music for entertainment and an idiom to be adapted to serious use. Then, in the background of the jiggling, hip-shaking, audacious minx who has danced her way into polite society, will be descried the mammy from whom she sprang, crooning a spiritual in one breath, a lullaby in another, a working song in still another, with a long breath left for a "shout." Her face is crisscrossed with wrinkles of resignation, paralleling lines of childlike laughter and gayety. The brilliant bandanna above and calico below her black face present a contrast as striking as that of her own moods. The spiritual-singing side of her might frown upon her jazzy daughter, but the other smiles tolerantly and remarks that gals will be gals.

CHAPTER IV

OTHER AMERICAN FOLK SONGS, THREE BAGS FULL

"WE have no American folk song," says the skeptic, comfortably sipping his Scotch and soda as he deplores his country's shortcomings.

"Oh, haven't we?" retorts the opposition. "I suppose that's one of the bedtime stories you learned at your mother's knee. And it's just about as wrong as rain is right, assuming the latter."

"But how can we have? We aren't really a nation. The only honest-to-God indigenous Americans we know of are the Indians, and we aren't even sure of them."

"Were the honest-to-God Germans planted on German soil

50

by Father Adam? Or the English in England? Or the French in France? Reminds me of the old, old riddle of the chicken and the egg. Yet when those people get to singing their folk song, I never seem to hear anyone complaining that it isn't really French, or English, or German."

"Perhaps not, but then they've been there so long, and their songs have so much character. They really *are* national, and no mistake."

"And how many centuries does it take for a nation to achieve a personality in music? Must it be a Methuselah to be a somebody?"

"No, but it must be a somebody, and reflect itself in its music in a way which is unmistakably its own."

"Aha! Then let's have a look around in different sections of our country, where folk songs have been collected, and try thinking of them in terms of Europe. Are you willing?"

"I'm willing."

"Very well. We'll start with the songs gathered in the mountains of Kentucky, North Carolina, Tennessee, Virginia, and Georgia. They've been pretty thoroughly explored for folk songs within the last twenty-five years, and hundreds have been tracked down. You've heard of mountain 'ballets'?"

"I believe so."

"Then you know that many of them are of English, Welsh, Irish, or Scotch descent, but have taken to going barefoot and in homespun, metaphorically speaking."

"I've heard of them."

"They've become American in spite of their origin, believe it or not. They're sung by Americans, as American songs. Then, too, they're supplemented by the original songs the mountaineers make up about their local feuds, heroes, and bad men. Those you'll concede to me without a struggle."

"I must."

"Take the play-party songs, of farther west, in the Ozarks, used in place of dance tunes. They wouldn't stand much transplanting. And as for the songs of the plains, and the cowboy songs—by the way, do you know any?"

"Everybody knows a couple."

"Then you're strongly of the opinion that the cowboy and his song have their counterpart all over Europe."

"Don't be sarcastic. You haven't proved that his songs are original with him."

"What if they aren't? By the time he gets through singing some Irish tune, with the words he makes up to it in his loneliness, he's branded it as wholly his as though it were a head of his own cattle. He does something to the tune he uses, like the negro and the mountaineer—like all our Americans. That's the kind of people we are. You couldn't even place the English ballads back where they came from, and expect them to fit, and they're probably most like the originals."

"I'm from Missouri. You've got to show me."

"I will. I'll show you how the French-Canadian songs of the northern border, the French-Creole of Louisiana, and the Spanish-American of California and the Mexican border become American, hyphen and all. I'll throw in the songs of the shantyboys, of hoboes, miners, sailors, and longshoremen, even jailbirds, and you'll have to admit they all belong to America."

"Shoot. I'm resigned, if not blindfolded."

This conversation represents a state of mind so general that the task of collecting American folk songs was shoved comfortably aside as not worth while, until comparatively recent years. American children were brought up on European songs, as though they had none of their own! When prospectors at last made an effort to "strike oil" in folk song, their astonished delight at the extent and value of their treasure trove sent others hot-foot on the trail. The hotter-foot the better, for civilization is upon the country to destroy its folk song. "Dirt and good music are the usual bedfellows; cleanliness and ragtime," was the discovery of one mountain prospector. Let us pray that the bathroom does not banish the folk song.

It was Cecil Sharp, English student of the folk songs of his own people, who first went as far afield as the Appalachian Mountains of America in search of material. He had the most modest hope of any result whatsoever, and made his decision to come here in 1915 on nothing more tangible than a hunch. His willingness to face the hardships of the expedition, with no assurance of reward, does him credit, for they were many, as he speedily discovered. His descriptions, as well as the later findings of Ethel Richardson, Josephine McGill, Howard Brockway, and Loraine Wyman, furnish a composite picture of the life of the Appalachian mountaineers, which indicates that if folk song thrives on solitude and privation it had no cause for complaint in these regions.

The people lived in log cabins, primitive little dwellings, usually guiltless of windows, admitting only such light and air as crept in through the doors. The spinning wheel and hand loom by the open fire, the Greek lamps with wick floating in oil, carried the visiting "foreigner" back several centuries. From the rocky soil the natives wrested corn, their only possible crop, which, in the form of corn pone and hoe cake, exercised their teeth and digestive juices to the utmost.

Razorback hogs, running wild over the mountain, provided them with the greasy bacon which was their sole meat. Their cabins were scattered over a large area, thickly studded with mountains that, viewed from afar, resembled a huddled herd of buffalo with humps going every which way. There were no man-made roads, and only a few natural trails, which were blocked by freshets and such manifestations of Deity often enough to emphasize the already marked isolation of the dwellers there. Horseback, or "nagging," was the only method of getting from place to place, and even that had frequently to be abandoned in favor of walking, so rough and impassable were the trails. Hardly any of the people could read or write, or had any kind of schooling. For them, wood and folklore took the place of book learning. They possessed a simplicity, and a straightforward, honest dignity which was heightened by the Archaic language many of them used, a Chaucerian-Spenserian-Shakespearean dialect, full of such expressions as "The moon fulls tonight," "The children pranked with the beastes, and throwed them to the ground," "He acted unthoughtedly." Cecil Sharp was keenly delighted at the farewell speech of one of his mountain hosts, "We hate to see you go, you are so nice and common." It is this well-hung, Old World flavor which gave the mountaineers the title of "our contemporary ancestors," and which imparted to their ballads the refinement of a bygone age.

In the acknowledgedly British ballads, words and tune were traditional, handed on by word of mouth, only rarely being "scripted down" on paper. Howard Brockway noted that the tunes have a "cumulative beauty." Although one version may differ from another, each singer is sure of the correctness of his own, and defends it jealously. It is for the collector to decide which is the most beautiful of those that are offered. He heard the ballad of *Pretty Polly*, for the first time, under most picturesque circumstances. Four little sisters, whom he asked for a song, shyly retreated into a dark and airless passageway. In sweet unison, their voices piped the tale of *Pretty Polly*, who eloped with her false sweetheart to the seashore, and there escaped the drowning he planned for her, as he had for six previous sweethearts, meting out to him the fate he had destined for her. While the song was in progress, the mother of the choir sat before the open fire, chewing tobacco and squirting the juice at rhythmic intervals into the fireplace. Mr. Brockway was enchanted with the song, and sang it as he then heard it to another mountaineer, to be told that the correct version ran quite otherwise.

Many of these old ballads do not confine themselves to major and minor modes as we know them. They make use also of the older modes, known as the Greek, but used throughout olden Europe, and predominant in English popular song until Elizabethan times. Thus Dorian, Mixolydian, and Aeolian modes flourish in these songs, a mark of antiquity comparable to the wormholes in old furniture.

The refrain is another caste mark denoting British descent. In *Lord Randal* it appears as a "hurtin' tune":

> "Mother, make my bed soon,
> For I'm sick at the heart,
> And I fain would lie down."

And, again, it is pure nonsense, as in *Bangum the Boar*, descendant of an English hunting ditty:

"There is a wild boar in these woods,
Dillum dan diddle, dillom dan diddle,
He eats our flesh and drinks our blood,
Tun a qui quiddle quo quum."

The ballad of Barbara Allen, the stony-hearted maid who repulsed her true love, saw him die before her eyes, and herself proceeded to languish and perish of remorse, is a narrative poem three hundred years old. Effective as a poem, it gained enormously when sung to its simple traditional tune, in unaccompanied unison, by mountain singers.[4]

Everybody sings—it is their way of keeping themselves company in their loneliness. The children sing as naturally as they talk, and a collector need not seek out the doddering old men in order to pick up "ballets," since they flow equally from the mouths of babes. They are of three sorts, the lonesome tunes, so-called by the mountaineers themselves, tragedies of desertion or betrayal; the fast songs, light and lively, sometimes humorous; and the love songs, in which the true knight, returning, finds his love awaiting him, years after their vows were plighted.

When adventurous spirits, wearying of the Appalachian hardships, decided to migrate to the Ozarks, they carried these "ballets" with them. They were such sticklers for the correct tune as they knew it, that all the wily collector had to do to elicit their version of a song was to sing it wrong in one spot and wait for the rush to correct it. *The Ballad of Edward*, printed in *Percy's Reliques*, became *Blood on the Pint of Your Knife* in the Ozarks, where it was sung with tears and genuine feeling. Presenting a "ballet" is a serious business, and though there are wags who venture to be funny once in a while, they dare not tamper with the traditional ballad in order to get a laugh.

A classic with the nonsensical twist beloved of the mountaineer in his hours of ease is *Sourwood Mountain*. How far back it dates, and where its first stanza became the nucleus of the many variants which followed, nobody seems to know. Yet its head is hoary enough to be its admission ticket to any folk-song collection.[5] *Frog Went A'Courtin', I Bought a Cow, They Gotta Quit Kickin' My Dawg Around* led by humorous stages to the typical play-party songs which were the substitute for dancing in the mountains. When the preachers put the ban on card playing and dancing, telling their congregations to lift their eyes unto the mountains instead, the letter of their commands was obeyed. But human sociability prevailed over church prohibition to the extent of providing a substitute for the dance. Whole families would walk for miles over the mountains to play *The Miller Boy*, or *Skip to M'Lou*, or *Old Dan Tucker*. Doing the grand right and left, swinging partners, marching or skipping in a circle were not dancing. Nor was the music provided by the clapping and singing of the bystanders, with possibly one fiddler, considered sinful. Though what with dancing lessons over the radio and young folks leaving home for the big cities, the play party is now dying out, the songs persist and are embodied in the literature of American folk song.

Songs which relate the story of a feud or a moonshining misadventure cannot be hung upon any family tree outside of their own locale. They celebrate the prowess of a *Wild Bill Jones,* or the *Pardon of a Sydna Allen.* They sing of *Jesse James* and *Cole the Younger,* who took from the rich and gave to the poor, and were heroes in the mountains, while a horse thief or a grafter always came to a bad end. The story of *Sam*

Bass, popular among the negroes, also freshened the air of the mountains. Probably originated by one enterprising individual, these songs were embellished by others until nobody knew who the original composers were. *On Smithfield Mountain,* the doleful legend of a youth who was bitten by a rattlesnake while "mowin' " in full view of his distracted sweetheart, is one of the very few whose composer signed his name. It was written by Nathan Torrey in Springfield, Massachusetts, in about 1761, and is the oldest local mountain song known.

White spirituals are also found in the mountains, where the religious gatherings, or foot washings, are comparable in a way to the negro's "shouts," with much song to precede the preaching. *The Hallelujah Christian, A Long White Robe,* and *Safe in the Promised Land* are some which have been noted. One commentator mentions tunes of a Moravian character, of haunting beauty, which he was unable to note down because of the extraordinary nature of the proceedings which followed the singing. He stood by while successive ministers, preaching in an incessant stream, worked the congregation into a "state of salvation," a form of uncontrollable hysteria terrible to behold. Since he who died "shouting happy" was sure of heaven, there was no attempt to check the crescendo of hysteria, and afterward the observer learned that at times those most affected became insane, even died at the height of their frenzy.

Temperance songs played their part in working up intemperately the emotions of hard-drinking yet salvation-seeking communities, and *The Drunkard's Child* was always sure of a hearing. Traveling preachers, representing various sects, were zealous. Not all sects were known, however, as witness the story of a woman in one of the remoter districts, who was asked if there were any Episcopalians in the mountains. She replied, "I dunno ef thar is. Jed, he has kilt about ever' kind of varmint thar is in the mountains. Ef thar's any of them you jes' mentioned, you'll find hit's hide in the shed out thar."

The fiddle is the favorite instrument, when an instrument is used, though mountain folks sing quite easily in unison with no accompaniment whatsoever. These are lonesome tunes, which do not invite harmony. The "dulcimore," which looks like the pocket fiddle of the early French dancing masters, is their very own instrument, related, perhaps, to the dulcimer which was the primitive ancestor of the piano. It has three strings, two tuned in unison, one a fifth below. It is laid upon the lap and plucked with a leather or quill, the melody on one string, a drone bass on the other two. The hickory limb, even more primitive, is strung with a single wire and twanged for rhythm. Banjo and an occasional reed organ complete the mountaineer's simple orchestra.

In contrast with the mountaineer and his English ballad were the men of the flat, wide-open spaces, the cowboy and shantyboy, the hobo, sailor, and all the other lone men who preferred singing to howling like coyotes when the solitude about them got on their nerves. Not that the cowboy spent all his life yodeling "Whoopee, ti yo, git along little dogie," or droning the sad tale of *The Buffalo Skinners*. He had rather the tendency to try a sea chantey or a ballad which took his thoughts away from "shop." Nevertheless, many of his best songs came to him in those moments when, no longer home on the range, he roamed the prairie, fighting wind and rain, dust storms of the alkali desert, Indians and horse thieves, cattle stampedes and marauding animals. The sadness and aridity of his daily existence are reflected in his songs, many of which are reminiscently Irish as to tune, but undoubtedly original as to words. Collectors have felt obliged to suppress many stanzas, as being too completely natural to be altogether proper. *The Lone Star Trail,* a cowboy classic, passed the censor only minus the conversations between the gallant knight and the squaw to whom he returned, but fortunately it included his modest description of himself:

> "My seat is in the saddle and my hand is on the horn,
> I'm the best damn cowboy ever was born,
> My hand is on the horn and my seat is in the saddle,
> I'm the best damn cowboy that ever punched cattle."

He allowed himself the luxury of indigo blues in *Poor Lonesome Cowboy,* where he indulged in a perfect orgy of self-pity, while *The Lone Prai-ree,* a minor plaint with a rhythmic snap, would draw tears from a stone.[6]

Some of his songs were composed in the democratic fraternity of the range, where boss, cowboys, horse wrangler and cook lived in close equality. When the group rode out on the trail, driving their cattle to market, the soothing songs they improvised to quiet down the herds at night, contrasting with the sudden, sharp yells to urge forward the stragglers, relieved the taciturnity enforced by their mode of living. They could always roar a bad-man song when all else failed, and frequently did, while they sought relaxation in the town saloon at the end of the long trail. Quick to draw gun to avenge or to defend, chivalrous in their own sentimental fashion, no wonder they enjoyed singing about *Bad Man Jones, Billy the Kid, Cole Younger, The Fightin' Booze*

Fighter, The Hell-Bound Train, and *The Highwayman.* The hero of the mountaineers, *Sam Bass,* also had his place in the heart and the song of the cowboys.

The cowboy's heyday was in the twenty years following the Civil War. The shantyboys of the lumber lands started their solitary wanderings earlier, in 1825, and for fifty years roamed the forests of Michigan, Wisconsin, Minnesota, and Maine. Machinery then came whirring in to do the work of men's brawny arms, and the silent places which had known only the sound of the ax and the song became alive with the snarling of saws and the hum of the motor. But in his long hours of intense physical activity, the shantyboy contrived to love and hate, to fight and play, to earn and spend, free as the air in all his activities. Song fell as readily from his lips as logs from his keen blade, and when he met his mates in the lumber camp for the night, he was eager to "swap songs" with them. In that way, he enlarged his repertoire to include sea chanteys, ballads brought from the mountains of Kentucky, hobo songs, songs of the prize ring and the battlefield. Back and forth across the Canadian border he went, picking up a French song here and there, to add a dash of Gallic seasoning to his basically Irish stew. His very name, shantyboy, is derived not from the humble quarters where he spent his nights, but from the French "chanter."

The oldest true song of the lonesome pine is the *Falling of the Pine,* "falling" meaning "felling." It was found in Maine, where it probably appeared impromptu, the inspiration of some forgotten man. A certain Billy Allen, who wrote under the pseudonym of Shan T. Boy, scattered many of his own products through the lumber camps, without claiming any of the glory of their composition, and certainly deserves much of the credit for perpetuating these songs.

The rollicking spirit came out with a roar in:

> "I am a jolly shanty-boy
> As you will soon discover,
> To all the dodges I am fey,
> A hustling pine-woods rover.
> A peavy hook it is my pride,
> An axe I well can handle;
> To fell a tree or punch a bull,
> Get rattling Danny Randall."

> *Refrain*

> "Bung yer eye; bung yer eye."

When minded to render a sea chantey, he would roar out

> "Oh, Tom, he was a darling boy,
> Tom's gone away."

or another favorite:

> "Then up aloft that yard must go,
> Whiskey for my Johnny."

In his more thoughtful moods, he dwelt, like the cowboy, on the possibilities of a sudden and unpleasant end being put to his existence by one of its many occupational hazards. *Lake Huron's Rockbound Shore* is one of many songs depicting the drowning of men in the discharge of duty:

> "Sad and dismal is the story that I will tell to you,
> About a schooner Persia and her officers and crew,
> They sank beneath the waters deep, in life to rise no more,
> Where wind and desolation sweep Lake Huron's rockbound shore." [7]

Old George Burns, whose voice was his fortune, staggered half frozen into a logging camp one evening during a blizzard.

When he had sufficiently thawed out, he offered to sing for his supper, and demonstrated satisfactorily that his strong tenor voice had not been frozen out of existence. The men kept him in camp all winter, and winked at his shortcomings as a logger as long as he would sing to them in the evenings. In the same way that Burns happened on the lumber camps, volunteer minstrels went wandering through the anthracite coal fields of Pennsylvania, carrying from mine to mine songs made up by themselves and others.

When San Francisco, known in olden days as Yerba Buena, welcomed settlers to her hospitable arms, they were mostly adventurous Spaniards or Mexicans. They rode in like knights errant, slinging their guitars from their saddles with the same fine free gesture with which they draped the serape from their shoulders. The songs they twanged were songs of the languorous night, of black eyes and alluring ladies and the torments of love. Sunlight silenced them, but they and the romantic moon understood each other. *Tus Ojos, Me Mue,* and *El Tormento* were some of the lays of these Spanish minstrels. San Francisco grew into a thriving seaport, and sailor chanteys and songs of the water front seeped in from the sea. Cowboys brought their songs from the prairie, shantyboys theirs from the tall timber. San Francisco became a veritable melting pot of folk song. Spanish romance, which thrives on *dolce far niente,* suffered from an overdose of activity, and either succumbed, or adapted itself to the changed conditions. But the influence of the original old Spanish songs can still be recognized in their modern descendants.

A dash more of the heady wine of Spain is found in the songs brought from Mexico into the Southwest. Love thy neighbor as thyself, especially if she is a pretty woman, is the burden to which were set the liltings of the vaqueros as they drove their cattle along the trail from Mexico into New Mexico, thence to Texas, Kansas, and farther north. *Mananitas, Lo Que Digo, El Abandonado,* and *Adelita* all croon of the love of man for woman. *La Cucuracha,* on the other hand, is a satirical song, somewhat akin in spirit to the Creole *Musieu Bainjo.* The double meaning of *Cucaracha*—cockroach and old maid—gives the wit a free hand in the verse, while the swing of the tune invites the stamping of feet and provocative shawl waving endeared by Spanish custom. The cowboys who rode shoulder to shoulder with their Mexican brothers speedily adopted their songs, changing a rhythm, a line, or a measure in the music, adding a stanza here and there to the words—naturalizing them, as it were.

To reproduce the words of folk songs without their accompanying melodies is to present the saucer without the cup, the tail without the dog. To print the tunes in a book intended to be read, not sung, is impossible. The little old Scotchwoman who pleaded that to print a ballad of the people is to destroy it was not merely trying to find an excuse for not offering one. She was right, in so far as she realized that its flexible body turns, if not to gold, to some equally unyielding substance at the Midas kiss of the typesetter. What she failed to realize is that not to write is equally to destroy them, since only so can they remain with us. Like canned peaches, preserved folk song is not so good as fresh, nor can it be served in as many appetizing forms, but it is infinitely better than none at all.

The folk festivals held yearly at White-Top, Virginia, offer a feast of folk song and dance. Ballad singing, banjo strumming, band playing, and solo fiddling, besides all kinds of dances, are presented by the mountain people, for the most part as they received them from their parents and grand-parents. In the cabin of Miss Jean Thomas, the "Traipsin' Woman" of Boyd County, Kentucky, *The Call of the Cumberlands*, an American grand opera depicting the life of the mountaineers, had its first hearing in 1935, with its youthful composer, Harrison Elliot, singing the lead. An old-time "singin' school" was reproduced at another of these festivals, and a "singin' gatherin'," as well, at which brethren sang old-time hymns. These are more or less local celebrations. The first National Folk Festival in America was held in the Municipal Auditorium in St. Louis, in the spring of 1934. It offered an excellent cross section of folk song in America, as follows: Spanish players from Albuquerque, New Mexico; lumberjacks from Michigan; Kiowa Indians under the direction of a leader from the University of Oklahoma; a ballad singer from Kentucky; nine old harp singers from Tennessee; cowboys from Arizona; singers, dancers, and old fiddlers from the Ozarks; Appalachian mountain folk in ballads and dances; negroes, a thousand of them, singing work, play, and plantation songs; singers from St. Genevieve, Missouri, and from Vincennes, Indiana, presenting old French songs; and ballad singers from Springfield, Vermont. This National Festival has become an annual event, its programs the only answer really needed for the doubting Thomas who questions the solid wealth in his inheritance of folk song.

CHAPTER V

RAH-RAH SONGS OF COLLEGE AND COUNTRY

WHEN the embattled farmer, having laid down the plowshare of ordinary song, girded on the sword of patriotic utterance, he was unconsciously doing more for his country than he knew. For the first time, he was asserting his nationalism, and that in ringing tones to which neither his own compatriots, nor his enemies, could turn a deaf ear. The timidity which had accompanied his political uncertainty, the hesitancy of the underdog, the shrinking of his inferiority complex, were forgotten as he roared his pledges of loyalty to his-country-right-or-wrong. There is a juvenile quality about national songs, which puts them in the same category with the songs of the college man.

The latter is an untried lad, exchanging the protective atmosphere of his home for the larger world of the university, and asserting in song his joy in living as a loyal member of the larger group. The composer of national songs similarly proclaims his exultation at emergence from the narrow conception of the individual and personal to the national, while the same youthful sentimentality pervades both in their more thoughtful utterances.

Either an old-fashioned emotional hysteria, or an overdose of alcoholic stimulation, is required to make the sophisticated city man-in-the-street carol aloud. He is inclined to be sheepish about being overheard, which is perhaps why singing in the bathroom is the American's great indoor sport. There, at least, he is safe from interruption or eavesdropping. Carl Sandburg once remarked pithily when he returned from one of his song-collecting tours, "The trouble with this country is, that when a man sings, everybody thinks he's drunk." But there are other ways of getting drunk than by imbibing hard liquor. When the American man goes patriotic, he is full of a headier stimulant than alcohol, namely, love of country. As a young collegian, whose patriotism is concentrated on his Alma Mater, he may be doubly intoxicated with love of college, plus actual liquor. No wonder that his musical outcries sometimes wax incoherent, if sincere, nor that their musical content is likely to be of no very high order. They are of interest chiefly as an elementary presentation of the rah-rah spirit which breaks forth with veritable fury in national song.

Collections abound, containing songs of all colleges, or segregating the Eastern from the Western, or the big three from the little three hundred, or the men's from the women's, or giving the favorite ditties of the fraternities within the colleges. Roughly speaking, college songs, like Ancient Gaul, are divided into three parts—the serious declaration of love for Alma Mater; the boola-boola cheering song; and the nonsense verse. It is natural that the spirit of youth and gayety should pervade them all, warming the cockles of hearts, old and young. It appears less natural, however, that they should display so little creative originality. What happened to the undergraduate, when he sat himself down to write an impersonal love song, a shout of triumph, or a bit of nonsense? After chewing the pencil for a while and deriving no inspiration from its splinters, he turned the paper face down, and instead of making up a tune, wrote words to one he already knew. Especially does this seem to apply to official Alma Mater songs, where one would least expect it. The tune of *Believe Me, If All Those Endearing Young Charms* became *Fair Harvard*. *Glory, Glory Hallelujah* passed over painlessly to *Pennsyl-Pennsyl-Pennsylvania*. *Yale's Bright College Years* is the German *Wacht am Rhein*. *C-o-l-u-m-b-i-a* is the undergraduate's version of *Vive la Compagnie,* while the Russian national hymn became *Hail, Pennsylvania*. The women did no better, for the lassies of Bryn Mawr sing her praises to the *Norsk Flagsang*, Vassar has taken *Auld Lang Syne*, and Goucher a negro melody. Although the student was only too willing to be cut into little pieces and fried to prove his devotion to his college, he appeared unable to register his sentiments while remaining in one piece. There are exceptions, such as Princeton's *Old Nassau,* and the Amherst *Sir Geoffrey Amherst,* both by undergraduates. But by and large, the student body was weak on tunes, though it had no difficulty in manufacturing such couplets as

"The burden of our song shall be
The love we bear to Genesee."

The intoxicating joy of creation was the collegian's when he opened his throat in a colossal cheer. If he could urge his team to victory, gloat over the fallen foe, or console the vanquished friend, he was truly in his element. At such moments he was not obliged to render articulate, as in the more sentimental Alma Mater songs, the affectionate tenderness which he hated to acknowledge even to himself. No manly reserve stood in the way of his being the small boy he wanted to be, noisy and carefree. Humor was not taboo. So he roared jeremiad and jubilation in his own rough and ready idiom. The Princeton *Tiger, Tiger, Siss Boom Bah,* the Swarthmore *Hip Hip for Old Swarthmore,* and the Brown cheering song are undergraduate products. The music of *Down the Field,* Yale's song of football triumph, was written by Stanleigh P. Friedman during his student years in 1904. He followed it with *Whoop It Up,* and in 1936, as a loyal alumnus, he sent his college a new song, *Sons of Eli.* Since 1906, Annapolis has been marching to *Anchors Aweigh,* by Midshipman Miles and Bandmaster Zimmerman, who wrote it to order for the Army-Navy game. Reserved for that annual event for twenty years, it was finally released in print and became almost a national song. Needless to say, the colleges are justly proud when their sons do crash through with a song, and honor them almost as highly as their football heroes.

Nonsense songs of the colleges can be passed over very quickly. By now, they are so traditional that nobody knows who wrote the tunes, although many of the words carry the diploma of higher education. *There Is a Tavern in the Town, Upidee, O, Who Will Smoke My Meerschaum Pipe, Sing*

Polly-Wolly-Doodle All the Day are the darlings of college groups addicted alternately to close harmony and rollicking unison.

Patriotic songs are rah-rah on a large scale. Take a sober American citizen who would rather die than be caught talking about his feelings. Add a pinch of patriotism, a dash of sentiment, a soupçon of exhibitionism. Shake well, together with the diatonic scale, and throw away the result. For that is what he does with it. Although the right sentiment may be there, its expression in serious musical phrases appears to him to be plain silly, and he will have none of it. The most he will do is to write a set of words. This is the case, whether the victim is a college lad bleating love and loyalty to the orange and pink, or a full-grown male with his eyes fixed fondly on the red, white, and blue. He takes his devotion too seriously to be serious about it in music. And so we shall find that our national anthems, dating back to before the Revolution, were foreign tunes decked out with native words. There are only a few among them which were wholly made in America, and those were usually not born to be national songs, but had that greatness thrust upon them.

War was the football game which intoxicated the national cheer leaders into writing melodies of their own. It is easy to understand how, under the impetus of waving banners and marching feet, tunes sprang spontaneously to the lips of the hitherto inexpressive. It has been said that if there were no uniforms, and no military bands, there would be no wars. If there were no wars, there would probably be no national songs.

During the days of psalmody, before the Revolution, the only loyalty expressed in song was, naturally, loyalty to the

English. Francis Hopkinson wrote a lengthy *Dialogue and Ode, with Words and Music Sacred to the Memory of George II,* and a companion piece upon the accession of George III to the throne. These are full of flowery compliments to England's reigning monarchs, quick and dead. Similarly, James Lyon's music for a pageant, *The Military Glory of Great Britain,* composed in 1762, conveyed a sugared tribute, untainted by the bitter flavor of taxed tea, which was, a decade later, to twist into a wry grimace the lips of the singers. The *Liberty Song* of Mrs. Mercy Warren, published in 1768, has been acknowledged as the first national song. The words of the chorus quaintly anticipate the later slogan, "Millions for defense, but not one cent for tribute."

> "In freedom we're born, and in freedom we'll live;
> Our purses are ready;
> Steady, friends, steady;
> Not as slaves but as freemen our money we'll give."

There is not much grace or charm to these noble sentiments, to be sure. And they seem to have been warbled to an English tune, *Hearts of Oak,* so Mrs. Warren's fame is not heightened by any contribution of original music. Still, hers is the distinction of having inserted the entering wedge of national song.

When the Revolutionary War was actually under way, there was a moratorium in psalm composition for a few years, while the fife and drum of the military bands earnestly tootled and beat melodies which roused the men at the time, but which have since sunk into oblivion. Good old William Billings, of fuguing fame, circulated his *New England Psalm Singer,* and his *Singing Master's Assistant* among the troops, setting to hymn tunes which everybody knew, words more ap-

propriate to the battlefield than the church. Under his treatment, the beautiful psalm *By the Waters of Babylon* became
a *Lamentation over Boston,* then regrettably occupied by the
British. And the men sang:

> "By the rivers of Watertown we sat down,
> Yea, we wept as we remembered Boston."

His paraphrases of psalms were surprisingly popular, considering the sacrilege involved in tampering with their lines.
But his chief song contribution to the Revolution was *Chester,* both words and music of which he composed some eight
years before the war, making a new set of words for war-time
use. In them, he made defiant proclamation of his trust in the
God of New England, and the beardless boys who fought for
her. Elementary as were both the tune and the words, Billings
was in deadly earnest, and the sincerity of his utterance, perhaps its very naïveté, endeared it to the troops.

> "Let tyrants shake their iron rod,
>   And Slav'ry clank her galling chains,
> We fear them not, we trust in God,
>   New England's God forever reigns."

Billings' *Chester* was probably the most popular war song
of the Revolution. Yet today it is mentioned only by historians, while *Yankee Doodle,* its contemporary, lives on.
That *Yankee Doodle* should ever have become a national
song is a compliment indeed to the American sense of humor.
It is not every man who will smile sweetly when an enemy
sings at him in derision and remarking, "That's a good tune
and catchy words," adopt the song for his national anthem.
Yet that is substantially what happened here, except that the
process of adoption was somewhat more deliberate.

During the French and Indian War, the raw colonial troops fought side by side with their elegant English cousins. They were a sorry-looking lot as to uniforms, and their military formations were, to say the least, architecturally unsound. When they appeared *en masse* in the streets of a town, they came in for their full share of ridicule. A certain Dr. Shuckburgh, who happened to be in Albany with the English when a contingent of colonial reinforcements marched through the street, stopped laughing at the sight just long enough to write down some foolish words to a tune which popped into his head. The words were:

> "Yankee Doodle came to town,
> Riding on a pony,
> Stuck a feather in his cap,
> And called it Macaroni."

A macaroni in England was a fop or dandy. Yankee was probably Anglais (French for English), pronounced with an Indian accent, while a doodle was a half-wit. Exactly what the tune was is still being debated. It sounds somewhat like the song of Lucy Locket in *The Beggars' Opera*. There are likewise a Dutch folk song which it resembles in part, a German street-tune, and a French popular melody. The one point upon which everyone agrees is that it was not composed by the Dr. Shuckburgh who wrote the words, or by any other American. In fact, Mr. O. G. Sonneck, for many years Curator of Music in the Library of Congress in Washington, prepared an exhaustive report on *Yankee Doodle, The Star-Spangled Banner,* and other national anthems, in which he cast doubt even on Dr. Shuckburgh's part in writing the song. He contended that the words are good-natured fun, without a particle of malice, and were probably written by a young colonial soldier to describe his first visit to town.

Whoever may have been responsible for its words and music, it was gleefully caught up by the English. Their ships' bands played it daily, and in the army they drummed miscreants out of camp to its mocking strains. During the seething months before the Revolution, they wreaked their malice on the pious church worshipers in Boston by singing the devilish air outside of the church doors. A secular song on Boston's blue Sunday was sacrilege indeed. And yet the colonists grew to like it, and in their turn began to sing and march to it. Around the melancholy campfires of Valley Forge, they stoutened their hearts with its merry tune. They never seemed to tire of it; it fitted every occasion. So completely did they make it their own that, as the cream of the jest, when the British band played the national song of the victorious army at the surrender of Yorktown, *Yankee Doodle* was rendered, by request, as the American national anthem. It has nestled securely in the affections of the American people ever since.

George Washington, father of his country, was also, according to one of his Birthday Odes, "parent of soothing airs and lofty strains." Two at least of his progeny are thriving members of the family of national song. *Hail, Columbia, Happy Land* was written to the tune of a march composed in 1789 for his inauguration. There were a number of such marches written, and the composer of this particular one is doubtful. Two German musicians, known respectively and affectionately as Philip Phile and Old Roth, have been named, with the balance in favor of Old Roth. No less a person than Judge Joseph Hopkinson, son of the famous Francis, wrote the words to oblige a friend. In 1798, the country was all of a dither as to the advisability of sending aid to France, then in the throes of revolution. Federalists and anti-Federalists came to blows on the question. Feeling ran so high that disputes were carried even into the theater.

A public performance of Federalist songs was a sure way to draw anti-Federalist fire, and vice versa, so that peaceful moments in the theater were few and far between. A piteous appeal from the musicians in a Boston theater was published in one of the magazines about this time, to the effect that "the musicians that perform in the orchestra of the Boston theater assure the public that it is not more their duty than it is their wish to oblige in playing such tunes as are called for, but at the same time they wish them to consider the peculiar poignancy of insult to men not accustomed to it. Thus situated, they entreat a generous people to so far compassionate their feelings as to prevent the thoughtless or ill-disposed from throwing apples, stones, et cetera, into the orchestra, that while they eat the bread of industry in a free country, it may not be tinctured with the poison of humiliation." Gilbert Fox, an actor in Philadelphia, was no more anxious than these Boston musicians to be hit by the slings and arrows of a patriotic public. (The appeal was not very effective, by the way.) But he wished to arouse enthusiasm with a nonpartisan patriotic song, which would at the same time liven up his act on the stage. He got his new song from his friend Hopkinson, and with it the personal success he needed to keep the wolf from his door. While *Hail Columbia* is not a work of genius, it seems to have filled a definite need when it was sung, and to have gone on filling some kind of need ever since.

The *Washington March* set the tune for *Hail Columbia*, and a stanza honoring Washington, to the tune of *God Save the King*, set the pattern for *America*.

> "God save great Washington,
> His worth from ev'ry tongue
> Demands applause.
> Ye tuneful powers combine,
> And each true Whig now join,
> Whose heart did ne'er resign
> The glorious cause."

The rhymes may be questionable, but the sentiment is as impeccable as the tune is imported. The tune of *God Save the King* is probably British. It is attributed to Dr. John Bull, one of the greatest composers of the sixteenth century, a brilliant organist, court musician to Elizabeth, and professor at Oxford. He is said to have composed his tune for so prosaic an event as a banquet tendered to King James I by the Merchant Tailors of England. However, it is also claimed by the Swiss as their national hymn composed in 1602 to celebrate the victory of Geneva over the forces of the Duke of Savoy, and Lully is said to have used it to glorify his *roi soleil*, Louis XIV. Still another claimant to the honor of its composition was Henry Carey, the English composer of *Sally in Our Alley*, who sang the words and music of *God Save the King* at a tavern in Cornhill, England, in 1740, with the remark that he had written them. Whoever may have written the music, plenty of people undertook to supply words to it.

It finally became *My Country, 'Tis of Thee* by way of Germany. The tune was brought from Germany to Lowell Mason by his friend, William Woodbridge. Mason was al-

ways on the lookout for fresh song material for his Sunday-
school classes, and, as he knew no German, he passed on the
book to Samuel Francis Smith, a young theological student
at Andover, asking him to make a few translations if he
found anything worth while. Smith was looking idly through
the book one rainy afternoon (rain seems to have frequently
set fire to the creative spark, instead of extinguishing it).
He hummed through the tune of *God Save the King,* liked it,
rapidly wrote the words of *America* on a sheet of paper,
shoved the paper into a desk drawer, and proceeded to forget
all about it. A few weeks later, however, he came across it,
and sent it on to Dr. Mason, who promptly took it around
and taught it to all his Sunday-school groups. Their childish
treble piped it in unison at a big Sunday-school festival at
the Park Street Church, in Boston, on July 4, 1832. Sung at
festivals, both Sundays and weekdays, ever since, it ran a
close second to *The Star-Spangled Banner,* when, in 1931,
Congress declared the latter to be our official national anthem.

If the Americans who have struggled manfully to sing the
tune of *The Star-Spangled Banner* knew upon what individual to throw the blame for its difficulty, they would gleefully
tar and feather him, in imagination at least. So perhaps it is
as well that the composer is unknown, and their acrimony of
necessity impersonal. The melody is that of an old English
drinking song, *Anacreon in Heaven.* The English in their cups
must have been more gifted vocally than when sober, for the
range of the song, five notes over an octave, and the awkward
intervals, make it hard sledding for the untrained singer.
Still, in the colonies, where they took delight in martyrdom,

it fitted admirably. Robert Treat Paine, in 1798, took the tune for his song, *Adams and Liberty*, with its awkward, if impassioned refrain:

> "And ne'er may the sons of Columbia be slaves,
> While the earth bears a plant, or the sea rolls its waves."

An anti-Federalist version, *Jefferson and Liberty*, appeared in Philadelphia a little later, while still a third celebrated Napoleon's defeat in Moscow to the same tune.

It is really America's bad luck that Francis Scott Key should have been so familiar with that unsingable tune, instead of any one of the hundreds of other simple folk tunes he could have used. For he wrote the words of *The Star-Spangled Banner* under the stress of overpowering emotion, using a melody which he knew so well that he needed to toss it barely a thought. During the War of 1812, he was sent by President Madison as his emissary on a delicate diplomatic mission. He was to negotiate for the release of a Dr. Beane, an American noncombatant who had been caught aiding and abetting the enemy. Key timed his arrival at the inopportune moment when the British fleet was planning to attack Fort McHenry. He was detained on shipboard for the twenty-four hours of the bombardment, and when he was released, on September 14, 1814, his relief at the sight of the flag still floating over the fort was inexpressible. Standing on the deck of the ship, feasting his eyes on the stars and stripes, he drew an old envelope from his pocket, and scribbled the words of *The Star-Spangled Banner* as they came to his mind. As soon as he returned to Baltimore, he made a clean copy of the scrawl, and, author fashion, showed it to a friend. Emboldened by the latter's enthusiasm, he took it at once to a printer, and had "broadsides" printed for immediate distribution. These were single sheets, very cheaply gotten up, and thrown about like handbills. The words were printed, "to be sung to the tune *Adams and Liberty,*" and were immediately so sung. Thus it happened that America is as British in the matter of the melodies of her two principal national songs, *America* and *The Star-Spangled Banner,* as England wished her to remain in her political affiliations.

The Revolutionary War left no lasting song souvenir excepting *Yankee Doodle,* which promises to continue to be sung as long as the nation remains one and indivisible. *The Star-Spangled Banner* was the most significant heritage of the War of 1812. Some others were composed at this time, glorifying the naval heroes of a war, much of which was fought at sea, but their tunes were so much less dramatic than their words that they do not today form a part of the education of the young patriotic singer.

Columbia, the Gem of the Ocean is sandwiched between the War of 1812 and the Civil War. It follows so faithfully an English melody of the day, *Britannia, the Gem of the Ocean,* that we have little sympathy with the controversy over its authorship. It hardly seems worth fighting over. A worthy gentleman, named Thomas à Becket, said that he had written words and music in 1843 for a friend, David Shaw, very much as Hopkinson wrote *Hail Columbia* for Gilbert Fox. Only the ungrateful Shaw claimed authorship himself, and had the song published under his own name, creating much unpleasantness until he consented to rectify the error.

All the songs thus far mentioned were very well in their way, but the real song-flowers of patriotism bloomed during the Civil War. Feeling ran high, from the prewar efforts of both sides to hold on to the stars and stripes as their own flag, and *The Star-Spangled Banner* as their own anthem, to the final split. When the Confederates ran up the stars and bars of their new nation, they inspired Henry McCarthy to write for them *The Bonnie Blue Flag*. Published in New Orleans in 1864, it proved mildly successful, but was so far surpassed by *Dixie* that it now figures hardly at all in a discussion of the war songs of the South.

Dixie came to the land of cotton direct from Byrant's Minstrel Show. A "walk-around" tune was needed, and Dan Emmett wrote words and music to order overnight. The swing, the sentiment, and the singability of *Dixie* came to be beloved of minstrel audiences from 1859 on. It was used in the political campaign of 1860, and the Southerners made it their own immediately upon the outbreak of war. They were not such sticklers for family background in their songs that they would refuse *Dixie* because of its Northern origin, for it suited them exactly. Its nostalgic gayety brought the old times on the plantations vividly before the boys who were fighting to perpetuate them, and put new strength into their sword arms. The Confederacy lost the fight, but they won for their own the best song of the Civil War—we had almost said the best national song of American history. Since the war, it has shed its skin of partisanship, and become a favorite of the entire nation.

Fair exchange being no robbery, the South returned the compliment of *Dixie* with *Glory Hallelujah*. A favorite camp-meeting song as soon as its composer, William Steffe, issued it in Charleston, it questioned earnestly:

> "Say, brothers, will you meet us,
> Say, brothers, will you meet us,

Say, brothers, will you meet us,
On Canaan's happy shore?"

From Charleston it traveled to the ranks of the Tigers, a battalion of Massachusetts infantry, by way of two homesick Southern boys. When they were singing it one lazy Sunday in quarters to raise their drooping spirits, their captain happened to hear them. The next time Pat Gilmore, the great band leader, came out to play for the Tigers, the captain gave him the tune. As his band played it, the men took it up. The words, however, were much too solemn to appeal to Tigers, who set their most irreverent wags to work to remedy that defect. A big Scotchman in the regiment, named John Brown, was the butt of many of the men's jokes; the other John Brown of Ossawatomie had just been hanged in 1859; result, the words, "John Brown's body lies a'mould'ring in the grave," designed to tease the living more than to glorify the dead. The song became the marching song of the Tigers, who generously passed it on, first to the other troops, then to the country at large. When Julia Ward Howe heard it chorused by men riding into battle outside of Washington, she was transported by it, and acquiesced gladly to the suggestion of Dr. James Freeman Clarke, who was with her, that she write more fitting words to it.

"Mine eyes have seen the glory of the coming of the Lord,
  He has trodden down the vintage where the grapes of wrath are
      stored,
  He has loosed the fearful lightnings of his terrible swift sword,
  His truth goes marching on."

Her poetical lines were received with as much enthusiasm as their irreverent precursors.

All the songs thus far mentioned became war songs more or less by chance. At the outset of the war, a prize of five hundred dollars was offered for a truly inspiring national song. More than twelve hundred contributions were received, enough to fill five wash hampers, and cause sleepless nights and gray hairs to the thirteen judges, especially as, after three months' deliberation, they found not one deserving of the prize. Fortunately, the country was not thereby doomed to fight in stony silence. War songs grew without the bottle feeding of prize awards. The words, *Maryland, My Maryland*, were set to the German folk song, *O Tannenbaum*, a melody so simple that anyone could sing it. *We Are Coming, Father Abraham, Three Hundred Thousand Strong* gave the North a strong boost at a time when she bitterly needed it. It was written in 1862, when Lincoln had just issued his memorable call for volunteers. James Sloan Gibbons, a Quaker abolitionist, replied to the call in these ringing lines, which came to him at dusk of a day filled with the tramp of marching feet, the blare of military bands, and the shouting of war extras in the streets.

The Battle-Cry of Freedom, with its stirring refrain

> "We'll rally round the flag, boys,
> Rally once again,
> Shouting the battle-cry of Freedom"

was another patriot's response to the same call. Only in this instance, the patriot was Mr. George Root, already a well-known composer of sacred songs. When his *Battle-Cry of Freedom,* dashed off hurriedly for a recruiting rally, became popular, Root immediately tried his hand at others.

"Tramp, tramp, tramp, the boys are marching,
Cheer up, comrades, they will come"

kept from despair many a boy languishing in a Southern
prison. *Just Before the Battle, Mother,* its less popular sequel,
Just After the Battle, Mother, and *The Vacant Chair* brought
sobs and sentiment to an already overwrought citizenry, who
bathed in them and cried for more. Henry C. Work, another
abolitionist composer, helped meet the demand. *Kingdom
Coming* was a highly humorous picture of the negroes on the
plantation having a grand time while Massa had to go away
to war. He followed it with *Babylon Is Fallen,* and *Wake
Nicodemus.* His best-known contribution, however, is *Marching Through Georgia,* an intensely partisan song, popular in
the North only. *Tenting Tonight on the Old Camp-Ground,*
by Walter Kittredge, had a more general application, and
had, besides, the luck to be composed by a young man with
a good voice, who could sing it around and make it known.
The night before young Walter Kittredge went to war, he sat
up writing *Tenting Tonight,* then went out and sang it to his
mates in the army and later to concert audiences. *When
Johnny Comes Marching Home Again* was another war hit.
Published in 1863 by Pat Gilmore, under the pseudonym of
Louis Lambert, it was worthy of this great band leader, who
preceded Sousa in his devotion to popular music of the better
sort. Johnny has come marching gayly home from two wars
since, to the tuneful *Hurrah, Hurrah* of Gilmore's song.

The four outstanding Civil War hits were *Dixie, John
Brown's Body, The Battle-Cry of Freedom,* and *Marching
through Georgia.* There is something about these songs which
sets them somewhat apart from the others. The very nature

of the domestic conflict which produced them created an exaltation unlike the usual flag-waving egotism of a warring people. Its expression was marked by rare sincerity, both as to musical utterance and words.

The Spanish-American and the World wars, on the other hand, were fought on alien soil. It is not surprising, therefore, that many of the songs with which the men whiled away the hours of inactivity struck a note of homesickness. Ragtime, too, was pretty well established by 1898, and asserted itself even in the songs sacred to battle. *On the Banks of the Wabash, Far Away,* written by Paul Dresser long before the Spanish-American War, but sung then *ad nauseam,* brought tears to the eyes of every homesick soldier-boy. And when Charles Harris' *Just Break the News to Mother* was given for the benefit of a troop off to the front, so many broke down and wept that another livelier tune had to be substituted. The fact that Charles Harris was also known as the composer of the gay *After the Ball Is Over,* and that the sad measures of *Just Break the News to Mother* occurred to him while he was comfortably seated in a barber's chair being shaved, robbed his sentimental lines of none of their poignancy. After all, there were more heartening ways of speeding the parting warrior than reminding him that the news of his demise would have to be broken delicately to the folks he left behind him.

A Hot Time in the Old Town Tonight was a blessed relief from tears and heart throbs, and ragtime though it was, its gayety shone through the clouds of war sadness with reassuring radiance. It was not written with the war in mind, but came direct from the minstrel show. As the story goes, McIntyre and Heath and their minstrels were passing through a village in Louisiana called Old Town. A house was on fire, and as they rode by it, McIntyre remarked to Heath, "They're certainly having a hot time in the Old Town to-night!" To which Heath's businesslike reply was, "That's a good song title." As such, he passed it on to his bandmaster, Theodore Metz, who agreed with him, wrote the music as we know it, and inserted it in the show. Metz liked it, although it made no particular hit with audiences, and when, a few years later, he deserted minstrelsy to become a music publisher, he published it with new words by Joe Hayden. W. C. Handy says the tune was an old negro tune, not original with Metz. He may be right. But Theodore Roosevelt's Rough Riders took it to their hearts so noisily that many Cubans thought it was the American national anthem. A French reporter, sending home to his paper the story of the entry of the American troops into Manila, stated that the bands played the two national hymns of the United States, *La Bannière Remplie d'Étoiles* and *Il Fera Chaud dans la Ville Ce Soir!*

By the time the World War was upon them, Americans had learned not to be too sorry for themselves because they were far away from home. They lived up nobly to the creed they warbled,

> "What's the use of worrying,
>   It never was worth while,
>   So pack up your troubles in your old kit-bag,
>   And smile, smile, smile."

They stuttered facetiously through Geoffrey O'Hara's *Katy,*

> "K-k-k-katy, beautiful Katy,
>   You're the only g-g-g-girl that I adore,
>   When the m-moon shines,

Over the c-cow-shed,
I'll be waiting by the k-k-k-kitchen door."

They paid jesting tribute to the girls they left behind them in

"Round her neck she wore a yellow ribbon,
Wore it for her sweetheart who was far, far away."

Will Callahan's *Smiles* sold more than two million copies, thanks to its pleasing blend of mirth and sentiment and its catchy tune. *Goodbye Broadway Hello France, You're in the Army Now, Hinky-Dinky Parley-Voo,* determinedly cheerful, were as far removed from the honest sentimentality of Civil War song literature as the younger generation from its elders.

The most rousing, and certainly the most popular song of the World War, was *Over There,* words and music by George M. Cohan. The French had their *Madelon,* the English their *Tipperary,* and the doughboys cheerfully joined them in singing these, but the darling of their hearts was *Over There.* Its snappy march rhythm, and the back-slapping vitality of its verse, beginning "Johnny get your gun, get your gun, get your gun," acted as an immediate tonic when they were in danger of becoming downhearted. Caruso lent his golden voice to singing it for gatherings all over the United States, as did Schumann-Heink and other great artists. No meeting during the war was complete without it; it electrified the dullest and least patriotic-minded. George M. Cohan put into this song his sense of the dramatic, his talent for writing ingratiating words and music, and his sincere devotion to his country. The title of one of his earliest songs fits him well, for as a song writer, he is America's own *Yankee Doodle Dandy.*

There were other songs of the World War, which are still popular, but perhaps the war is not yet far enough in the past to predict their lasting quality. Irving Berlin's *Oh, How I Hate to Get Up in the Morning,* with its hits at the routine of an army camp, brought down the house at *Yip Yip Yaphank,* the show given by the enlisted men at Camp Upton, Long Island, about 1917. It traveled overseas with the next detachment of departing soldiers, and enlisted in the army of war songs for the duration of the war. *There's a Long, Long Trail a-Winding into the Land of My Dreams,* another exceedingly popular tune of the times, has as explanation of its immartiality the fact that it was written for a college fraternity banquet, not a battlefield. When young Zo Elliott, Yale undergraduate, set down the tune and the words, he had no notion that his few fraternity brothers would grow into an army of soldiers full-throatedly proclaiming the existence of the long, long trail. But so it was, and no dugout deprivations could rob that vision of its appeal.

The songs of the Revolution and of the War of 1812 were somewhat inept and clumsy, those of the Civil War were on the whole sad, although a great improvement over their predecessors. Sentimentality and Spanish-American War were synonymous, while the World War injected jazz and bravado into the national idiom. The great national song of America is yet to be written, and we cannot but hope that, despite the precedent of battle as the great stimulus to national song, it will be a peace product. One expression of the ideals of postwar America, which seems to point the way, is Katharine Lee Bates' poem, *America, the Beautiful.* Miss Bates, poetess, idealist, educator, for many years president of Wellesley College, wrote her poem in 1893, when no war was being waged.

It strikes a note of fine seriousness, a prophetic vision, which has inspired numerous musical settings.

> "O beautiful for spacious skies
> For amber waves of grain,
> For purple mountain majesties
> Above the fruited plain!
> America! America!
> God shed his grace on thee,
> And crown thy good with brotherhood,
> From sea to shining sea."

CHAPTER VI

THE sentimentality of the nineteenth century, which started as a timid pianissimo, worked itself through a powerful crescendo during the Victorian era and Civil War, into a double fortissimo of mawkishness in the mauve decade. Emotional overstatement drips especially from the songs of those years from 1890 to 1900, to form a kind of stalactite which souvenir hunters of today break off and carry away to preserve among their musical curiosities. Curiosities they are, if not objects of art, for they represent a whole outmoded school of thought and feeling. And they have additional significance in that their emotionalism exerted a strong influence on Stephen Foster. Whenever he had lived, Foster would undoubtedly have produced, for his was the spontaneous urge of the born creator. Coming when he did, in the heart of the sentimental era, it was inevitable that whatever he wrote should have been affected by the contemporary output, and that, like other writers of the period, he turned out sentimental ballads in profusion.

There were sentimental ballads long before Foster and his contemporaries, however. A little song collection published in Boston in 1798, entitled *The American Musical Miscellany*, bore, as a preface, the following exposition of the editors' intentions: "Their aim has been to cull, from a great variety of ancient songs, such as have been, at all times, generally approved; and have endeavored to avoid such as would give offense to the delicate ear of chastity itself."

In the first half of the ensuing century, similar collections appeared in numbers. The preference then was for light, handy little volumes which could be stuck into a man's pocket, to be drawn forth nonchalantly, perhaps with the remark, "Unaccustomed as I am to public singing." These songsters contained no music, and the words were printed in atrociously small print on bad paper. The tunes were considered relatively unimportant, something that one knew by heart and did not have to read from a book, except when new songs were included. In *The United States Songster*, "A Choice Collection of about 170 of the Most Popular Songs as Sung by [a list of three dozen names], To Which is Added *The Piʒing Sarpent, Settin' on a Rail,* and a Number of New and Original Songs Written Expressly for this Work," a single line of melody is printed for the *Piʒing Sarpent* and other novelties, in the old-time square-shaped notation. The round notes, in use a little later, did not find their way into this collection. One of many verses it contains worth quoting is from *The Woodpecker*.

> "By the shade of yon Hawthorn, whose red berry dips
> In the gush of the fountain, how sweet to recline,
> And to know that I sighed upon innocent lips,
> Which ne'er had been sighed on by any but mine."

A collection published somewhat later, *The Musical Carcanet,** "A Choice Collection of the Most Admired Popular Songs," prints words and music of all songs, thus going one step farther than the *Songster*, but there is no mention of who composed either words or music. The absence of copyright laws probably accounted in part for this indifference. What did it matter who wrote them, as long as any publisher could make money printing them? Hence, the same songs are found again and again in collections of that time (1832). Some were favorites from overseas; nobody knew who had written them in the first place, and nobody seemed to care.

They rubbed shoulders amicably with English importations in *The Musical Carcanet*. Presently, the *Virginia Warbler* came out boldly in the preface to the collection with the statement: "It was thought best to include a liberal share of the strains of our native bards, who, to say the least, do not fall much below their transatlantic contemporaries." Considering that some of the most sentimental of these songs came direct from those transatlantic contemporaries, the apologetic tone seems quite misplaced. Mother England has never ranked as a specialist in lush expression, but the two sons she sent to America at this time, Henry Russell and Thomas Knight, pulled out the *vox humana* stops in their respective organs, figuratively speaking, to the very limit.

* A Carcanet is a collar of jewels.

Henry Russell was in this country from 1833 to 1841, and was idle for very little of that time. He composed and sang one song after another for the huge audiences who sobbed wholeheartedly over his *Woodman, Spare That Tree.* In his description of his concert tours here, he remarked with repeated amazement upon the lack of musical culture, particularly in the West. In illustration, he related an incident in a small Western town. The rural choir leader came to call on him in his hotel before the evening concert. He asked for a wholesale rate on tickets for his numerous family, and then inquired what the program was to be. Songs by Martin Luther, Rossini, and Russell had been announced. The caller was much disgruntled to learn that both Luther and Rossini were dead, and was not sure that he cared to come, even when Russell offered him free tickets for his entire family. He was not interested in songs by dead composers, and had no hesitation in saying so. In another town, Ole Bull, the great Norwegian violinist, played a concert to which Russell conducted one of the local luminaries. At the end of the program, Russell exclaimed with enthusiasm, "There, isn't he wonderful?" To which his companion drawled, "Waal, he may be all that, but he's a damned long time tuning. Tell me, when is he going to play?"

What Russell did not realize, when he criticized the benighted hinterlands, was that their very benightedness worked in his favor, for the rosy sentimental light he threw into the darkness was welcomed the more eagerly. Here was something which people could understand. His songs were extremely simple. Since his own voice had a range of only about five notes, he never wrote large intervals or sensational high notes, otherwise he could not have sung them himself.

In catering to his own weakness, he catered at the same time to his public's. When the subject of his song touched a matter close to their hearts, as it usually did, they could not have enough of it.

The tune of *Woodman, Spare That Tree* was the result of a country drive with his friend, George Morris, a poet. Morris started to tell the story of a tree he had watched his father plant on the family estate near by when a very little boy, and went off into a flood of reminiscences about his youth. He ended by suggesting that they drive over to see the historic tree. With dramatic timing worthy of the cinema, the two friends arrived at the moment when the farmer-caretaker on the estate was sharpening his ax to cut down that very tree for firewood. A ten-dollar bill averted the tragedy. And many a ten-dollar bill accrued to Russell as a result of the incident, after he had set to music the poem with which Morris commemorated the event. It begins:

> "Woodman, spare that tree,
> Touch not a single bough,
> In youth it sheltered me,
> And I'll protect it now."

His *Life on the Ocean Wave*, written during a stroll beside the water along the Battery in New York, was hardly less popular.

The other Englishman who visited these shores at the same time with Russell was Joseph Philip Knight. At a benefit concert of the Indigent Female Assistance Society, he was moved to sing a little thing of his own, *Rocked in the Cradle of the Deep*, first cousin to Russell's *Life on the Ocean Wave*. Apparently the indigent females and their friends liked his watery cradle song, for it settled down and builded its home in American song collections, although its writer returned to England. He did not sail, however, until he had given other works to his public here, among them his setting of T. H. Bayly's poem, *She Wore a Wreath of Roses,* in which pink roses, orange blossoms, and widow's weeds succeeded each other to appropriate melody on the exercised brow of the heroine.

A wreath of laurel was placed on the brow of John Philip Hewitt by some appreciative contemporaries, who hailed him as the Father of the American Ballad. But the laurel withered, the title was forgotten, and of the three hundred songs written by Hewitt in his eighty-nine years probably the only one which arouses a gleam of recognition in the average person is *All Quiet along the Potomac Tonight.* Hewitt was American by birth, born in New York of an English father. He gave that father plenty to worry about, for he was a rolling stone, and when, at twenty-four, he burst into ballad writing with *The Minstrel's Return from the War,* his family seem not to have regarded it as a sign that he had ceased to roll. His brother James, a music publisher, printed it with such fraternal skepticism as to its merits that he did not even bother to take out a copyright on it. He had the sorry satisfaction of seeing it pirated and sold to the tune of thousands of dollars. After that, James no longer thought of his brother's songs as "only John's," but scrupulously insured the copywriting of every one, including *All Quiet along the Potomac.* This was John's best. The homesick sentry who wiped a furtive tear from his eye at thought of wife and child at home, just at the moment that the enemy sniper decided to use him as a target, had an appeal which could not fail, especially coupled with the simple tune which Hewitt wrote to his own words.

Probably the most popular sentimental song in all our wealth of such literature is *Home, Sweet Home*. But, alas, it is American in its touching lyric only. The tune is a Sicilian air, presumably taken from Bishop's *Melodies of Various Nations*, a collection which appeared long before 1823, the date of the song. John Howard Payne, American actor and playwright, who is responsible for the words, became a wanderer while still in his teens, which presumably qualified him as an expert on nostalgic hankerings. While living in London, he was commissioned to make an opera from the ballet, *Clari, Maid of Milan*. It contained a scene wherein the lowborn heroine, after her elopement with the designing duke, hears a company of players from her native village singing one of its familiar songs, and decides forthwith to return to her sorrowing kinsfolk. Needless to say, the decisive song supplied by Payne was *Home, Sweet Home*. His positive statement,

"Through pleasures and palaces though we may roam,
Be it ever so humble, there's no place like home,"

and the sense he displayed in selecting a tune which everybody could sing, won him more glory than all the rest of the opera and his other works together.

When *Clari* was performed in England, two prima donnas almost came to blows for the privilege of appropriating its best song for their own use. Maria Tree, creator of the title role at Covent Garden, lost out to Kitty Stephens, spoilt darling of the opera. After Kitty, arrayed in virginal white, had successfully advertised the joys of "Home, Sweet Home" at the York and Birmingham festivals in 1823, she simply made the song her own, her public demanded it whenever she appeared on the concert stage, and it won her a rich and noble-born husband besides. Yet, when the opera was produced in America seven months later, there was no special pleading for the song hit, either in the advance publicity, or in the critical notices of the performance afterward. The public simply fell in love with it at first hearing. Their clamorous demand rushed the publishers into printing hundreds of cheap copies for "home and fireside" consumption. Thus, *Home, Sweet Home* became one of the classics of sentimental song in America by popular acclaim. Not even the custom of playing it to mark the end of a ball or party has embittered the sweetness or dimmed the light it shed upon its hearers.

The songs of Russell, Knight, Hewitt, Payne, and a few others, are the well-born aristocrats of the half-century from 1800 to 1850. But what of the vast army of illegitimates, claiming no father, yet surviving because of the wistful appeal of their sentimental words and music? The handy little songbooks and cheap sheet music are full of them. In a collection of so-called "parlor songs," "tender, elegant, and chaste, and designed to produce a sob," there appears one which, in its concluding lines, summarizes a whole philosophy:

> "Then, stranger, if thou fain would find
> This rose no storm can sever,
> Go seek it, stranger, in the mind,
> The ray that beams forever."

Despite this good advice, there were still those who persisted in seeking the eternal ray, not in the mind, but in the heart, as in *Eliza:*

> "The shadows of eve 'gan to steal o'er the plain,
> To Eliza my heart I confessed,

Love sanctioned the moment, she smiled on my pain,
On her lips a soft kiss I impress'd.
I saw her warm cheek like Heav'n's canopy glow
When Aurora empurples the morn;
She loves me! Oh, Heaven, let me never forego
The faith on her lips I have sworn."

From courtship to marriage, love wound its way. Bride and bridegroom came in for many reminders of their duties.

"Remember, 'tis no common tie
That binds her youthful heart;
'Tis one that only truth should weave
And only death can part."

The height of that platitude is equaled only by the touching sentiment of this lament for a lost beloved, entitled *Encompass'd in an Angel's Frame:*

"With yew and ivy round me spread,
My Anna there I'll mourn;
For all my soul—now she is dead—
Concentres in her urn."

When hard-hearted parents interposed between young lovers, the song consequences were dire. One sighed reproachfully:

"The world may think me gay, for my feelings I smother,
Oh, thou hast been the cause of this anguish, my mother."

Some tender maids died for love, others because they were simply too good to live. One by one, *Rosalie the Prairie Flower, Little Nellie, Hazel Dell, Amber Lee,* and *Lily Dale* went to "the land of rest."

It might be an insinuation of old age to ask the reader, *Oh, Don't You Remember Sweet Alice, Ben Bolt?*, yet one of the belles of this period was "sweet Alice, with hair so brown." The lines describing her sad career were indited by Dr. Thomas Dunn English in response to a request from *The New York Mirror* for a roaring sea chantey. Dr. English got as far as the line "Ben Bolt of the Salt Sea Gale," then trailed off into five eight-line stanzas about his youth and sweet Alice. He did remember to tack on four lines about the sea before sending it to the newspaper. It was published, nevertheless, just as he wrote it, on September 2, 1843, and two or three musical settings were made for it at once. Nelson Kneass, a minstrel, has been given credit for writing the melody, but it now seems pretty positive that he merely tailored a German melody to fit a garbled version of the words as he remembered them. Two lines, incidentally, were deleted from the original lest they cause embarrassment when sung in the presence of the fair sex. These are the shocking lines:

> "And the shaded nook by the running brook,
> Where the children used to swim."

Dr. English never was paid for his words, but he achieved plenty of notoriety, especially when Du Maurier immortalized the song in his novel, *Trilby*.

With the passing of the mid-century mark, there was no passing of the sentimental song. On the contrary, the vapors and fainting spells of the Victorian Miss in England traveled to the hardy American lassies, to change the manners of a whole generation. The Civil War produced its quota of sentiment, as well as nationalism, in song. *Weeping Sad and Lonely*, or *When This Cruel War Is Over*, music by Henry Tucker, words by Charles Carroll Sawyer, gave many a raw recruit an itching desire to turn tail and run back home. Sawyer also inquired, to the music of C. F. Thompson, *Who Will Care for Mother Now?* and there were many who undertook to answer his question. One of the replies came from Septimus Winner, who wrote under the name of Alice Hawthorne, saying, *Yes, I Would the Cruel War Were Over.* His songs, *Listen to the Mocking-Bird, What Is Home without a Mother,* and *How Sweet Are the Roses* are advertised in John F. Ellis's *Musical Almanac for 1863* as "well adapted to the taste of the family circle, the sentiment being of the most moral and refined character . . . free from all negro absurdities and lovesick sentiment."

Children were not neglected in song, but were made to suffer acutely, if resignedly. Here is one called *Nobody's Darling:*

> "Out in this cold world alone
> Walking about in the street,
> Asking a penny for bread,
> Begging for something to eat.
> Parentless, friendless and poor,
> Nothing but sorrow I see,
> I am nobody's darling,
> Nobody cares for me."

In the temperance songs which came with a rush after the Civil War, tots in frilly white dresses were used with telling effect to sing persuasively:

> "Father, dear father, come home with me now,
> The clock in the steeple strikes twelve."

The Drunkard's Child wailed:

> "Ragged and hungry, alone in the street,
> Walking about in the cold and the sleet,

Wild is the tempest,
I've nowhere to go,
What will become of me,
Out in the snow?" [8]

The deluge of imaginary woe increased in the decade 1890–1900. Sarcastically dubbed the "naughty nineties" because of the complete propriety of the mores of the day, these were naughty years in the sense that the good people of America skirted as closely as they dared the borderline between vice and virtue, with delicious shivers at their own temerity. They never quite crossed the line, not publicly, at least. But they poured into their sentimental ditties all their righteous indignation on the subject of original sin, and derived a pleasant sense of vicarious wrongdoing from singing about it.

It was Charles K. Harris who, in 1898, had the bright idea for the song, *After the Ball Is Over* which opened the gate to a new flood of sentiment. *After the Ball Is Over* was nothing new. It told the story of an old bachelor confiding to a child upon his knee his disillusionment after the ball, where he had seen the girl of his dreams kissing another. He had not waited to hear her explanation that it was her brother, but had broken the glass of water he was bringing her, her heart, and his own, in one fell swoop. A simple tune, words of one syllable, and a commonplace sob story, constituted Harris' recipe. It was his proudest boast that "I have never in my life written any vulgar stuff. Most of my compositions are sweet, simple love ballads. It's the clean songs that are never forgotten. All the rest pass on." [9]

The songs of the nineties were undeniably clean, for punishment always overtook the villain. The wronged lady who was offered gold as balm for her lost virtue, melodiously protested *Take Back Your Gold*. She asserted that, if she could not have a wedding ring, she was definitely off the gold standard. Her sister, whose "beauty was sold for an old man's gold" suffered through many stanzas, to die broken-hearted in the last one, of *She's Only a Bird in a Gilded Cage*. Some splendidly dramatic songs dealt with a bigamous bridegroom. In the *Moth and the Flame,* the banns were being called when the wronged wife appeared in church to halt the proceedings. The startled husband-to-be-for-the-second-time promptly struck her. Bride Number Two informed him that he was no gentleman, a triumph of understatement, and he retreated, a broken man. In the *Fatal Wedding,* wife Number One went a step further. After forbidding the banns, she held up to the shocked gaze of the wedding guests her pretty babe, who obligingly died on the spot, having completed its destined work in the world. Its wicked father retired to shoot himself in remorseful privacy, there was a double funeral the next day, and the two near-wives lived together ever after.

A song of the same period which sentimentalizes with more dignified restraint on the subject of old age is Henry P. Danks' *Silver Threads among the Gold*. He was a writer of gospel hymns, but did not disdain turning his talents to sentimental song when it paid. *Silver Threads* undoubtedly paid, and never has lost its appeal, despite minstrel-show harmonizations and barbershop quartettes.

We have waded so determinedly into the sticky stream of nineteenth-century sentiment because we were assured that presently we should come upon Stephen Foster, standing ankle-deep there, like St. Christopher, bearing aloft upon his shoulder the infant, American folk song. True, according to strict definition, the infant should not have been christened "folk song." Stephen's songs were composed; they did not spring spontaneously from a group or a nation. But in form, feeling, and popular appeal they could not have been more folksy had a hundred minds, instead of one, concentrated on their creation. So, however loosely the appellation may have been bestowed in the first place, it has stuck.

Stevie, as his family called him, was admirably fitted for his role. He had natural good taste, which enabled him to skim from the boiling caldron of sentiment the impurities of exaggeration and bathos, leaving a clear and comforting draught. He was sensitive by nature, emotional, not over-sophisticated, and moderately cultured. Content with small pleasures, simple in his tastes, he was imbued with the copy-book precepts of the Victorian era in which he lived. When he waved his wand, or we might say his flute, over the pale chiffon of sentimentality in the magician's hat, behold, a strong fabric of red, white, and true-blue American song emerged.

Foster's life was short, and not too merry. He was born July 4, 1826, of a hard-headed business father, and of a mother gentle and well bred, but singularly obtuse in the matter of her son's talent. The rambling white house in Lawrenceville, Pennsylvania, which received the wailing Stephen on the waves of the thunderings of an Independence Day salute was the home likewise of four brothers and three sisters, Charlotte, Ann Eliza, Henry, William, Henrietta, Dunning, and Morrison. A comfortable home it was, its occupants bound together by ties of affection which marriage, distance, and differing ideas never sundered. Steve was undoubtedly the Bohemian square peg in their round bourgeois hole. In view of his later development, it is not difficult to credit the stories of his leap through the schoolroom door with a wild war whoop on his first day in the halls of learning, nor his later mischievous infractions of school discipline, though he was always a good student.

He evinced his talent for music quite by accident. When he was a little boy of seven, he went shopping one day with his mother, and while she was busy about her purchases, picked up a flute from the counter and began idly to blow upon it. Presently he found himself playing a tune, to the edification of the crowd which rapidly gathered to hear the infant prodigy. As a result, he was permitted to play the flute, and later the piano, becoming reasonably proficient at both, and a very agreeable singer as well. His mother, to judge from some of her published letters, deplored his absorption in music, and welcomed the few occasional symptoms of his becoming more like a solid citizen. Stephen adored her so wholeheartedly that his love of music must have been strong indeed to outweigh his fear of displeasing her.

His first known attempt to compose was *The Tioga Waltz* for four flutes, written for his college commencement. He did not repeat that experiment, but tried a song for his next effort, and at sixteen produced *Open Thy Lattice, Love*. A credit to any ability, not alone that of a sixteen-year-old, *Open Thy Lattice, Love* has a page in every reputable collection of songs that has been published since its appearance. It was Stephen's springboard to song writing.

A group of young men used to meet semiweekly to sing together in harmony. Stephen was of their number. What more natural than that he should try his budding talent on his friends? For their gatherings, he wrote two of his best, *The Louisiana Belle* and *Old Uncle Ned*. Both are colored songs with a new slant. *Old Uncle Ned,* in particular, was arresting in its depiction of an aged darky, pathetically lovable, not devoid of humor, yet not a caricature. *Uncle Ned* sang his way out of the little group and into the big public in a very short time. The minstrels took him up, and introduced him to their society, where he was as well liked as *Jim Crow* and his humorous antics had been. For a young man who had never been South, who knew the negro only by hearsay and by acquaintance with the few local characters in his town, Stephen caught their spirit extraordinarily well.

It must have been a relief to his parents when he went, in 1846, to be bookkeeper for his brother Dunning in Cincinnati. That was really the proper thing for a Foster to do. But he wrote

"Oh, Susannah, don't you cry for me,
I'm just from Alabama, with a banjo on my knee,"

in an interval between totting up rows of figures. Everybody knows *Oh, Susannah.* But not everybody knows that Stephen generously presented it, along with *Old Uncle Ned,* to a family friend, a Mr. Peters, who published them both, cleaned up ten thousand dollars, and established his publishing firm on a solvent basis while Stephen gained nothing but glory.

When he returned to his father's house at the age of twenty-three, having found bookkeeping not to his taste, he took a room at the top of the house, fitted it up as a study, and withdrew to it for many hours daily to study French, play the flute, and write. His notebooks, in which he jotted down song ideas as they came to him, show painstaking attention to details of words and music. He labored diligently to achieve the apparent spontaneity and simplicity of his output. *Nelly Was a Lady,* another colored song with a lovely melody, *My Brudder Gum, Dulcy Jones,* and *Nelly Bly* duly appeared. The year of his marriage to Jane Mac-Dowell, 1850, was a fruitful year for him. He poured his happiness into song. The minstrel shows were made the gainers by *Camptown Races,* originally issued as *Gwine to Run All Night.* Its insistent rhythm and nonsensical refrain of doo-dah-doo point the way to ragtime. *Way Down in Cairo, Oh, Lemuel, Go Down to de Cotton Field,* and *Angelina Baker* were others which he composed for his minstrel friends, thus keeping his domestic pot at a comfortable boiling point. By now, he had learned that publishers paid royalties. He tried his hand, too, at ballads of the type of *Open Thy Lattice, Love.* Experiments in sentiment of that year of wedded bliss are *Ah, May the Red Rose Live Alway, Lily Ray,* and *Dolly Day.*

He had moved to New York after his marriage. Within a year, however, he became too homesick to remain. Did he have an actual mother complex? It appears highly probable. It must have been a well-nigh irresistible pull that drove him to uproot his little family avowedly in order to be near his mother. His wife was none too pleased with the move, one of the first rifts in their wedded happiness. But just as Stephen's talent had bloomed during his first year with his wife, it now bloomed afresh in his mother's dear vicinity. *Swanee River,* or *Old Folks at Home,* was written after he had renewed his acquaintance with his own home surroundings.

On the subject of *Swanee River,* his brother Morrison related that Stephen appeared breathless in his office one morning, demanding, "What river do you know of with two syllables to its name? I *must* have a two-syllable river." "Pedee," suggested Morrison helpfully. "Won't do." "Yazoo?" "Worse still." "Here's an atlas. Let's see what we can find." Morrison's questing finger fell upon Suwannee, a tiny stream in Florida. It had three syllables, but they could be telescoped, and Stephen liked the sound. "That's it!" he shouted, hastily scribbled the name in the blank space of the first line staring from his notebook as "Way down upon the   river," and rushed out of the office with as little ceremony as he had rushed in.

A hardly less popular song, *My Old Kentucky Home,* Stephen was said to have written while on a holiday visit to a favorite uncle in Bardstown, Kentucky. The story has it that he jotted it down on a scrap of paper while he and his sister were sunning themselves on the front lawn, and that she took it from his hand and sang it through. John Tasker Howard, after sifting masses of evidence, decided that *My Old Kentucky Home* was the revised version of another Foster song, *Goodnight, Poor Uncle Tom, Goodnight,* and that it never saw the Rowan mansion in Kentucky at all. It was one of a group—*Hard Times Come Again No More, Old Black Joe,* and *Massa's in de Cold, Cold Ground*—in which Foster, with loving tolerance, presented the negro as an object, not of ridicule, but affection. He himself had learned so to regard them when, as a small boy, he was smuggled into colored prayer meetings by the mulatto "bound maid" who worked for his mother.

Stephen's best-known works are his negro songs. Yet the largest proportion of the hundred and seventy songs he brought forth in his twenty productive years are sentimental ballads which he himself preferred. Some are good, many are weak; all have the savor of the crinolines and hoop skirts of his day. They seem to miss the hearty universality of his negro songs. Still, *Old Dog Tray* (1853), with the nostalgic yearning for past happiness which was Stephen's obsession, is one of his most beloved songs. *Come Where My Love Lies Dreaming,* which he whistled absent-mindedly after a family dinner at his brother's (would that all family dinners provoked such melodies), became a vocal quartette. Someone defined a quartette as "a tenor who thinks he can sing, and three others." Stephen fed such groups royally, on what one critic calls "pale, melodiously weeping heart songs of strict propriety." *Willie, We Have Missed You* is exceptional in possessing a masculine hero, but, to compensate, Foster sings of a whole harem of ladies—*My Alice Fair, Nell and I, Katy Bell, Ellen Bayne, Gentle Annie, Jeanie with the Light-Brown Hair, Little Belle Blair, Jennie Dow.* How did he find names for them all? If these are not his most distinguished works, they at least make healthy use of the unhealthy sentimentality running riot about him.

After the death of his mother, in 1855, his output decreased. In 1860, he again drifted to New York. He had written a temperance song, which might have been prophetic.

> "Comrades, fill no glass for me,
> To drown my soul in liquid flame,
> For if I drank, the toast would be
> To blighted fortune, health and fame."

He was bitterly lonely in New York. By this time, his wife and little girl were living apart from him. He went about very little, made no friends. His songs, *Farewell, My Mother Dear, Farewell, Sweet Mother, A Dream of My Mother and*

Home, Leave Me with My Mother, all four of this New York period, are the expression of his grief and loneliness. He took to drinking more and more steadily, tortured by self-disgust after each lapse, but unable to resist. Always generous and easygoing, he had spent his royalties as fast as they came in. Finally, he reached the point where he scribbled songs on scraps of paper, sold them outright for a few dollars, and hastened to the public house to drink up the proceeds. Such an existence could not long endure. Alcohol had afforded a temporary escape. In 1864, death effected the final release. America's Troubadour, as John Tasker Howard has named him, died alone in the charity ward of Bellevue Hospital. In his wallet was no money, but a scrap of paper, with the scribbled words, "Dear friends and gentle hearts." The first line of a song? A message to absent friends? Or a reverie on bygone days?

If Stephen Foster was great—and he is certainly one of the great figures in American music—it is because he was born so. He did not slave at his craft, nor pore over the works of other masters, in order to push the development of his own gift to its utmost. One of his finest songs was written at sixteen. Those he wrote at thirty-six are no more mature. His productive life shows no Beethovenesque three periods— there is but one. Into that one, however, he crowded the America of his day. His sentimental ballads and Ethiopian melodies have become our folk song. Even his less significant temperance and war songs are not forgotten. Simple to the point of naïveté, his songs at their best have a poignancy which carries them straight to the heart, and there keeps them pulsatingly alive. The melodies are fresh, wide of range, tremendously appealing. The words are made to fit the music; their healthy sentiment blows like a current of fresh air upon the heavily scented jasmine-and-honeysuckle liltings of his day. He is associated with the banjo, but his is rather the voice of the flute—plaintive, clear, sensitive, loving and tender—soaring above the other instruments because of these qualities of its sound, not because of its ability to deafen or defy.

CHAPTER VII

AMERICAN grand opera may be regarded as a blushing bride, shy, unaware, poised on the brink of life. A composite bridegroom appears in the person of imported opera—English, Russian, Italian, German, and French. His predatory eye lights up at sight of the maid who is heiress to all the wealth of a great country, for he is the fortune-hunting foreigner familiar to millionaire fathers of daughters. She is intrigued by his warm exotic quality, *savoir-faire,* and man-of-the-world ease. The strange tongue in which he woos her falls sweetly on her ear. His tights and armor contrast favorably with the homespun of her native swains. She falls in love, bestows her hand, her wealth, and her talents upon him.

Presently she discovers, like many another bride, that her

husband is of a decidedly dominating nature. In his insistence upon possessing her, he alienates her from her family, her friends, even her mother tongue. At first, she is too enamored to resist, and gives herself up to him completely. She learns to speak his polyglot languages, and masters his musical idiom, making little or no effort to preserve her own. But when the first flush of passion is past and she awakens to a realization of her plight, she starts to struggle to be herself, American opera, with her own spoken and musical language. It is difficult, for she really loves him, and does not wish to divorce him. She is young, unsure of herself, possessed of few traditions. He is, in comparison, a Methuselah, virile and energetic despite the four centuries behind him. Their union spells struggle. The bride's awakening occurs with the production of William Fry's *Leonora* in 1845; as she grows increasingly sure of herself, her husband assumes less and less importance.

Opera-in-America emigrated from the mother country to the American colonies when they had been in existence barely a hundred years. It was not grand opera as we know it today, but ballad-opera, the form most popular in England at the time. Historians point with pride to the advertisements, which have been preserved, of *Flora,* or *Hob-in-the-Well,* produced in Charleston in 1735. This is the first opera performance to be recorded, though others may have preceded it. It was a mixture of song and recitation, the songs being already-known popular ballads sung either as originally written or with new words. The ballad-operas were plentifully besprinkled with spoken dialogue, and most closely resembled the "stunts" put on today at family parties and club gatherings, with their parodies of popular songs and personal, somewhat rowdy repartee.

Once here, ballad-opera settled down for a stay of many years. Even after the Revolutionary War cast its shadow on articles marked "Made in England," this particular product throve. New York, Philadelphia, and most of the Southern colonies found ballad-opera blessed both to give and to receive. Boston and the New England colonies, always the last to pull up the green blinds and admit the sunshine of life, got along for years without such entertainment. Even in the less rigid communities, the fear of compromising with the devil nagged persistently, as witness a letter in *The Pennsylvania Gazette* of November 10, 1773, stating, "It is a matter of real sorrow and distress to many sober inhabitants of different denominations to hear of the return of those strolling comedians, who are traveling through America, propagating vice and immorality. And it is much to the disreputation of this city that more encouragement is given here than in any other place on the continent." Even in easygoing, pleasure-loving Charleston, the theater was deprecated in some quarters as "the Devil's Synagogue." However, perhaps because of the rugged endurance of original sin in original settlers, ballad-operas were drawing cards, especially after Gay's *The Beggars' Opera*, with its bright, popular tunes and somewhat coarse comedy, had come to the stage of the Nassau Street Theatre in New York in 1750. That jolly entertainment enjoyed repeated revivals there and elsewhere right down to the present day, and set the ballad-opera mode for years to come. When Lewis Hallam, who had transported his troupe from London to Williamsburg, Virginia, a few years previously, heard that New York had a usable theater building in Nassau Street, he decided to pick up his company and move it to that metropolis. To his disappointment, the Nassau Street Theatre did not come up to his high standards, although the dirt floor which originally gave the pit seats their name, "par terre," the flickering wax candles set in a barrel hoop by way of illumination, the uncomfortable backless wooden benches, were all carry-overs from the English theater. So he set an example followed, to their sorrow, by many subsequent managers, and put up his own theater, making New York the headquarters from which he sallied to other cities, presenting ballad-operas along with "consorts and musickall entertainments." As head of the company, he drew the munificent salary of sixteen dollars a week, while his leading lady received nine. When the schedule became heavy, and receipts larger, he was raised to twenty-five and she to sixteen. Only a hundred and fifty years later, Enrico Caruso "obliged" the management of the Metropolitan by singing six performances in seven days when another tenor was ill. For this concession, he received twenty-five hundred dollars per performance, and extra emolument in the shape of a diamond-studded wrist watch from the management! It is a far cry to this from the ballad-opera, and the simple souls who unquestioningly sang their nine performances weekly, doubling besides as wardrobe women, scene painters, carpenters, and property men.

The first operas to depart from the English ballad type were found in New Orleans, and were sung in French. A bit of a town of five thousand inhabitants, the New Orleans of early days was so steeped in French thought that it was known as the Little Paris of the New World. A corner of the luxurious court of Louis XIV was broken off and exported, to form, in a comparative desert, an oasis of culture whose inhabitants drank thirstily from its wells of French language, literature and music. The very cobblestones in the streets were brought from Paris, that the émigrés might pick their high-heeled way the more daintily through their city. At a very early date, New Orleans had its own theater, Le Spectacle de la Rue de St. Pierre, described as "a long low wooden structure, built of cypress and alarmingly exposed to the danger of fire." Hither, in 1791, came a company of French refugees, fleeing from revolution in San Domingo, who presented "comedies, dramas, and operas of the second class." When the theater was closed for a while for repairs, its reopening with a row of boxes, a pit, and a gallery was a great event. There were no lights other than flickering oil lamps. No programs were printed, the manager bowing before the curtain as he announced the names of the performers and their roles. But the actors and singers had their hearts in their work, and the operas they sang were by Grétry, Monsigny, and Dalayrac, French to the marrow. They became as familiar to the citoyens and ci-toyennes of New Orleans and their children as, later, *Yankee Doodle*. A second house, the Théâtre de St. Philip, presently accommodated overflow audiences. The first ballet to be given in New Orleans was danced here; and here, some years later, Adelina Patti made her debut in Meyerbeer's *Dinorah*, or *Le Pardon de Ploërmel*. So strong a hold did opera have upon the people of New Orleans that they could not bear the thought of missing a single performance. In proof whereof, when they erected the Théâtre d'Orleans in 1817, a vastly more pretentious structure, they provided special seats behind a grille in order that those in mourning, whom convention prohibited from being seen in a place of public amusement, but whom grief had not wholly prostrated, might not be deprived of operatic alleviation of their woe.

This theater was burned down and rebuilt; it had to close for months during the yellow-fever epidemic of 1821; a whole company which was being transported from France to appear there was shipwrecked and lost. A volume could be written about the tribulations of the impresarios of those days. But still New Orleans had its opera. The forties were the golden age, when cotton was king, and chicken à la Creole simmered in every pot. Leaders of society rallied to each performance, making of it a social as well as musical event. Not to be seen there in best bib and tucker was a mark of social ostracism. Hoop skirts and jewels, ribbons and satins and flowers and furbelows were an indispensable adjunct to the enjoyment of the music. People came at six and left at twelve to attend Mass in the Cathedral. The beaux of the day actually fought duels on behalf of their favorite prima donnas. Here Jenny Lind, the Swedish Nightingale, sang in *L'Élisir d'amour,* to an audience throwing bouquets, stamping, and yelling their applause. Here were sung *La Juive, Guillaume Tell, Lucia di Lammermoor,* and others.

All the larger cities have a chapter devoted to the excellent performances of the companies which came a-visiting from New Orleans in those years before the Civil War. The entire repertoire of French opera effected a peaceful penetration into every city of any importance, via this company.[10] After the Civil War, there was a difference in the social tinsel in which the opera of New Orleans was wrapped, but the musical standards remained high as ever, and the visiting companies continued to visit. In December, 1919, catastrophe descended upon it. After a glorious performance of *Carmen,* the theater took fire, and opera in New Orleans died in the conflagration which destroyed its opera house. The loss was irreparable. A whole tradition perished in the flames. But the love and knowledge of French opera lived on, not only there, but in half a dozen other cities. If audiences today relish Charpentier's *Louise,* Dukas' *Ariane et Barbe Bleue,* Debussy's *Pelléas,* it is because of the people of New Orleans, who established the first permanent opera company in America and educated a whole nation to the enjoyment of French opera.

Meanwhile, other cities were not wholly blank on the operatic side. Philadelphia suffered sporadic attacks of ballad-opera, beginning with the Hallams and their company struggling bravely to amuse. They put on *Theodosius,* or *The Feast of Love,* at the old Southwark Theatre in 1759, and enjoyed enough of a success to follow it with *The Beggars' Opera,* whose bright music by Gay and words by Dr. Pepusch were then already known to New York. The woes of Pretty Polly proved as entertaining in one place as in another. Despite the drawback of a law in the Quaker City against "theatrical performances and other vain diversions" during the years when every man was expected to concentrate on the struggle to free his country from English rule, the Hallams managed to carry on. They undoubtedly received theatrical aid and comfort from the enemy, for the British army officers stationed both in Philadelphia and New York liked ballad-opera well enough to put on their own, and were only too happy to supplement their amateur efforts with the professional offerings of the Hallams. Much later, the Woods and Seguins, other English troupes, came over to reap some of the crop of popularity sown by the crude but enthusiastic performances of early days.

When the new Chestnut Street Theatre was opened, after

the War of Independence, the opera business took a distinct turn for the better. Alexander Reinagle, an Austrian musician indefatigable in the wooing of the muse, played the harpsichord and took charge of the musical direction, while Thomas Wignell, English actor and singer, shared the labors of production. Dr. Arne, William Storace, Henry Bishop, Dr. Arnold, English composers all, were responsible for the important offerings there, which were so very, very English that they influenced Reinagle and others, imposing their accent on such native operatic vernacular as there was.[11] The records of the time have frequent and flattering mention of Mrs. Oldmixon, who sang all the leads, and was a favorite on the concert stage also. With her husband, Sir John, who played the violin, she seems to have graciously dominated the vocal scene in her city from her first appearance there as Clorinda in *Robin Hood* in 1794 until her death, many years later.

The city of Philadelphia was then, as now, most hospitably inclined, and a delightful place to visit. Traveling companies from other cities appear to have found it so, for they faithfully included it in their itineraries. The rivalry between it and its neighbor, New York, for the honor of first performances, a rivalry which still persists, did not rob Philadelphia, always music-minded, of any of her gusto when, presently, foreign companies came to grace the Chestnut Street Theatre with their presence. There is every indication that the Philadelphia public had the musical taste to pronounce opera "grand" in the days when it was a rare treat, like champagne—expensive, reserved for state occasions and for the social elect, sparingly served, but, like champagne, sparkling, stimulating, and intoxicating.

In Chicago, the gateway to the West, opera made a late

start, but once under way progressed by leaps and bounds. Its first home was in the New Theatre, a wooden building of modest proportions erected in 1847 with Mr. J. B. Rice as its patron. After all the visiting companies had their turn, Chicago for a number of years maintained its own, with a foreign repertoire closely parallel to the Metropolitan's, and with singers largely recruited from there. Under the successive managements of Andreas Dippel and Campanini, followed by Mary Garden and later by Herbert Witherspoon, notable performances were given. Strauss' *Salome,* Massenet's *Le Jongleur,* Février's *Monna Vanna* had their American premières there. A by-product of the Chicago Opera Company was the outdoor opera given in Ravinia during the summer months, a unique experiment. However, the crash of 1929 robbed the Ravinia Company as well as the Chicago, of the financial underpinning essential to survival, and both were temporarily discontinued. Not, however, before a whole generation of those who dwelt in Chicago and points west had learned to open their mouths, shut their eyes, and smack their lips when a spoon laden with imported nectar and ambrosia was held before them.

Long before the Metropolitan became the autocrat of opera in the United States, New York seemed to afford a firmament in which opera stars, even of small magnitude, twinkled with the greatest amount of satisfaction. The post-Revolutionary efforts of Reinagle and Wignell in Philadelphia were paralleled at the same time in New York by those of James Hewitt, George Gilfert, and John Hodgkinson, who followed the prevailing style and presented one ballad-opera after another. James Hewitt, father of the ballad writer, John, who gave us *All Quiet Along the Potomac Tonight,* was a well-trained

English musician who could compose new music or arrange old with equal nonchalance. Gilfert was an organist and music teacher who turned to the stage, while Hodgkinson was an actor-manager. They had things all their own way, and had for a while, besides, the assistance of Victor Pelissier and Benjamin Carr, both of whom later removed to Philadelphia. All these men were Europe-trained in music, and the ballad-operas they put on, simple and unaffected as they were, paved the way for the brilliant efforts to come. New York was prepared by them for the part she was to play.

But the day that Manuel Garcia came to New York with his troupe, to throw a good handful of Italian garlic and dried red pepper into the simple, unseasoned English operatic cookery in vogue, marks a true dramatic climax in the life of imported opera in this country. Americans took to his garlic, for all its pungent atmospheric assertiveness. It was different from their accustomed mild fare, brought tears to their eyes, and a burning sensation to their throats, and made their other food appear tasteless and unpalatable. But they liked it. Italian opera was "different," new, exciting, tantalizing, its piquancy heightened by the foreign language, sophistication, and otherworldly fashion of those who came to present it here. The people of New York would have liked to have a theater worthy to house their exotic guests, for the Park Theatre, to which the visitors repaired, was a cheerless retreat for so glittering an assemblage.

In an article in *The Century Magazine*, March, 1882, Richard Grant White draws upon his recollections of "the good old days" when Italian opera first appeared in New York, with the following description of the boards trod by Garcia and his company. "Across them [the boxes] were stretched benches consisting of a mere board covered with a faded red moreen, a narrower board, shoulder high, being stretched behind to serve for a back. But one seat on each of the three or four benches was without even this luxury, in order that the seat itself might be raised upon its hinges for people to pass in. These sybaritic enclosures were kept under lock and key by a fee-expecting creature, who was always half drunk except when he was wholly drunk. The pit was . . . in the Park Theatre, hardly superior to that in which the Jacquerie of old stood upon the bare ground (*par terre*). The floor was dirty and broken into holes; the seats were bare, backless benches. Women were never seen in the pit; and although the excellence of the position . . . and the cheapness of admission took gentlemen there, few went there who could afford to study comfort and luxury in their amusements. The place was pervaded with evil smells, and not uncommonly, in the midst of a performance, rats ran out of the holes in the floor and across into the orchestra. This delectable place was approached by a long underground passage, with bare whitewashed walls, dimly lighted, except at a sort of booth, at which vile fluids and viler solids were sold. As to the house itself, it was the dingy abode of dreariness."

Garcia was about fifty years old when he decided to bring his wife, his son Manuel, his daughter Maria, and an assorted company to present Italian opera in these surroundings. Himself a distinguished singer, he had worn his voice so hard on his European tours that all the nap was gone from its velvet. Consequently, his reputation abroad was on the wane, but he trusted that the unsophisticated public here would overlook his vocal lacks in view of the novelty of his offering. His hopes were realized beyond his fondest dreams.

When, on November 29, 1825, he opened his season, it was to a Park Theatre bulging with important personages. His first offering was Rossini's *Il Barbiere di Seviglia*, in which he himself sang the role of the sportive barber. In the four weeks which elapsed between his arrival and the performance, Garcia had done three men's work. He had had to rehearse twenty-four local orchestra men, not the most gifted, in the difficult score; to drill the chorus of local English-speaking singers in Italian words and music; to solve the thousand problems of his company of homesick Italians in a strange cold country. How he did it all is his secret. There are many stories to attest his caliber.

At a performance of *Don Giovanni*, he is said to have rushed madly down to the footlights, with drawn sword, as the first act came to a close. Singers and orchestra were shouting and blaring with blatant disregard of one another's proceedings. At the point of his property sword, Garcia demanded a repetition of the finale. He got it, with improvements, and a round of applause to boot. He knew how to get his own way, in his own way. Someone passing his house in Paris, hearing sounds of violent weeping, decided to investigate. He inquired of the servant at the door, "Is anything wrong?" "Oh, no," was the reassuring reply. "Nothing at all. That is only Mr. Garcia giving a singing lesson."

Whether or not his singers learned their roles in *Il Barbiere* with sobs and tears, that opera reduced the audience to groveling admiration. Rossini's *Tancredi* and *Otello*, and Mozart's *Don Giovanni*, later added to the repertoire, were as wholeheartedly acclaimed. When Garcia put on *Otello*, his daughter Maria was to sing Desdemona. The role was new to her; she had to learn it in a few weeks, and she told him she feared she might not have it ready in time. In his mild way, he threatened to kill her if she failed to be letter-perfect on opening night. At the first performance, his menacing advance upon her when, as Otello, he played the jealousy scene with her, was so realistic that, terrified, she whispered to him in Spanish, "For God's sake, Father, don't kill me!" It would have been shortsighted on his part if he had, for he knew that no small share of the applause was for Maria. Her voice has become almost a legend. It was fresh, clear, admirably trained, and eighteen years old. Its possessor was not only beautiful, but had an indescribable allure which won all hearts. New York might not have been quite so receptive to its Italian opera without the sugar-coating of Maria. When the Garcia company went to Mexico, Maria was left behind. Papa Garcia had arranged a marriage with the elderly M. de Malibran, who was supposed to bestow wealth, a title, and security upon her, instead of which it was she who had to support him. She learned English, and took part in the opening performance of opera in English at the New York Theatre in 1826. A year or two later, having divorced her unsuitable spouse, she sailed back to Europe without him, there to duplicate her triumphs. The opera *Maria Malibran* by Robert Simon and Robert Russell Bennett, produced at the Juilliard School in 1935, pleasantly dramatized her life.

At this writing, when the itinerant organ grinder and Italian arias have developed distinct associations of commonplaceness, it is difficult to envisage how new and different the tunes, the language, the whole Italian set-up appeared then. Newspapers vied with one another in pointing out its beauties, people in boasting of their discrimination in appreciating them. An Italian discovered America in 1492.

America returned the compliment, and discovered Italian opera, in 1825.

Now that the ball had been set rolling, Lorenzo da Ponte, a figure second in picturesqueness only to Garcia, gave it another push. For some time previous to the advent of Garcia, Da Ponte had been a monomaniac on the subject of opera in Italian. He knew whereof he raved, for he had written the Italian librettos to Mozart's *Figaro* and *Don Giovanni*, and had put in a long and adventurous period knocking about Europe in one musical capacity or another. He settled in New York in 1805—as much as Da Ponte could settle. He was the Garcia troupe's Man Friday during their entire sojourn in New York, and as soon as they were gone began to make propaganda for a permanent company to sing Italian opera.

He persuaded the French tenor, Montresor, to gamble with him on one season at the Richmond Hill Theatre. And, having lost every dollar at the end of an artistically successful year, he hypnotized a group of capitalists into building the Italian Opera House. This really looked like the white and gold answer to Da Ponte's prayer. No expense was spared to deck the house, with hand-painted panels on the walls, crimson silk hangings in the first boxes New York had seen, velvet-cushioned seats instead of benches. On the opening night at least (November 18, 1833), when Rossini's *La Cenerentola* was given, the house was crowded to the doors, and the applause was prolonged and sincere. As the season went on, since Italian opera was considered to be any sung in that language, Da Ponte's company gave Mozart's *Don Giovanni* and *Figaro*. They took their wares to Philadelphia, and were made welcome there, like Garcia and Montresor before them.

However, even Da Ponte could not pay his bills with applause, and money was not forthcoming. He had a formidable rival in the company giving opera in English at the old Park Theatre, which despite its discomforts, was accessible and familiar. *The American Musical Journal* of October 1, 1834, in commenting on the reason for Da Ponte's two fiascos, had this to say: "We regard the Opera in a higher light than a mere place for amusement. . . . It should be an establishment in which will be exhibited the perfection of vocal and instrumental performance, and in which our amateurs can assemble, and from living examples learn the refinements of style, and hear what, in the estimation of the best judges, is the best music."

Thirteen years after Da Ponte's failure, which he did not long survive, being eighty-three years old at the time, there came a group described by Max Maretzek as the greatest ever assembled. When Señor Francesco Marty y Tollens, a Havana millionaire who had amassed an enormous fortune, sent his opera company to New York in 1847, his object was not to educate the New Yorkers, but to get his stars out of Havana during the yellow-fever season. Apparently, he made so much money in the winter that he considered the summer a good season to lose some of it. He engaged singers and orchestra regardless of expense. Bottesini, one of the greatest of contrabassists, and Arditi, distinguished Italian conductor and composer, shared the musical direction of the company. They presented Verdi's operas in New York, giving *Ernani* and *I due foscari,* also Bellini's *Norma* and *La Sonnambula,* and Rossini's *Mose in Egitto.* They returned for the next three years, visited Philadelphia, New Orleans, Chicago, and other cities, and revived and enhanced the interest aroused by earlier experiments, while they paved the way for later ones.

When the first of the true foreign impresarios, Max Maretzek, came to New York from London in 1848, he remarked that "the failure of Italian opera has flourished for twenty-five years." He attended a rehearsal at the Astor Place Opera House, which he found being conducted in one large room, where carpenters were hammering, wardrobe women sewing, scene painters daubing, singers and orchestra going through their parts, the whole a pandemonium. Even at the performance of the *Barber* for which they were rehearsing, the orchestra leader played first violin throughout with no attempt to beat time, and no regard for either singers or orchestra. In his book of memoirs, Maretzek painted a humorous but disillusioned picture of his difficulties at the Astor Place Opera House, when he changed this haphazard order of things and tried to establish the rehearsals and performances on the dignified footing of those abroad.

Even when he had finally brought order from chaos, and was giving excellent performances, there was Marty's Havana troupe competing with him, selling tickets at half the usual price for performances of twice the usual merit. Another competitor was Fred Niblo, who attracted audiences to his Gardens near by with ices and sherry cobblers and strolls in the shaded walks between the acts of the Italian opera presented there by a visiting company. In attempting to freeze out this rival, Maretzek ruined himself. He put on a novelty, Meyerbeer's *Robert le Diable,* with the most expensive singers and production. The audiences crowded his performances and developed a liking for Meyerbeer, sent the Niblo Gardens to Coventry and the visiting company, too. But Maretzek's gesture proved a boomerang, for he went bankrupt, and suffered the ignominy of seeing the Astor Place Opera House taken over by Niblo, who, as a humiliating flourish, replaced the opera company with Donetti's Troupe of Performing Dogs and Monkeys.

When the new Academy of Music was opened in New York, October 2, 1854, its avowed purpose was to house productions of Italian opera in the grand manner. It is pleasant to picture the hoop-skirted ladies and long-coated gentlemen who fought their way, always genteelly, of course, into the first-night performance of Bellini's *Norma* there. Mario, the great Italian tenor, and his wife, Giulia Grisi, headed the troupe. That the company, like its predecessors, failed to pay expenses as time went on, is no slur on its artistry. Nor can it be held against the managers who succeeded one another that the ball given there for the Prince of Wales on his visit to this country in 1860 was much more enthusiastically patronized than their operatic offerings. Ole Bull, Norwegian violinist who had settled in America and who passionately labored for better music in his adopted country, was one of the most distinguished managers to direct the Academy for a year or so. He offered a prize of a thousand dollars for an opera on an American subject, by an American composer, thus breaking away from the original Italian theme on which he was supposed to produce variations. But even that attempt to secure a following by an appeal to patriotism was fruitless. His tenure expired before any prize-winning work was offered, and the placard, "Transients Accommodated," was hung on the Academy of Music, implicitly, if not literally.

Every few months now witnessed a different troupe there,

with Italians in the ascendant. *Tannhäuser,* the first Wagner opera to be heard in America, was given there by a German company. Weber's *Der Freischütz,* and Beethoven's *Fidelio* had been given in English, but opera in German was a comparative novelty. It did not revolutionize public taste; people continued to prefer French and Italian, if anything. A French company presently brought the opera bouffe of Offenbach and others. New Orleans liked Offenbach and his light operas, *La Vie parisienne, La belle Hélène,* and *La grande duchesse,* and New York was mildly receptive. But in 1878, with the advent of Henry Mapleson, who came from London to manage the Academy of Music, grand opera as we know it today began to take form. The star system was introduced. Clever showman that he was, Mapleson assembled a company of bright lights, with Adelina Patti as twinkler-in-chief. He seems to have had a way with him in handling refractory stars and creditors. They were always threatening proceedings, but seldom executed their threats. He himself related with glee how, at the end of the season, when he owed Patti six thousand dollars, he persuaded her to sing at a benefit to raise the money to pay herself! Deficit or no deficit, he took his company on tour, and somehow they avoided being stranded, always by a hairsbreadth, and even created the illusion that they were engaged in a prosperous undertaking. And so, thanks to Mapleson, Chicago and Boston, Cincinnati and St. Louis, Philadelphia, Washington, and other big cities heard fine presentations of Italian opera.

Meanwhile, the Metropolitan Opera Company had been formed in New York. A group of wealthy enthusiasts put up a splendid opera house, and when it was finished (1883) invited Henry E. Abbey of England to be their impresario. It was Abbey *vs.* Mapleson from the very first moment. The Metropolitan opened with a brilliant performance of Gounod's *Faust,* presenting Christine Nilssen, Swedish prima donna, as Marguerite. Mapleson countered with an equally brilliant performance of *La Sonnambula,* featuring Etelka Gerster. Stars were pitted against stars, and people were heard to ask, "Who is singing tonight?" not, "What is being sung?" With a nucleus of Patti and Gerster against Nilssen and Sembrich, both managers started bidding for European artists. They played a game of London Bridge, each attempting, by offering greater inducements than the other, to persuade the strongest artists to line up behind him for the final tug of war. The outcome, as might have been expected, was the deadlock of financial ruin for both. Abbey went back to England, and Mapleson retired temporarily.

It appeared a favorable moment to add to the existing list of foreign operas produced at the Metropolitan a solid German element, and Leopold Damrosch undertook the task. An occasional guttural had been uttered by visiting companies, and there had been a number of performances in translation. But this was the first serious attempt to make German opera a part of the standard repertoire. It proved so serious for Damrosch, who worked zealously, training his singers in their new roles, and drilling the orchestra in the difficult scores of *Tannhäuser* and *Fidelio,* that he fell ill, and actually died of pneumonia contracted at a prolonged rehearsal. His son Walter, then aged nineteen, carried on for a while. Later, Anton Seidl, a friend of Wagner's and probably his most intelligent interpreter, took the baton, and with it pointed the way to a whole new realm of unexplored delights in German opera. In fact, for almost a decade after

1884, when Damrosch made the initial attempt, there was a growing group of enthusiasts with the motto *"Aut Wagner aut nullus"* ("Either Wagner or nothing"), yet public sentiment eventually swung back to Italian as first choice. Maurice Grau, who was then impresario, sensed the change. He noted that the limpid strains of *Il Trovatore* and *Rigoletto* were attended by more satisfactory box-office receipts than *Tannhäuser, Der Ring,* or even *Die Meistersinger.* He cut down the German dosage, and the Metropolitan entered upon a period of artistic and financial success which has become a legend in musical circles. The story of the years from 1897 to 1902 should be bound in a hand-tooled leather volume, with hand-illuminated manuscript pages. Through the successive managements of Grau, Conried, and Gatti-Casazza, hundreds of operas were given, including a number by American composers. Operas by foreigners found in the Metropolitan a sort of Ellis Island, which received them when they came in as immigrants, checked up on their antecedents and their fitness for citizenship, and finding many of them to be of distinguished ancestry and high cultural value, received them with open arms.[12]

It was necessary to step carefully in the matter of producing the works of unknown or obscure composers, even attractive foreigners. The occupants of the Golden Horseshoe, who footed the bills, were definitely conservatives, who vastly preferred operas they already knew or knew about. Unless a novelty was presented to them well ballyhooed, invested in easy melody, glittering with Old World glamour, or as a vehicle for a favorite singer, they could not be persuaded to patronize it. Edward Johnson, who became director of the Metropolitan in 1935, put their viewpoint in a nutshell when he said, "It is better to produce standard works with a great cast than to experiment with great cost."

There are always some hardy fighters, however, who are willing to take the bull by the horns even if they are gored. Such a one was Oscar Hammerstein. He opened the Manhattan Opera House in New York in 1906, and administered a bitter dose of competition which proved dismaying to the Metropolitan. During his first season he gave only Italian operas; during his second he featured the French. His stress was consistently upon popularizing opera. He had his subscription list, indispensable if he was to carry on, but he also had many seats at popular prices for all performances. Following the Metropolitan Company to Philadelphia like a thirsty gadfly, he joyously plunged his sting into the plump bankers of the Quaker City who were supporting his rival there. Eventually they had to buy him out, in self-defense, leaving him only the Manhattan Opera House in New York to play with. At the same time, they paid him the compliment of exacting a promise that he would not manage opera in Philadelphia, Boston, Chicago, or New York, for the next ten years. He did not abide by the letter of his promise, but his later attempts were short-lived and financially disastrous.

Oscar Hammerstein was a dynamo. He had come to New York without a cent in his pocket in 1863, found a job as a cigarmaker, and later became a manufacturer of what is known as the filthy weed, casually inventing a machine which brought him good returns. He took money from his cigar pocket and put it into his opera pocket—only he never came out even. Gayly he proceeded from one financial debacle to another, with his big cigar and his silk hat at an equally rakish angle, whatever the condition of his cash register. Opera came to life when he was there. Composers were happy to give him first rights at reduced royalty rates because they felt assured of an artistic production at his hands.[13]

When Hammerstein was asked, during a performance at the Chicago Opera House, not under his auspices, how he liked the work of the chorus, he replied, with a cocky tilt to his cigar, "I ought to. I trained them myself." Certainly, his vivid presence egged on the Metropolitan to its best efforts, and besides, brought modern French and Italian opera as a living thing to Philadelphia and Chicago, where it appreciably increased the number of opera enthusiasts.

In the opera houses which have sprung up through the country, as well as on radio broadcasts and in movies, foreign opera is considered "standard repertoire." Opera in English is still something very special, and a new American opera is heralded with great fanfare. When San Francisco opened her own Civic Opera House as a war memorial on October 15, 1932—the first municipally owned opera house in the United States—the chosen opera was Puccini's *La Tosca*. With repertoire and cast recruited from the Metropolitan, which means largely from Europe, San Francisco followed the Italian trail. Philadelphia, long chafing under the necessity of operating on the same principle, tried a season of independent opera in conjunction with her own Philadelphia Symphony Orchestra in 1934–35. This proved a joyous, brilliant, and artistically satisfying experiment, but it could not be repeated for the same old reason—lack of funds. Other cities have acquired opera—Cleveland, St. Louis, Detroit, Cincinnati, Minneapolis—with partial, if not complete seasons.

The titled foreigner takes Horace Greeley's immortal advice and goes West. The number of châteaux to which his American wife can invite him grows steadily, and his welcome there is unquestioned, while hers, still in the making, grows each year more cordial.

CHAPTER VIII

AMERICAN OPERA—THE BRIDE

AMERICAN opera is less than a hundred years old, reckoning 1845, the date of Fry's *Leonora*, as her natal day. *Leonora* was the first native grand opera whose librettist and composer were both born here. Before *Leonora*, there were half-and-quarter-breed indigenous works, only partially preserved, almost forgotten, but admirably catalogued by Mr. O. G. Sonneck. These efforts are evidence that the early musicians here were far from dead to operatic

hummings in their souls, though the tunes were brought by
the foreign suitor when he came a-wooing.

In the beginning, the libretto was considered much the
most important part of the opera, and was frequently preserved when the music, sometimes even the composer's name,
had been lost. Such a one was Francis Hopkinson's semi-
operatic allegory, *The Temple of Minerva,* performed in
1781. A record of the fact of performance, and the words, are
all that remain, but their elegance takes the sting out of the
fact that *The Disappointment,* by Andrew Barton, announced for performance fourteen years previously, had been
forbidden, and withdrawn because its robust humor and
personal allusions were too pronounced even for the none-
too-squeamish ears of the day. The play was ostensibly written to discourage the wild searches for buried treasure very
prevalent at the time, and pokes ribald fun alike at those
who go and those who fear to go. On the title page, Barton
wrote, in *Beggars' Opera* style:

> "Enchanting gold! Thou dost conspire to blind
> Man's erring judgment, and misguide the mind;
> In search of thee, the wretched worldling goes;
> Nor danger fears, though fiends of night oppose."

When Mrs. Hatton, of Philadelphia, wrote a libretto based
on the story of *Tammany,* or *The Indian Chief,* for which
James Hewitt supplied the music, she led the red man on the
American operatic stage, where he has since appeared a number of times, without, however, convincing the public that the
opera of America, like its nickel, requires the impress of the
Indian's head to be genuine. A companion piece to *Tammany,* in subject at least, *The Indian Princess,* or *La Belle
Sauvage,* was given in Philadelphia in 1808. It made effec-

tive use of Indian themes in its relation of the touching tale
of Pocahontas and Captain John Smith.

Between these two operas, there were a number in ballad
form by transplanted, but acclimated, foreigners. Benjamin
Carr of England, Victor Pelissier of France, and Alexander
Reinagle of Austrian descent, are a trio who placed their very
considerable gifts at the service of the music of their day in
divers ways, and did not even flinch from the writing of
operas, as that term was then understood. They created not
only a certain amount of pleasant entertainment, but a great
deal of discussion in after years as to where in the American
scheme their product truly belonged. It was so American in
one sense, so foreign in another.

Alexander Reinagle was the sort of man who left in his
trail a flashing wake of music. Of Austrian parents, but educated in England, he had Bach and Haydn in his system
before he hung out his shingle in New York announcing his
willingness to teach violin, piano, or harpsichord. For many
years, he distributed his activities between New York and
Philadelphia. It was he who introduced four-handed piano
music to America, to the delight of amateurs of a later generation. He composed ballad-operas—*The Sicilian Romance,*
Slaves in Algiers, Columbus, and *The Savoyard*—and possibly others which were not preserved.

Benjamin Carr, English pianist, singer, and organist, composed the music for a ballad-opera, *The Archers,* or *Mountaineers in Switzerland,* in which William Tell and his famous
apple played the leading parts. Carr sat in his Musical Re-
pository, the first music store in Philadelphia, like a benef-
icent spider sending out filaments in every direction to weave
a web of music which would catch the public. His own

Musical Miscellany and *Musical Journal for the Pianoforte* disseminated and preserved useful musical material. He was, besides, one of the moving spirits in founding the Musical Fund Society, so important in the growth of Philadelphia's Symphony Orchestra.

In *Edwin and Angelina,* the next ballad-opera of importance, which was performed in New York, December 19, 1796, there is, for the first time, positive evidence that both words and music were composed here. Hence some writers call it the first American opera. But it was still not grand opera. Victor Pelissier, who turned his French Conservatoire training prolifically to the uses of music in his adopted country, was responsible for the score, while Elihu Hubbard Smith, of Connecticut, provided the words. The cheery little Pelissier, between the exactions of his job of playing the French horn in the theater orchestras of New York and Philadelphia, made numerous arrangements, in addition to writing several original opera scores.[14]

The ballad-opera form stuck like a burr to our native composers. *The Saw-Mill,* or *A Yankee Trick,* which was composed and written by one Micah Hawkins, had genuine local flavor. It was American in subject, and the music was original. A grocer who keeps a piano under his counter and gives his customers a tune or two with each brown-paper parcel must have more musician than grocer in his soul. Hawkins is said to have composed his entire score in the shop, trying the individual tunes, as they popped into his head, on his delighted customers. It took him several years to assemble them all, but he did, and *The Saw-Mill* was produced and ran at the Chatham Garden Theatre in New York all through the season of 1824. Hawkins himself played fiddle in the orchestra, and when calls for "author" became insistent, appeared on the stage in his pepper-and-salt suit, violin in hand, blushing like a schoolgirl, and unable to make the customary speech. Had he not died shortly thereafter, but lived to taste the delights of the Italian opera brought to New York by Garcia that same year, he might have been the man to write the first American grand opera.

That event was deferred until twenty years later, twenty years during which the Marty Company from Havana, the French Company from New Orleans, and other visiting companies had carried on the work of converting America to grand opera. William Fry, of Philadelphia, was one of the most ardent converts. The many performances he heard in his capacity of music critic familiarized him, perhaps too intimately, with the works of foreign opera composers. When he wrote the music of *Leonora,* he could not forget what he had heard. *Leonora* was a family affair. One brother, Joseph, supplied the libretto; another deserted his profession of bookkeeping and went into opera management in order to produce it. Nevertheless, the newspaper critics refused to be impressed by the lavishness of the first performance in Philadelphia, paid for by Fry himself, and were unanimous in pointing out that while there was plenty of melody it was not intrinsically Fry, but warmed-over Donizetti and Bellini. They intimated, furthermore, that Fry did not even know when he was composing and when remembering, that he probably composed by heart.

Much of this may have been true. Nevertheless, Fry was as important to American opera as Garcia to opera in America. He supplied the first grand opera on the European plan, with both words and music by native Americans. Indeed, he dwelt upon that fact, stressing the nationality of his work *ad nauseam*. He argued that any composition by an American should be given consideration for that reason alone, regardless of its merits. He expressed himself in many newspaper articles to that effect, before being sent abroad as foreign correspondent for *The Tribune*. During the six years he spent in Paris hobnobbing with Berlioz and other musical celebrities, he continued to argue, adding to his original thesis the importance of placing American works on French programs. He brought a grievance back with him because he had not succeeded in gaining his point. On his return to this country, he staged a series of lecture-recitals, in which he dealt with "the subject of musical composition, its scientific relations, its history, its ethics, its aesthetics." This gave him ample opportunity to bring in special pleading for the American composer. His remarks sound today as reminiscent as his music did then; there has since been so much of the same. But he actually was saying something new to the ears of 1845 when he demanded passionately, "Shall our muse chant in a foreign tongue?"

Fry was seconded in his pro-America hue and cry by William Bristow, a rival as a composer but an ally as a flag waver. Bristow had also written the music of a grand opera, *Rip Van Winkle,* which was given in New York three years before Fry managed to have his *Leonora* raise her voice in that city, although ten years after she had been heard in Philadelphia. Fry's self-esteem was undoubtedly wounded at having the first opera thus given second place. Furthermore, the fact that he was obliged to have *Leonora* translated into Italian in order to have it sung in New York at all must have been a bitter pill. But he proved himself big enough to rise above personal difficulties and pettinesses, and to fight shoulder to shoulder with Bristow, whose opera proved, after all, to be no more original than his own.

Yet the appearance of *Rip Van Winkle* close upon the heels of *Leonora,* and the newspaper articles which Bristow wrote backing up Fry, strengthened the position of both of them, and of American opera composers to come. They did a superlative job of road breaking. To be sure, as Mr. Elson remarked in his *History of American Music,* there was a certain humor in their protest against what they stigmatized as "the systematized effort for the extinction of American music," when they themselves were the only Americans of any prominence on the scene, and one of them copied Italian, the other English, models. Fortunately, they were quite oblivious of any such implications. Fry died, still fighting, in 1864. Bristow lived on until 1898, to a ripe old age.

The squatter system of opera then flourished unquestioned for another thirty years. Whatever of American origin was written during that period was doomed to blush unseen. High hopes were expressed in an article in *The Herald Tribune,* reprinted in *Dwight's Journal* of April 23, 1853. Commenting on the building of large opera houses in Boston, Philadelphia, and New York, and the project to make the Academy of Music in New York a temple of Italian opera, the article stated: "We are of opinion that no fine art can flourish in a country at second hand. We believe it must be rendered National, and in the case of music, be presented through the language the people understand. . . . We further believe that Europe cannot supply this country habitually with singers. Whatever may be the first and absorbing use to which the opera house may be put, it should be obliged to educate artists, and to produce original works. In this view, it becomes an object of national consideration."

The National Conservatory of Music and American Opera somewhat belatedly adopted these ideas, and in 1886 issued a prospectus which promised an operatic Utopia:

1. Grand opera sung in English by most competent artists.
2. The musical guidance of Theodore Thomas.
3. The unrivaled Thomas orchestra.
4. The largest chorus ever employed in grand opera in America, and composed entirely of fresh young voices.
5. The largest ballet corps ever employed by grand opera in America.
6. Four thousand new costumes, for which no expense has been spared.
7. The armor, properties and paraphernalia made from models by the best designers.
8. The scenery designed by the associated artists of New York, and painted by the most eminent scenic artists of America.

Mrs. Jeannette Thurber, a zealous patron of the arts, staked one hundred thousand dollars on her belief in that program.

Theodore Thomas, although he had his hands full with his crusade for better symphonic programs, consented to direct the new National group, because he believed in it so wholeheartedly. Failing original opera in English, he put on translations of such standard works as *Faust, The Flying Dutchman* and *Tannhäuser, The Magic Flute* and *Martha*. No expense was spared, and that is where Thomas made his error. He labored under the delusion that he had only to ask, and it would be given unto him. His disagreeable awakening occurred with the stoppage of his own salary check at the height of the season. Incredulous at such a turn of affairs, he kept going without pay, thinking to weather the storm. It proved to be not a squall, but a tornado. He was obliged to admit defeat, and resigned at the end of the season, without having realized half of his cherished plans. The company was stranded in California, where they might still be had not Mr. Thomas provided them with meals and transportation out of his own pocket. A year later, after a few grudging and insufficient financial life preservers had been thrown them, the company went into bankruptcy and dispersed.

The sun of the Metropolitan Opera, which had risen three or four years previously, shone the more effulgent for the failure of what was erroneously termed American opera, though in reality merely opera in English. Leopold Damrosch had set the German fashion, and after him there was a long period when German, Italian, and French opera monopolized public attention. That period is hardly yet completed. Star performances by foreign artists were preferred, which is not surprising, as American artists were not so well trained, nor could they hold the attention of a public languishing for the exotic. Nevertheless, they continued to try, with varying degrees of success. The Castle Square Opera Company, of Boston, toured a few years later, and held their own for five years by presenting mostly light operas, charging a low admission rate, and being more canny as to cash. The Bostonians, another excellent company, followed their example. Their wagon was hitched to a less exalted star than that of the Century Opera Company, which was formed in New York some years later, with a list of comfortably solvent backers to insure its permanence. It, too, enjoyed only a season or two of opera in the vernacular before it hauled down the stars and stripes and ran up the flags of many nations.

Then a Society for the Production of Opera in English was announced. At the inaugural meeting, attended by opera stars, newspaper critics, and all the musical luminaries of the day, Tito Ricordi, Italian music publisher, came out with the statement that, next to Italian, English was the most singable of languages. It took more than his assertion to convince the public, however, and nothing came of his speeches or the others which flowed on this convivial occasion. The Eastman School in Rochester sent out companies of young American singers for several seasons; the Juilliard and Curtis and others have persevered in their efforts on behalf of opera in English with native talent, and if possible native composers.

One of the most recent attempts, an opera bouffe entitled *Amelia Goes to the Ball,* written by a young Italian-American, Gian Carlo Menotti, was produced by Curtis School opera students in Philadelphia and New York in the spring of 1937. Charmingly written light music, and sly humor couched in clear, singable English, provided an admirable combination which seemed to satisfy the American concept of operatic enjoyment, though it was considerably lighter than grand opera.

Another novel experiment of 1937 was a three-act opera written expressly for children, *The Second Hurricane.* Aaron Copland composed a tense, staccato score, employing some of his best jazz technique at certain points, while rising to heights of dramatic intensity approaching tragedy at others. Edwin Denby supplied a colloquial, occasionally slangy, but always vivid and comprehensible book. Partly sung and partly spoken, *The Second Hurricane* struck an original, yet strongly American, note in its initial idea, pattern, and method of presentation.

It was not until 1896 that an American grand opera actually came to roost in the august precincts of the Metropolitan. Then Maurice Grau, casting about, impresario-fashion, for novel ideas, decided that it would be distinctly a feather in his cap to put on a grand opera of native origin. This momentous decision was not so difficult of execution as may appear, for Walter Damrosch was on the scene. He not only had an opera already "set" to produce, but he was there to mention the fact. At the age of nineteen he had inherited from his father, Leopold, the baton of the Metropolitan orchestra, and with it the solemn charge to bring Wagner's works into the operatic family group. He had done his conscientious best, and it was a great deal. He had given lecture-recitals on the Ring, put Wagnerian overtures on the programs of the New York Symphony Orchestra, of which he was also the conductor, and continually urged the production of Wagner's operas. No wonder, then, that when he wrote one of his own, even on a wholly American subject, it came out laden with Wagnerisms. He selected Hawthorne's tale, *The Scarlet Letter,* and commissioned the author's son-in-law, G. P. Lathrop, to write the libretto. Lathrop, unfortunately, gave the composer a highly diluted Hawthorne. The vivid scarlet of Hester Prynne's letter appeared in the libretto and score as a discreet pastel pink, which after a few performances faded out completely, along with Hester and the opera. It was a noble experiment, the first of a royal line, each hailed before its performance as the "great American opera," each shelved after a few presentations. The later ones have been less cavalierly handled, either because they are better, or because, as time went on, the public has become more aware of the complex problems to be surmounted in writing a music drama, more appreciative of even a partial solution, and more eager to see one of "our boys" achieve success in that field. The Metropolitan has extended the hand of encouragement, and the history of American opera is contained, in large part, in the annals of performances there, of which *The Scarlet Letter* was the first.

The Pipe of Desire, an opera fantasy in one act by Frederick Converse, sounded its call in Boston in 1906, and traveled to the Metropolitan four years later. When that pitiless spotlight was thrown upon it, the enthusiasm was so tempered as to be negligible. Lawrence Gilman, in an article in *Harper's Weekly,* April 9, 1910, paid tribute to Converse as a musician of skill, taste, and experience, but deplored the absence of good dramatic straw in the bricks with which he built, and the lack of convincing individuality in the piece as a whole.[15]

Most favorably known as a writer of symphonic works, Mr. Converse was for many years director of the New England Conservatory, and assistant professor of music at Harvard University. He was hampered in his creative activity by no financial struggle, but after sound training at Harvard and in Munich, was able to divide his time as he liked between his wife and family, poetry and romance, golf clubs and music.

The Pipe of Desire was followed by another professorial opera—doubly professorial in that both words and music emanated from Yale pedagogues. *Mona,* which won the ten-thousand-dollar prize offered in 1912 for the best American grand opera, was the story of a descendant of Boadicea, Amazon queen, as told in blank verse by Brian Hooker, and clothed in musical armor by Horatio Parker. Parker had established himself as America's outstanding choral composer; but when he applied his choral technique to opera it was unsuccessful, and his *Mona* could not fight her way to popularity, Amazon though she was. What with the cloudy diction of the singers, and the difficulty of the libretto, the only line which seems to have been comprehensible to the first-night audience was "I do not understand." They echoed it heartily. Henry Krehbiel dismissed *Mona* as "The firstling of inexperienced men, of fine capacity and high ideals."

Their second-born, *Fairyland,* for which they received a similar prize award two years later, failed equally to convince audiences that theirs was the ideal combination, the Gilbert and Sullivan of Grand Opera. Perhaps there was too much beans and biscuit in Horatio Parker's New England blood to feed the dramatic fire of operatic composition. He was born in Auburndale, Massachusetts, September 15, 1863, and received all his early education in New England. Having studied in Munich, he came back to his own country for a quiet life of teaching and composition, with occasional trips abroad to conduct his own works. His choral compositions appealed so strongly to the English, who make a habit of large choral festivals, that he was invited to conduct the *Hora Novissima,* his finest achievement, at the Worcester Festival. Furthermore, he was specially commissioned to write *The Wanderer's Psalm* for the Hereford Festival the following year, a signal honor for an American. As professor of music at Yale, a position which he held for many years, he reorganized and drilled a large singing group, and aroused and fostered an appreciation of choral music in America, which lived on after his own death in 1919.

When both *Mona* and *Fairyland* failed to please, Walter Damrosch, who had adjudged both of them to be prize winners, offered another opera of his own, *Cyrano de Bergerac*. Given an excellent libretto, made from the French of Edmond Rostand by W. J. Henderson, music critic, Damrosch had worked for nine years on the musical score. This time, he was much more successful in writing humorous, entertaining, dramatic music than in *The Scarlet Letter*. The wholetone scale which accompanied Cyrano's exits and entrances, symbolizing his nose, stuck out from the score as the enormous nose which was Cyrano's bane stuck out from his face. The general feeling, however, was that there was too much of it; too much, in fact, of the whole opera. Although its model was Italian, the too, too solid German writing remained.

The Man without a Country, a two-act opera written by Dr. Damrosch at the ripe age of seventy-five, to a libretto by Arthur Guiterman, was given several performances during the 1937 spring season of opera in English at the Metropolitan. It is still too soon after the event to pass upon the merits of the work, which was received by critics and public with the cordial respect and appreciation due to its venerable composer.

After *Cyrano,* a man famed for his light operas took the torch which Damrosch passed on. Victor Herbert, the irrepressible, who had come to America from Dublin via Munich some years previously, had been turning out operettas which set everyone to humming their lyrics. When the word went forth, in 1911, that he had written a grand opera, *Natoma,* which was to be produced in Philadelphia by the Chicago Civic Opera Company, hopes ran high, for he and his music had a head start in popular favor over other composers. But the public did not reckon on a highly ridiculous story cloaked in an unbelievable libretto. Natoma is an Indian girl who, as Krehbiel succinctly stated, "shows her love for an American naval officer by killing a man who is seeking to abduct her mistress in order that the mistress may . . . marry the man whom the Indian girl also loves." When an admirer said of Herbert that he "could compose a perfectly singable tune to any given column in the telephone directory" he described a talent of which Herbert had need in writing this opera. He succeeded surprisingly well; in fact, his music seems to have been much too good for the material it had to work with. After the furore of the first performance in Philadelphia on February 25, 1911, and the less enthusiastic response a few days later at the Metropolitan, it was seldom heard. Yet Herbert had no need to hang his jovial head in apology for his contribution to the slowly growing body of American opera. In spirit, it was closer to the native character than any which had yet appeared.

It was a great deal more successful than his *Madeline*, a one-act operetta produced several years later. Taken from a lighter-than-air French story, this should have been the very thing to bring out a fine crop of the charming lyrics which Herbert wrote so well. Instead, it brought upon itself the characterization of "futile, far-fetched, frivolous, fuliginous, fumid fustian in score, inept operatic idiom in text."

When Reginald de Koven, also known primarily for light operas, brought *The Canterbury Pilgrims* for a brief moment to the Metropolitan, he was not so successful as Herbert. Percy MacKaye had made the tales of Chaucer into a blank verse play in modern English, which De Koven essayed to set to music. But opera was not the vehicle for missionary work in English literature, and *The Canterbury Pilgrims* is remembered less for its music than for an incident which occurred at one of its few performances. News of the sinking of the Lusitania came to the Opera House just as Margaret Ober, who was singing the Wife of Bath, was on the stage. She was so affected that she fainted, and had to be carried off, supplying the most dramatic incident of the opera. *Rip Van Winkle,* De Koven's other grand opera (1920), did not hold a candle to his lighter works, especially the oft-revived *Robin Hood,* if public response is any criterion.

The next American production was *Shanewis,* by Charles Wakefield Cadman. This was carried over and sung in two successive seasons, 1918 and 1919, which argued well for it. In selecting his story, Cadman was thoroughly at home, for he had spent much of his life in the study of Indian tribal lore and song, and had already done much musical modeling in red clay. Furthermore, his librettist, Mrs. Nellie Richmond Eberhart, had previously written the words to some of his most successful songs. Henry T. Finck, in *The Evening Post* of April 20, 1918, wrote: "At last the Met has a novelty of American origin which is worth preserving for future seasons, *Shanewis,*" and pronounced it the best opera composed in America except *Natoma.* Another critic called it "an American *Madame Butterfly.*" Opposing voices murmured that *Shanewis* was too facile to be great, that it had neither originality nor distinction, that the story was outlandish and absurd. But the public understood its music, as they had that of *Natoma,* and accepted it with much better grace than heavier attempts in imitation of the European.

It was not Cadman's first opera. From the cabin in Estes

Park, Colorado, where this Pittsburgh boy went when the fever of creation was upon him, had issued *Daoma, the Land of Misty Water,* an opera in which he incorporated forty-seven Indian themes; it was produced in the West. But whether or not his works appeared before the public made little difference to this indefatigable composer. He shoved the closely written sheets into desk drawers, and thus salted away a number of operas against a boom in the American market. *The Sunset Trail,* a story of the last stand of the Indians against the conquering whites, was produced by the American Opera Company at the Gallo Theatre in New York in January, 1928, a singable opera which is never sung. Of late years, he has ceased to walk the trail of his Indian friends. *A Witch of Salem,* given its première by the Chicago Civic Opera Company on December 8, 1926, did not seem as typically American as his earlier works, for all its New England subject and background. But the driving pen of Cadman will bear watching. He is one of the few composers alive in America who combines a technique of choral writing, a feeling for melodic line, and a sense of drama, with a talent sufficiently prolific to produce many operas of sustained merit.

In the ballet by Henry F. Gilbert, *The Dance in the Place Congo,* which was given at the Metropolitan along with the two-act *Shanewis,* the juxtaposition of barbaric negro themes with the dignified Indian songs of the opera proved Gilbert as eloquent a spokesman for the black man as Cadman for the red. Originally designed for the concert hall, *The Dance in the Place Congo* proved to be so dramatic that Gilbert embodied one of George W. Cable's stories in it and turned it into a ballet. He piled up sharply cut barbaric dance rhythms, alternating them with tender Creole love songs, the whole a work of tremendous vitality, almost overpowering at times in its plethora of life and color, but never dull.

Henry Hadley (1871–1937) was the next knight to tilt with the operatic windmill. *Cleopatra's Night*, a two-act opera performed at the Metropolitan January 31, 1920, was his ninetieth work. The stars must have been propitious, for Hadley had an unusually good libretto, taken from the French of Théophile Gautier by Alice Leal Pollock; he had the artistic stage settings of Norman Bel-Geddes, and a splendid cast who actually enunciated their lines so they could be understood. There was then nothing to detract from his score, which showed to the best advantage as a skillful and artistic piece by a man who knew his modern harmony. Trailing clouds of Massenet, Saint-Saëns, Strauss, and Wagner adhered to it from its infancy in the heaven of European culture, but it contained passion, action, clash, and color. Hadley had previously won a thousand-dollar prize with another opera, *Bianca*, had seen his *Azora* produced at the Chicago Opera House in 1917, *The Garden of Allah* in New York the following year, and had other works in readiness to spring at the proper moment, whose coming he never doubted. In a recent address on *Idealism in American Music*, delivered at Columbia University, he informed his hearers that "young composers in America are writing music which reflects joyousness, buoyancy, indomitable courage, and a wholesome belief in life." He attributed to others the qualities which were his own, and which brought him success in his threefold career as composer, conductor, and teacher, until his death in September, 1937.

John Alden Carpenter's ballet *Skyscrapers*, must be mentioned in passing, like Gilbert's *The Dance in the Place Congo*, because, like that unrestrained composition, it defied the proprieties of the opera house. Into the dignified atmosphere, saturated with correctitude, it brought the darkling gleam of true jazz. It was well liked for its setting, angularly expressive of modernity at its most modern, for its frank and joyous jazz, and its interpretation of the spirit of that collection of Towers of Babel, reaching toward an unattainable heaven, which calls itself New York. Carpenter is a Chicago lumber merchant, most of whose musical works are gently poetical in feeling, and French in manner. To write *Skyscrapers*, he shut himself up in a Southern farmhouse, and produced music which was the essence of New York.

An opera by a New York man on a subject miles removed from that city now caused the critics to sharpen their pencils. Deems Taylor was commissioned by the Metropolitan to write an opera, because they knew and liked his earlier works.[16] Mr. Taylor met the chronic difficulty of a libretto by tightening his belt, assuming his most engaging smile, and asking his friend Edna St. Vincent Millay to write one for him. She produced a libretto on the story of *The King's Henchman*, more worthy as poetry than as lines to be sung, it appeared, for when the opera was given, in 1927, much of the beauty of the words was lost. But the music was favorably received, and the opera enjoyed fourteen performances over several seasons, more than any previous American opera. In writing for the voice, Taylor made great strides toward that happy marriage of the English tongue and a corresponding musical line which was his dream when he undertook his task. Modestly, he did not allow his head to be turned by the undoubted success of *The King's Henchman*.

No sooner had the excitement subsided than he began looking around for another libretto.

Du Maurier's sentimental but infinitely touching story,
Peter Ibbetson, fell in with his idea of what he wanted. It was
admirable—if anything too much so—for there was such
poignant drama in the story, and exquisite beauty in the
stage pictures, that they tended to take precedence over the
music. The inner life of a man was revealed as distinct and
separate from, and almost more real than, his outward existence. Sleep and dreams bridged the gap between the two.
On this theme, set forth in an intelligent libretto by Con-
stance Collier, Taylor produced noteworthy music. The
happy melodies of Peter's childhood at Passy; the waltzes of
the ball at which he met again his beloved Mimsy, grown to
womanhood as the stately Duchess of Towers; the tragic discord to which he murdered the uncle who had wronged him;
the music of conflict and resignation during his life imprison-
ment—all were of the utmost expressiveness. In his dreams
in prison, he was united for many happy hours with Mimsy,
and when she died, his spirit followed hers almost immediately. The dream music was never absent—it was there as a
continual background, softened but never silenced by the
events of his outward life. *Peter Ibbetson* was a distinct advance over *The King's Henchman.*

It was followed by an opera strongly in contrast in subject
matter and treatment, although, like *Peter,* it contained so
much drama as to give heavy competition to the music.
When Louis Gruenberg wrote music for Eugene O'Neill's
play, *The Emperor Jones,* he was really applying burnt cork
to an already ebony skin. The play did not require the emphasis of music. Such as was needed had already been indi-

cated by the playwright in the persistent tom-tom. As its throbbing swelled and diminished, it beat out the whole story of the flight, pursuit and defeat of the colored porter in the African jungle, who masqueraded for a brief span as the Emperor Jones. Gruenberg made skillful use of the tom-tom and provided a chorus of black natives, who remained constantly upon the stage, intoning a polyphonic commentary upon the action until, in the tragic finale, they closed in upon Jones with barbaric cries. The negro spiritual, *It's Me, It's Me, It's Me, O Lawd, Standin' in de Need of Prayer,* was inserted at a most effective moment in Jones' agonized trek through the forest. But all the considerable skill of the composer could not make the music to such a play as this appear other than extrinsic and superimposed. When Gruenberg turned his attention to a lighter subject, in the two-act opera *Jack and the Beanstalk* produced by the Juilliard School, his craftsmanship was displayed in a more grateful, if less ambitious vehicle.

Howard Hanson's *Merrymount,* produced February 10, 1934, concerned itself with the particularly torrid hell fire which crisped a Pilgrim Father who allowed the Devil to catch his soul with the time-honored bait of an alluring maiden. The music was too carefully cerebral for its stormy subject, and although the composer feelingly described in words his own identification with the hero, Wrestling Bradford, and the agony of spirit with which the opera was wrung from him, he did not communicate that agony in music. There was fine choral writing in the modal songs of the Puritans; the arias, too, were dramatically effective, though vocally difficult; and in the Hellish Rendezvous of Act III there was a powerful attempt to achieve a dramatic climax.

As a whole, however, the opera won lukewarm approbation.

More's the pity, since its composer, Howard Hanson, is the modern William Fry, champion of American music and its indefatigable interpreter. At the Eastman School, of which he is Director, he has instituted annual festivals of American music, over which he presides with wit and wisdom. His contention that organizations paid by American money, catering to American audiences, should produce American music has logic on its side. Hanson is well fitted by birth and education to champion the American composer. Born in Nebraska, October 28, 1896, he had the energy and ambition to become Dean of Fine Arts in San José, California, at the age of twenty-one, to win the Prix de Rome, to become President of the National Association of Music Teachers, to compose abundantly, and to make himself a welcome guest conductor with all the large symphony orchestras. As he is still under forty, the cause of the American composer may look for leadership to his optimism, energy, and sound knowledge for many years to come.

The chorus of disapproval after *Merrymount* was as naught compared with the reaction to an opera by Lawrence Seymour, a California composer, produced the following season, entitled *In the Pasha's Garden*. Used as a debut vehicle for a young and beautiful American singer, this served its purpose and disappeared from the scene. Richard Hagemann's *Caponsacchi*, previously produced abroad, and brought to the Metropolitan with high hopes in the season of 1937, fared little better.

Limiting the discussion of opera by Americans to Metropolitan productions is arbitrary but necessary. We dare not digress into the field of light opera, with Victor Herbert, De

Koven, Sousa, Friml, Jerome Kern, and many others, making contributions which were wholly delightful of their genre, and more popular than the grandest of opera. Besides, there are enough records of splendid performances throughout the country, both of grand opera and opéra comique, to fill a book of their own. Opera with no spoken dialogue is known as "grand." In the case of opéra comique, the composer supplies serious music, but spoken dialogue also enters in. For example, Virgil Thomson's *Four Saints in Three Acts,* a fantastic and imaginative setting of a play by Gertrude Stein, produced in 1934, was straight grand opera in that sense, one of the most interesting of the modern experiments in that field because it treated nonsense in terms of serious recitative and aria. George Gershwin's *Porgy and Bess,* on the other hand, composed to a libretto by Du Bose Heyward, was technically opéra comique, though A. Walter Kramer wrote of it: "I am not sure that it is an opera, nor that it is a folk-opera; in fact, I do not know just what it is, nor do I think that placing it in a category makes any difference." Neither it does, save to insure its inclusion in the growing list of American operas worthy of consideration.

In its freshness and originality, the sense of vitality it conveyed, the clever blending of operatic and popular writing, *Porgy and Bess* opened a new avenue. Along it, the young wife, American opera, finds temporary refuge from her exacting foreign husband. She may remain there for a while. She may decide rather to go in the more somber direction indicated by *Mona.* The sunny Indian trail of *Natoma* is not distasteful to her. She has her choice of pursuing one of these paths already opened, or of finding a new one, as yet untouched. As more operas are written, she becomes more broad-minded, less hampered by the ideas of foreign relatives, more resourceful in seizing new opportunities for expression. More and more, she is thinking for herself, asking no one's opinion. And her thought processes are leading her away from the husband at her side. Whither, remains to be seen.

CHAPTER IX

THE CARE AND FEEDING OF THE SYMPHONY ORCHESTRA

TIME was, not long ago, when many a conscientious young American mother went out of her way to secure a German nurse for her offspring. For she felt sure that, if she did, her baby's formulas would be properly measured, its bottles scrubbed clean, hours for rest and feeding scrupulously observed, the disciplinary regime followed to the letter. There was the danger that her child might be weaned from her maternal Americanism, and might even speak with a German accent for a while. But she could anticipate with reasonable certainty that he would shoot up in height and gain in weight, would honor his father and mother almost as much as his nurse, and grow up to be a credit to them all.

When the symphony orchestra was in its infancy here, it had the good fortune to be tended by such nurses. The conductors who received the puny infant from its American parents' hands knew what its every cry meant. If the pin of popular disapproval was sticking into it, if it was hungry for a different kind of nourishment, or just plain mad, they had the proper remedy. So even when anxious relatives attempted to dictate, even though there was not always enough money for things they deemed essential, and despite the occasional rebelliousness of their charges, they did a complete job. The impress of their uncompromising German discipline in the formative years is still evident in the magnificently trained orchestras of today.

It is a pity that the two who did most are not alive to glory in the results of their labors. Gottlieb Graupner was responsible for the first permanent orchestra here. Theodore Thomas worked out the feeding formulas which caused orchestras to increase and multiply, finally becoming so healthy and wealthy that they dared to thumb the nose at their European cousins, in defiance of their competition. If Graupner and Thomas were still alive, and someone were to hand them the list of American orchestras of today, they might remark, with justifiable pride, "How that child has grown!"

For there are now at least eighteen major professional orchestras: Chicago, Boston, Cincinnati, Cleveland, Detroit, Kansas City, Baltimore, Pittsburgh, Los Angeles, Minneapolis, Washington, New York, Philadelphia, Portland, Rochester, St. Louis, San Francisco, Seattle—the roll call sounds like a list of baseball teams. The orchestras consist of from eighty to a hundred pieces. They not only give concerts in their home towns, but go on tour, make gramophone records, and play over the radio, spreading symphonic music broadcast. Their individual claims to preeminence are taken much to heart, and although we know of no duels fought with rapiers over the respective merits of the Boston Symphony, the New York Philharmonic, and the Philadelphia, we have seen glares and heard gnashes aplenty from their loyal supporters when the question was raised. These star orchestras, moreover, are only a part of the whole. A recent development has been the formation of large symphonic groups, sponsored and paid by the Federal Government, in order to give employment to musicians deprived of their means of livelihood by the financial depression of 1929. These excellent groups are rapidly becoming so forceful an element in the musical life of the country, what with their free and popular-priced concerts, and their generous interest in the works of new and native composers, that it is to be hoped they will become a permanent feature of the musical landscape. The Government also sponsors brass bands, in addition to those already in existence, which do their bit at outdoor concerts in the summer. For those who sit on hard park benches, as for those who recline luxuriously on plush seats, symphonic music is to be had for the listening. According to George King Raudenbush, young American conductor, "there's hardly a town in this country that hasn't the makings of an orchestra." Mr. Raudenbush's experience in building in Harrisburg, Pennsylvania, an orchestra of one hundred men from an original semi-amateur group of thirty-five can be duplicated the more readily, in his opinion, due to the educational work done by radio broadcasts, and the widespread interest aroused by the prowess of high-school bands and orchestras. A recent computation shows two million boys and girls playing in school brass brands; there must be at least as many in school orchestras. In Dayton, Louisville, Indianapolis, Richmond, and elsewhere, small orchestras of fine caliber are formed or forming, to attest the validity of Mr. Raudenbush's statement.

It is impossible to enumerate the number of small ensembles of from sixteen to sixty. The radio broadcasting studios are nurseries wherein they thrive. The country today is literally honeycombed with orchestras, so much so that Percy Grainger, Australian composer-pianist, recently indulged in an amusing outburst against them. When asked whether he favored the establishment of one in Melbourne, Australia, he exploded: "The symphony orchestra is one of the worst musical combinations ever thought of. The whole idea is that everything must be screaming and high. . . . The symphony orchestra is only a small part of music, and symphonic music is far too much emphasized at present. Choral music is much more important. And so is chamber music."

Boston housed the first permanent symphonic group, after having for many years hubbishly resisted the allure of opera and light music. When the infant crowings of the small instrumental ensemble were first audible there, choral music was already perched aloft on the Plymouth Rock of psalmody. The Stoughton Singing Society was founded by William Billings as an offshoot of his singing school back in 1786. Hardy as its founder, it weathered all storms, and survived down to the present day. There is mention of small singing circles and an occasional instrumentalist here and there. But no record appears of a group of instrument players until Johann Gottlieb Christian Graupner took a hand.

With himself and his oboe as a nucleus, Graupner rallied to his support the half-dozen professionals and all the willing amateurs he could find in Boston in 1799. A trial orchestra, in more senses than one, this was dissolved after sundry meetings. The Phil-harmonic Society, his second venture, made in 1810, proved more tenacious of life. During the fourteen years of its existence, its public concerts, which were well attended, gave Bostonians the pleasing conviction that "God was in his heaven, all was right with their world," so long as they had their orchestra. The Phil-harmonic men were characterized in a journal of the day as "a useful nursery of music," inasmuch as "in their small way, they practiced Haydn symphonies."

Graupner, indefatigable promoter of the orchestra, hailed from Hanover, North Germany, where his oboe talent had flourished in an army band. He played contrabass, clarinet, and piano, and had a good understanding of the other instruments of the orchestra. The vocal side was also represented in his family circle, thanks to his marriage to a singer during his early days in Charleston. Perhaps as a tribute to Mrs. Graupner, he took a prominent part in establishing the Handel and Haydn Society, Boston's great choral group, in 1815. There are many hundreds of such groups today; a whole volume could be devoted to them alone. Early in its history, the Society was honored by having Beethoven consent to write an oratorio for it—a promise made in good faith, although for some reason left unfulfilled. But Handel and Haydn afforded plenty of material for the eager singers of Boston, and the concerts of their namesake society were, and are, given in the grand manner, with Mendelssohn, Mozart, and others represented on its programs. Aside from its concerts, the Society sponsored the publication of valuable works such as Lowell Mason's collections of hymn tunes, used for years in churches and schools.

Most significant to the development of the symphony orchestra, the Handel and Haydn Society afforded the young organization so dear to Graupner's heart the experience of playing the necessary accompaniments at its concerts. Thus, it put nourishing sandwiches into the lunch box of the orchestra, now in its schoolboy stage. Until the break-up of the Phil-harmonic in 1824, Boston was unique in that it boasted both a flourishing singing society and a symphony orchestra. Graupner did not die until twelve years after the demise of his group, but he had apparently no time to waste in repining over its discontinuance. He gave concerts, ran a music store where he both sold and published music, traded in piano-fortes, and composed piano exercises and other pieces. He was one of the pioneers in American music, who flew in the face of all the adages about doing one thing at a time by doing many, all of them well. He undoubtedly brought the joy of music, as well as the sterner aspects of its cultivation, to his young charge, and to the staid city of his choice.

After his death, Boston marked time, and waited for another Graupner. Meanwhile, the interest in group music had not died. Harvard harbored a number of young men who breathed out their musical yearnings on the flute. They had formed themselves into a club, called the Pierian Sodality, which met weekly for a ration of music and beer, both presumably from Pierian springs. So regular were they in the observance of their duties, that a veteran member relates with a chuckle how at one period, when it happened that there were not many flute players at Harvard, the only active member of the Pierian found himself the sole attendant at meetings. Conscientiously, he read the minutes of the last meeting aloud to himself, played the flute a bit, and fortified himself with beer and pretzels, until the group again took on more sociable proportions.

Graduates who remembered their Pierian days with pleasure, later, in 1837, founded the Harvard Musical Association, which gave concerts of great length, weight, and dullness. In fact, they vied, in this respect, with those of the Musical Fund Society, an orchestra founded by a group of amateurs. In the story of the symphony orchestra, the much maligned amateur comes into his own. He was expected to shut up, play up, and put up. He did all three.

The concerts of the Musical Fund Society were led by James Webb, an associate of Lowell Mason, who interests us because of one bold act, emulated with a sigh of relief by subsequent conductors. He was the first American to wield the baton without playing the violin at the same time. Up to his time, concert master and conductor were one and the same, and such leadership as there was came from the first stand. The pianist would have the only score, and was much too busy playing his own part to bother about the rest. The concert master waved an occasional bow to establish tempi, but there was no director on the podium to divert audiences and direct players. Webb introduced that innovation, and made conducting a full-time job.

A new German impetus now came to stir musical Boston. The date of 1848 is almost as important in American as in European history, for it underlines the foreign, particularly the German, influence here. A group of young revolutionaries, fleeing from oppression, reached these shores. Among them were twenty-four Germans, all of them competent musicians. Some were recruited from Gungl's band in Berlin. Their ex-leader, who came over a year or two later, gave several concerts with such chill results that he withdrew in disgust at the insensitiveness of this barbarian country to the beauty that was Gungl. He even wrote a letter home which, though it can be discounted to a certain extent as the impression of a disgruntled individual, indicates how much was still needed here in the matter of care and feeding of the orchestra. Bitterly he commented: "Madame Musica in America lies still in the cradle here, and nourishes herself on sugar-teats. How much soever the American as a business man surpasses most European nations, just so much, perhaps in all departments of fine arts, but especially music, is he behind all . . . and not capable of enjoying instrumental music. It is a matter of course that only the so-called anti-classical music can in any degree suit the taste of the American public—such as Waltzes, Galops, Quadrilles, and above all, Polkas." He added that the symphony soirées of the New York Philharmonic had small audiences, which dwindled successively, while Fry's Italian opera "with a troupe at least as good as that which visits Berlin every winter, is not making much money."

This goes to show that the young German refugees, who in 1848 banded together into the Germania Orchestra, offshoot and at the same time rival of Gungl, did not have things all their own way. They had to employ many expedients to persuade audiences to give ear to their offerings. But they persisted. They were not above such heavy-footed humor as having a toy locomotive, with black cotton smoke, run across the platform during a piece called the *Railway Galop*. They played a piece called *Panorama of Broadway, New York,* which included fireworks, an imitation of Barnum's Band, and a fight between two fire companies. These were the tidbits with which they enticed audiences to listen to Mendelssohn's *Midsummer Night's Dream,* Hérold's *Zampa Overture,* Rossini, Johann Strauss, and others. During the six years that they journeyed up and down the land, they did a splendid job of educating audiences, a little at a time. When, in 1854, the Germania was disbanded, its members were sown about the country, like the dragon's teeth planted by Cadmus, and an army of orchestra men sprang up where they fell.

Carl Zerrahn, one of the members who settled in Boston, was selected to lead the new Philharmonic Orchestra, which continued the honorable line from Graupner's, the Harvard Musical Association, and the Musical Fund Society. After six years with them, it was natural that he should go on wielding the baton when the Harvard Musical Association in 1865 formed the symphony orchestra which is the precursor of the present Boston Symphony. Zerrahn was a choral conductor as well, led the Handel and Haydn Society for many years, and was guest conductor at many choral festivals. William F. Apthorp, a music critic of the day, records that he never heard a well-balanced symphony orchestra until the Handel and Haydn Festival of 1865. String players from New York were called in then to augment the Bostonians, and for the first time he understood why the strings in an orchestra were the main power.

The programs, practically all German, on which Zerrahn fed his orchestra, were never aspersed as being either too short or too light. However, the audiences of those days did not consider a concert truly high class unless they got a bit of a nap there, while the rare feeling of superiority over those not privileged to attend compensated for the boredom of listening and the discomforts of public sleeping. The ponderous programmatic precedent endured for some time after the formation of the present Boston Symphony Orchestra in 1881. It was only gradually altered, much of the improvement being due to Theodore Thomas, feeder-in-chief of a balanced menu. Meanwhile, the Boston Symphony inherited many of its predecessor's virtues, besides the tradition of heavy programs. Colonel Henry Lee Higginson, its founder, was a cultured capitalist with a passion for music. He won general love and respect by the high ideals from which he never swerved, for he felt that the orchestra was essentially not a mere commercial enterprise, insisted that its members should be adequately paid, and enlisted the interest of the most cultured circles in Boston. It was his boast that every man of the ensemble was an artist. Under Serge Koussevitzky, its present conductor, the tender young composer of every nationality, including American, has been dished up with consummate artistry. In symphony, as in psalmody, Boston has led the way.[17]

New York followed hard upon her heels. In truth, the New York Philharmonic was founded before the Boston, but took longer to get into its stride. Ureli C. Hill, a New England violinist who had studied with Spohr in Germany, formed the first considerable orchestra in New York. He had the wit to realize that the city's musical needs were not fully satisfied either by foreign visitors or local organizations. One of the latter, the Sacred Music Society, he directed. The Euterpean Society, an amateur group of instrumentalists who practiced all year in order to give one annual concert, suffered from the shortcomings implicit in its personnel. A letter from a German musician to a friend abroad described music in New

York in 1828. He wrote: "The Orchestra is as bad as possible to imagine. It is incomplete; there is usually one clarinet; no bassoon, oboes, trumpets, drums; but one oboeist in North America" (probably Graupner). "The trombone and double bass are best paid. The conductor accompanies every solo with the violin; one never hears a solo performed alone. Such is the condition of music in New York. I am going now to see if it is better in Boston—I have my doubts."

This was written twenty years before the German influx of 1848, which the Philharmonic antedated by six years. Hill's first act was to form a cooperative association of professional musicians, and try to establish a professional attitude. In this, he was only partially successful, for when Theodore Thomas later took command, he found the men attending rehearsals or not, as they pleased; inviting their friends as to a social event, and smoking and talking with little regard for the conductor. He changed all that. But meanwhile, poor Ureli Hill had discovered that it takes more than one to make a cooperative enterprise. In 1854, the organization almost broke up, when Fry and Bristow, those professional pro-Americans, exploded violently against the prevalence on programs of such foreign upstarts as Beethoven, Haydn, Mozart, Mendelssohn, Schumann, and Schubert. In their vociferous protests they all but unionized, struck, picketed, and sat down. Fortunately, they took out their feelings in talk, and the Philharmonic infant, exposed on the hillside to die, survived the chill blasts of Fry-Bristow disapproval. From Hill, it passed to another nurse, and again a German hand fed and sustained it. Poor Hill died, a suicide, in 1875, but not before he had seen his baby toddling, at least, and with a fair chance of growing up.

"Hier wird Deutsch gesprochen und gespielt" might well have been the motto over the mantelpiece in the Philharmonic rooms in the early days. It was only after some years that guest conductors of different nationalities came, bringing fresh foods to the Philharmonic larder. Under the baton of Arturo Toscanini, who arrived in 1926 as a guest and remained as a member of the family until 1936, the orchestra gave some of the most notable performances of its entire career.[18]

The Damrosch family has been assiduous through thick and thin in developing symphony orchestras in New York. When the New York Symphony was formed in 1878, first father Leopold, then son Walter presided over it, until its amalgamation with the Philharmonic in 1928. They gave Theodore Thomas' own orchestra, as well as the Philharmonic, a very healthy brand of rivalry. Not only did they set up keen competition for audiences, but they bid against Thomas for the compositions of the new young composers Wagner, Rubinstein, and others. Walter, who succeeded his father in 1885, took his men to tour the West, following Thomas' footsteps. At the Young People's concerts, which he inaugurated in New York, he seized upon the truism that the children of today are the audiences of tomorrow, and made it his business to train them for that vocation. In words of few syllables, he explained, illustrated at the piano, and then played with the orchestra, the masterpieces of symphonic literature. Many white-haired occupants of seats at concerts today listen to the César Franck Symphony through memories of the sonorous Damrosch voice, as it intoned, "All is lost, all is lost" to the main theme, approximately thirty-five years ago. He still continues his educational work on the radio, broadcasting music appreciation on a coast-to-coast network, and directing his broadcasts specifically to the schoolroom and Young America.

In every city, the story of the growth of the orchestra is more or less the same. From the amateur acorn springs the professional oak, almost as the mango tree is whisked into being by the Indian fakir. Almost, but not quite. For it takes considerable whisking to create and maintain a body of eighty men capable of interpreting with sincerity the great music of the masters. Much honor is due the pioneers to whom the modern orchestra owes its existence.

Tribute must be rendered, also, to the foreign groups who provoked America into orchestral growing pains. The Germania, one of the most stimulating and tireless, was dissolved in 1854, but two years previously a French import had come, seen, and conquered. The conductor, Jullien, a graduate of the Conservatoire, was a character—almost a caricature. He brought with him a band of forty well-trained French musicians, and increased the number to ninety in the bracing American climate, bracing to Jullien's pocketbook as well as his imagination. A sophisticated note of showmanship new to America came with him. To Theodore Thomas, who played first violin in his orchestra for a while, he appeared "the charlatan of all the ages," and in truth his antics must have affronted the forthright Thomas. Yet there was good musicianship behind the circus stunts.

For example, Jullien handled his men literally with gloved hands, in the presence of the public. The gloves were pink kid, and the hands they encased waved a jeweled baton with gesticulatory ardor which apparently exhausted their owner, for a crimson and gilt chair was placed behind him at every concert, in readiness to receive his plump little form. Into it he would sink at the end of a number, gloved hands clasped theatrically upon his chest, grinning like a Cheshire cat, as if with satisfaction at his own performance. Concerning his appearances in London before coming to this country, the *Illustrated London News* of November 25, 1843, commented as follows:

"Jullien is not a silent man; his *coup d'archet* is a proclamation, his most piccolo fiato is a whirlwind, and his very look indicates the presence of somebody determined to 'do something' and make a noise in the world. Well, he does, and most effectively does, something. He lethargizes his auditory to the most magnificent compositions of Beethoven, Weber, et cetera, but has the magician's power of awaking them to the highest and most attentive *qui vive* on striking up an English quadrille." (This piece was written in London, of course.) "This is mesmerism at command. But, badinage apart, Jullien is a man of considerable ability, and highly deserves the patronage bestowed upon him. It is not his fault, that the people will not relish the delicious fare he provides for them in the principal dishes he serves up; and if it be their penchant to 'feed more scurvily,' we can only exclaim, with Timon, 'Uncover, dogs, and lap!'"

In England, then, as well as in America, Jullien used quadrilles and polkas, in addition to his stunts, to sugar-coat the unpalatable pills of Beethoven, Weber, et cetera. His programs, lengthy as they were—for it was part of his popularity to give people their money's worth—were well played. Mendelssohn, Mozart, and Beethoven jostled schottisches, polkas, and galops. The works of American composers, too, such as they were at the time, were bait on his hooks. That was shrewdly done. He muzzled Fry and Bristow by giving excellent performances of their works; and others, forgotten today, had their chance, too. He gave them the boost which their own countrymen withheld, and he gave audiences some of the same symphonic works, with vaudevillian trimmings, that they were to hear later, without the trimmings, on Thomas' programs.

Another foreigner, who pursued somewhat similar tactics, was as broguishly Irish as Jullien was French. Patrick Sarsfield Gilmore was a bandmaster in the old country. So when he emigrated to Boston, he formed his own brass band with little delay, and led it on its tootling way from state to state, playing semipopular programs. The Civil War gave him his great opportunity. His band will be recalled as the one which introduced *John Brown's Body* as a marching song. He is also believed to have written *When Johnny Comes Marching Home Again*. Having made this contribution to the Civil War, he turned around to show what he could do for peace. A mammoth symphony orchestra was one of the instruments with which he celebrated the cessation of strife.

He put on two huge festivals, one in 1869, one in 1872, with sound effects which rocked Boston like an earthquake. The first was the more successful. He collected instrumentalists for the event until there was an orchestra of a thousand, with Carl Zerrahn and Julius Eichberg alternating at the conductor's stand. An organ was built into the hall which had been especially erected to hold fifty thousand people. A drum corps, military bands, and all the bells of the city swelled the orchestra, while an enormous chorus of the best voices in Boston held up the vocal end. A hundred red-shirted firemen struck real anvils in the chorus from *Il Trovatore*. Cannon volleys exploding in rhythm with the national songs on the program were touched off by electric buttons. The din must have been terrific, but the audience liked it. Gilmore was emboldened to try again in 1872, but his balloon had been inflated to the bursting point, and when he tried to blow it even bigger by doubling the number of participants, it burst.

Although the popular Irish bandmaster embarked on no conscious campaign to raise the level of musical taste but played what he liked, he had no call to apologize for the programs he put on in his own sensational way.[19] People came from all over the country, taking advantage of the excursion fares thoughtfully provided by the railroads. Many of them had never heard a symphony orchestra, so that however small the residuum of music, however large the percentage of ballyhoo they carried home with them, they were the better for the experience. Even those who sense deeply the lofty message of Beethoven are not necessarily without a bit of Barnum, a dash of Whiteman, perhaps even a touch of Duke Ellington, in their make-up. Jullien and Gilmore recognized this homely truth, and inveigled audiences into listening to high-brow music by presenting it in low-brow fashion, as entertainment.

Gilmore was a famous bandmaster. John Philip Sousa was another, who followed hard upon him. Both administered symphonic sustenance to nonsymphonic audiences. Band concerts have always been immensely popular, their informality making its special appeal to those who do not consider themselves quite up to a symphony concert. Sousa conducted the United States Marine Band for many years. He built it into a superorganization by impressing the men with the fact that a band *can* play softly, brasses or no brasses.

That alone was an achievement. Furthermore, he had them playing Wagner, Puccini, Verdi, and others, in excellent arrangements. He wrote many stirring marches for them, including the famous *Washington Post, Stars and Stripes Forever, El Capitan,* and *Hands across the Sea.* No band concert, no important event of the nineties, was complete without a Sousa march. The title of March King was well bestowed upon him. When, in 1892, he formed his own band, he worked with them as he had previously with the Marines. He took them abroad and showed the European potentates that a superlative brass band could be equally successful with the classics, with semipopular music, and ragtime. His efforts to popularize good music here with band concerts were unremitting. The heir to his ideals, Edwin Franko Goldman, the present protagonist of symphonic band concerts, like Sousa, has written and arranged a great many pieces for his band.

The Messiah of symphonic music in America, however, was Theodore Thomas—a Messiah with a testy temper, and with ideals so uncompromising that he raged like a lion at let or hindrance to his plans. When previously Thomas appeared in these pages, his coat was off, his back was up, and he was fighting for the life of the American Opera Company and opera in English. He was worsted in that fight for the time being. He admitted it. But it was only a minor incident in a career crowded with symphonic adventure. His life's work, pursued passionately, unwearyingly, selflessly, was to feed what he knew to be good music to the people of the United States, and to make them want it. He found them listening unintelligently, when at all, to a weird jumble of pieces, planned, like Jullien's and Gilmore's programs, mainly to attract the crowd. When Thomas acquired his own orchestra, he packed them onto a train, installed a diner of musical foods of the highest caloric content he knew, and went traveling with them. Back and forth they went, from East to West, weaving their way from towns where the only concert hall was the railway station, to towns which threw open an opera house to receive them. The line of march came to be known as the Thomas Highway. In truth, he took the high way, while others took the low way. It was a lonesome road, illumined by little of the sunshine of popular favor or financial success. All he had to light his path most of the time was his unswerving faith in his own mission, and his Joan-of-Arc-like conviction that he was the one elected to carry it through.

Thomas' whole life of seventy years was lived in music. At the age of ten, he came to New York from Esens, Germany, where he was born in 1835. He described the Gotham of those days as "a provincial town of two-story houses, where the pigs ran through the city and ate the refuse." But the provincial town offered young Thomas jobs by which he could help support his family. There was a market for his good German violin technique in dancing schools, theater orchestras and cafés, at weddings and banquets. At fourteen he took to the road, all alone except for his instrument, a box of clothes, and a lot of homemade posters announcing a concert by "the talented violin prodigy, Theodore Thomas." He put up his posters, collected the tickets at the door, then slipped back to the stage and gave his concert. No wonder he was asked to leave one little town in Mississippi because the authorities there believed the devil was in his fiddle. So it was— the devil of energy and ambition. They were clever to recognize it.

His career as a soloist ended with his return to New York. When Henrietta Sontag, Giulia Grisi, Mario, Jenny Lind, and other artists came from Europe, some kind of an orchestra was always hastily assembled for their concerts. Thomas was invariably to be found somewhere in the violin section. He kept his eyes open, and carefully noted the vagaries of all the conductors he played under, from Jullien up and down. It may have been negative education, a course in what not to do, but he stored it up carefully for future use. He had his first chance to conduct as a pinch hitter for Anschutz, who was directing the orchestra during the opera season at the Academy of Music. One night, December 7, 1860, to be exact, Anschutz fell ill just before the performance, an illness, it was said, aggravated by certain differences with the management. Theodore Thomas, his concertmaster, aged twenty-five, insouciantly conducted a performance of Halévy's *La Juive*, of which he had never even seen the score. When Anschutz resigned, shortly afterward, Thomas held the job. From then on, his right arm and the baton were one. In 1862, he formed his own orchestra, and drilled it, thoroughly, sternly, without mercy, until he felt that he could play upon it as upon his own violin. This was the famous Thomas Orchestra. It broke up now and then, due to financial hard sledding or public indifference, but the alumni always reunited loyally at the first call from their leader. Of the eighty he employed in New York, Thomas took forty on the road with him when, like Kim's Lama, he went out to seek converts and dispense musical wisdom.

The Thomas Orchestra was but one, though perhaps his pet project. In New York, he conducted in Terrace Garden and in Central Park Garden "pop" concerts out of doors, the programs of which rose as steadily in quality as did the mercury in the midsummer heat. From 1866 on for a number of years, he led both the New York Philharmonic and the Brooklyn orchestras. At one time, he was conducting his own and the New York Philharmonic in New York during the same season, making the concession to so arduous an undertaking of planning somewhat lighter programs for his own organization. Meanwhile, he was playing first violin in the Mason-Thomas Quartette, introducing into the aristocratic Dodworth salon the little-known chamber music of the masters.[20]

So much for Thomas in New York. If he had not been a musician, he would have made a first-class traveling salesman. He sold Boston; the formation of the Boston Symphony Orchestra by Colonel Higginson is directly traceable to the Thomas concerts which galvanized Boston out of its Harvard-Musical-Club lethargy. He sold Cincinnati; the music festival, which he directed annually for years, and the Cincinnati orchestra, organized and directed by him, resulted. The Cincinnati College of Music was one by-product. He headed it for a year, resigning because the free hand he had been promised was denied him. He conducted the Centennial Concerts in Philadelphia in 1876, for which no less a person than Richard Wagner composed a *Philadelphia Centennial March*. The success of this celebration led to his giving a series of subscription concerts there later. Although box-office receipts at a depressingly low level led to their discontinuance, a nucleus of music lovers who profited by the Thomas education wrote a letter to Santa Claus asking for a symphony orchestra in their Christmas stocking. The wish was not granted until 1900, but Santa then made up for the delay by providing a fine organization. Since 1912, when Leopold Stokowski took command, the Philadelphia Orchestra has been ranked among the best. A group of businessmen from Minneapolis heard the Thomas orchestra in Chicago, went back home determined to have their own, and did. And so it went. As time went on, more and more cities included in the itinerary of Thomas' orchestra became independent of his visits. The number of orchestras increased, the number of places on his route decreased. This was just what he wanted.

His own big opportunity came, according to some accounts, because a wealthy gentleman, name unknown, having nothing else to do, wandered idly into a "pop" concert in Chicago, and came forth to sing its praises. One day some weeks later, as Thomas was walking along the street in Philadelphia trying to figure out how he should pay his bills, whom should he meet but the selfsame gentleman, who entered into conversation with him.

After a while, "Would you go to Chicago if you were offered a permanent orchestra there?" he asked.

"I'd go to hell for a permanent orchestra," replied Thomas, fervently.

It was not required of him. In a short while, he received an invitation from a little group of sponsors, headed by his wife's brother, Charles N. Fay, to travel to Chicago for a meeting with them. He lost no time in availing himself of their invitation, which appeared heaven-sent. With all his apparent success, he was generally in financial hot water, thanks to his kindly habit of paying his men out of his own pocket when receipts were low, foregoing his own salary if there were no funds, and scrupulously meeting all bills, whether or not the responsibility was his. This was one of the dark times when he had disbanded his men, who had been "out" for three years. New York had shortsightedly let him go. In 1878, when Anton Seidl was conducting the Philharmonic, Leopold Damrosch the New York, and Thomas his own orchestra, the rivalry had been keen. Thomas, who was more or less of an old story by that time, had ceded to the others. Of course, as soon as Chicago had Thomas safely under contract, New York, Philadelphia, and probably other cities as well, would have given their eyeteeth to have him back. Too late. They had not killed him with kindness while they had him, and had in fact given him plenty of occasion to sob himself to sleep. Now he was lost to them.

Chicago was a bed of roses in comparison, roses not wholly without thorns, for Thomas always found thorns where any existed. But the three-year guarantee he was assured when he came was scrupulously observed, and the fifty guarantors paid the inevitable deficit each year without a murmur. He was free to organize his own orchestra and to plan his programs without interference. True, at the beginning of his stay there, a critic demanded to know, "Why does Mr. Thomas play the soggy tunes of Bach, Brahms and Bruckner? Has he never heard of Victor Herbert and Sousa?" And another asked him why he played so much Wagner. "People don't like it," he complained. "Then we must play it until they do," thundered Thomas.

One of the sore spots of his Chicago years was the Columbian Exposition of 1893, for which he had planned a mammoth program, with no expense spared. Paderewski was to play. American composers were to have a hearing. Thomas Paine, George W. Chadwick, Arthur Foote, Mrs. H. H. A.

Beach, and Dudley Buck had been commissioned to write new works. When the commercial and artistic elements clashed, as they so often do, Thomas found himself with his appropriation cut, with the advertisers at the fair aligned against him, and his artists in high dudgeon. He resigned, to sulk, like Achilles in his tent, until matters were smoothed out. When he returned to take up the baton, he had been vindicated, but as usual impoverished. He lived just long enough to conduct a few concerts in the beautiful new auditorium with which his services to music were ultimately rewarded. When he died, January 4, 1905, his assistant, Frederick Stock, took over the spirit, as well as the letter of the commandments laid upon him, and continued to feed Chicago its balanced ration, as prescribed by Thomas.

The ration was worked out on a simple theory. It is paradoxical that if a piece is heavy, it is *over* the heads of the audience, yet such seems to be the case. When Thomas played a symphony, usually esteemed the high point of heaviness, he placed on the program lighter pieces which bore, in theme or mood, some relationship to the symphony. If the audience sat quietly, without fidgeting or giggling, through the sermon, they received their peppermint drop as a reward. This took the form of a song or an instrumental solo, and the program would end with a rousing march or an overture. To more advanced listeners he occasionally administered another symphony as a closing number. Thomas' was more than a "five-year plan." A whole lifetime was not long enough for the steady advance he envisaged.

There are many "first times" on the list.[21] He stuffed Wagner and Brahms down people's throats until they ceased to choke and gag, and took to swallowing voluntarily. He played the music of Rubinstein as fast as that composer wrote and dispatched it to him; he introduced Tschaikowsky and Dvořák. The American composers Paine, Chadwick, Bristow, Buck, Converse, Gleason, Goldmark, and Pratt, besides others today forgotten, had generous encouragement from him.

By this time, the works of most of the composers introduced by Thomas are so familiar that the confirmed concert addict permits himself the privilege of an occasional murmur against the reiteration of their sonorities on one program after another. He says he knows them by heart and wants something new, although this does not prevent him from looking with a jaundiced eye on new works as they are tentatively offered. He is always ready to bring up the good old days of Theodore Thomas, forgetting that Thomas' pioneering was done against the same odds—indifference, lack of understanding, ultraconservatism, which afflict the musical pioneers of today. The one essential difference is that, thanks to Thomas, where there were but three orchestras when he started his work, there are hundreds today, equipped to give a fair field and no favor to the composer—that is, an adequate performance of works that seem to merit it. American composers are bending their backs to the task of providing such works.

CHAPTER X

SYMPHONIC COMPOSERS, OUR MUSICAL ARISTOCRACY

SYMPHONIES have come more trippingly than operas to the pens of American composers. Just as there is, according to the dramatists, hardly a literate individual who has not a cherished play hidden away in a desk drawer, there is hardly a composer, whatever his preferred form of writing, who has not succumbed at some time to the lure of the symphony.

The fact that the orchestras of the country are waiting to devour symphonic nourishment as it is fed to them furnishes a tremendous incentive to native composer chefs, who rejoice to see orchestra men and audiences turn from the familiar table d'hôte of foreign foods to dishes prepared according to the local recipe. As yet, too many cooks have not spoiled the broth. They have, however, by their number, made it difficult to fasten upon any one, or in fact any half dozen, as *cordons bleus*.

In the sixty years since the first American symphony was penned, no native Beethoven has arisen to furnish a comforting touchstone of musical values. In 1929, William Arms Fisher stated his belief that the great American symphony will come as the culmination of all the efforts of all the men who have written, and are today writing, music expressive of "the robust, smiling spirit of true Americanism." Aye, there's the rub. For that spirit, slow in emerging to any form of musical expressiveness, is here held especially in check by the very training which made it possible for American composers to write symphonies at all—that is, the influence exerted upon them by foreign teachers and by the hearing of foreign compositions.

So powerful was this influence that, in the beginning, inferiority complexes came out like a rash at the thought of competing with the foreign product in anything so ambitious as a symphony. American composers needed a sea voyage to give them the courage, as well as the technique, to proceed, and it was not until they had started to go abroad in great numbers that one of them took symphonic pen in hand.

John Knowles Paine (1839–1906), who wrote the first American symphony, was trained in Berlin, like most of his generation, and frankly followed German models. He was already well known, and the Handel and Haydn Society had produced his oratorio *St. Peter,* before Theodore Thomas, in 1876, gave his *C minor Symphony* its first performance in Boston. Paine did not suffer from neglect, the first symphony achieving eighteen performances in Boston alone during his lifetime. Theodore Thomas was naturally eager for the success of a work written on the lines of the German masterpieces which were his meat and drink. He commissioned

Paine to write several other works for the Philadelphia Centennial that same year, and for the Chicago World's Fair of 1893.[22]

In Dwight's Journal of February 5, 1876, the First Symphony was estimated as follows: "We listened to the whole work with pleasure and surprise. It is beautiful, it is earnest; it is learned and yet not manufactured but flows naturally as from a deep, full source, and it affects you as one live, consistent whole. What most struck us as a mark of progress . . . was the much greater freedom with which it was composed. . . . Whether it is a work of genius is a question always better left to time." The moderate, tolerant tone of this criticism was characteristic of John Sullivan Dwight, whose *Journal of Music* flourished from 1852 to 1881 and is probably the most valuable record in existence of the musical life of that period. Dwight was a conservative, who held his own uncompromising ideals before his readers, pointing the way to selective listening in a day when there was no music criticism worthy of the name. His carefully calculated estimates of his contemporaries, both native and foreign, won him the title of Father of American musical criticism.

He looked with a kindlier eye upon the products of that other parent, the Father of the American symphony, in that they were of the conservative school approved by him. Actually, the only startling fact about Paine's symphony is that it was the first. Occasional historical concerts dutifully feature one of his works on that account, without arousing audiences to any high pitch of enthusiasm for their musical content. In fact, as John Tasker Howard summarizes Paine's contribution, "It is but honest to admit that as a creative artist he was something of a pedant, wholly dominated by

European composers of the day," with a flair for the imitation of those composers, whose works he analyzed so ably for the wide-eyed students in his classes at Harvard.

He taught those students without salary for several years, while music was on trial at Harvard. When finally, in 1875, he and his subject were accorded a recognized place in the curriculum, Paine occupied the newly created chair of music, the first in an American university, and held it for thirty years. The course in organized music which he instituted served as a model for other universities which later followed Harvard's lead. Many of the students whom he led thoroughly, if not always ingratiatingly, through the mazes of theory and composition, achieved more or less renown, notably Daniel Gregory Mason, Arthur Foote, Frederick Converse, John Alden Carpenter, and Louis A. Coerne.

His contemporaries, William Wallace Gilchrist, Silas Gamaliel Pratt, and Frederick Grant Gleason, produced symphonies in addition to their other works, which, like Paine's, were in the best European tradition, but, unlike Paine's, were not the first of their kind in America, hence their value is chiefly as indices of the rising tide of courage to compose.

The task of giving American symphonic composers their due would be rendered a great deal easier were it possible to classify them neatly in groups, according to their style of composition, as are the great Europeans in Thomas W. Surette's book on *The Development of Symphonic Music*. Here, in a pigeonhole labeled "Classic," are filed Haydn and Mozart; "Epic," Beethoven; "Lyric," Schubert; "Realistic," Tchaikowsky; "Folk," Dvořák; "Neo-Classic," Brahms; "Mystic," Franck. It all works out admirably. But the generation of composers since Paine and his pupils cannot be disposed of in that fashion. They belong in a shoe with the little old lady who had so many composers she didn't know what to do. Having no desire to "spank them all soundly and put them to bed," but, on the contrary, to praise them all roundly and push them ahead, she found herself with a difficult problem.

To mention even the names and chief works of all those who have produced symphonic music in America requires an encyclopedia. It has been necessary, therefore, to select the few, with apologies to the many, and the reservation that they are chosen, not because in the opinion of this writer or any other they represent the best, but because their works exemplify definite trends, have been found worthy of performance by major orchestras, and have already assumed a certain importance.

There have been, for example, a large number of composers who believed that the fact that they lived and wrote in America was sufficient to impart a native bouquet to their symphonic wine, though it be pressed from the grapes of the Rhineland, of Malaga, or the Loire country. They write conservatively, much as they have been taught, taking no chances on novel tonal effects or experiments in form. The good old days, which Deems Taylor dubs the bad old days, are good enough for them. The composers immediately following Paine were naturally of this school. George Chadwick, Arthur Foote, Horatio Parker, Arthur Whiting, Mrs. H. H. A. Beach, Edgar Stillman Kelley, and Edward MacDowell all wrote symphonies together in Boston at the turn of the century; those of them who are living are still actively producing. Harold Morris describes their work as "more learned than inspired," being "too far from the heart-throbs of America." They might be called the Ivory Tower group, who leaned out from their lofty elevation to survey the American world they wrote about, but turned back to their European masters in attempting to interpret that world.

Edward MacDowell was the big man of the group, and his extra-wadded cosy corner in the Hall of Fame is among the composers of songs and piano works. Yet his orchestration of his *Piano Concerto* is as masterly as the solo part; his symphonic poems, *Lancelot and Elaine, Hamlet and Ophelia,* and *Lamia,* the fragments of the symphony he planned to write on the *Chanson de Roland,* and most decidedly of all, his two *Suites,* possess all the lyric beauty associated with his other writings. The Second or *Indian Suite* represented the first successful attempt by an American to use the red man's song as Dvořák had used the negro's. Lawrence Gilman described its Dirge as "the most profoundly affecting threnody in music since the Götterdämmerung Funeral March."

George Whitefield Chadwick wrote three symphonies and numerous symphonic poems along sturdily conservative lines. Since he was just as successful in the field of song, wrote virile and imaginative choral music, and many clear, melodious chamber works, he is one of those who present most acutely the problem of classification according to the type of composition favored. Apparently, he liked them all! The charm and sincerity, as well as the large quantity of his output, made him a beloved member of his group.

Arthur Foote, reminiscing about that group, and about the days in Boston when the writing of a symphony by one was an exciting and novel event calling for the support of all, mentions weekly meetings with Chadwick, Parker, and Whiting, at which they tore one another's work to pieces. When Foote played a movement of his new orchestral suite on the piano at one of these meetings, he waited tremulously for their reaction. Silence. Then up spoke Horatio Parker, "It is all in D minor!" So it was, and this explained a certain monotony in the piece. Foote made the necessary changes, was grateful for the criticism and came back for more.

Mrs. Beach's *Gaelic Symphony* is hardly less well known than her many songs. Edgar Stillman Kelley's symphonies, *Gulliver* and *New England*, his symphonic poem, *The Pit and the Pendulum*, and symphonic suite *Alice in Wonderland*, vie for favor with his oratorio, *The Pilgrim's Progress*, and the incidental music to *Ben Hur*.[23] The works of this entire group are never so highly seasoned as to cause indigestion. They are substantial and solid, and are served up with the German sauces which are known to render even flat foods palatable.

If MacDowell had a tendency to romantic self-expression, checked but not wholly curbed by intellectual censorship, the same may be said of the writings of a number of men who were partly his contemporaries, partly successors, among them Henry Hadley, Frederick Converse, Daniel Gregory Mason, Rubin Goldmark, John Powell, Charles Skilton, and Charles Martin Loeffler.

Loeffler, who left his home in Alsace-Lorraine to come to Boston at the age of twenty, lived there until his death in 1935, a matter of fifty-four years. In a memorial article in *Modern Music* in December, 1935, Edward Burlingame Hill of Harvard, himself a composer, wrote: "Already Loeffler has taken on the aspect of a legend. As a highly scrupulous, if exacting teacher, as a virtuoso in whom subtlety of detail never obscured vigor of interpretation, as an erudite and witty companion with a rich background of experience and anecdote, as a man of acute and varied tastes, and, in his music, as a master of finesse and almost eerie delicacy, equally at home in moods of robust vigor, Loeffler remains an unparalleled figure in our recent musical life."

All the while he was earning his living playing the violin in the big orchestras of New York and Boston, his true love was composition, and to composition he devoted himself from the moment of his retirement to his farm in Medfield in 1903. His disciples called him the Sage, but he was better pleased with the simple title, Farmer of Medfield. The crops raised by this "farmer" proved a source of nourishment to the American orchestra, inasmuch as they consisted of half a hundred compositions of high integrity. *La Mort de Tintagiles, La bonne chanson, La Villanelle du Diable,* for orchestra, and the *Pagan Poem* for voice and orchestra, are familiar to concertgoers. In them, Loeffler displayed his musical kinship with Franck, Chabrier, Debussy, and D'Indy, while the poems of the Frenchmen Verlaine, Baudelaire, Rollinat and Gustave Kahn inspired his somewhat melancholy muse in other works. He made a study of plain song, and used it with distinction in an unpublished symphony in one movement, in the *Hora Mystica,* and the *Hymn to the Sun* for voice and small orchestra. Yet he was fond of jazz, and believed it could be used in the interest of higher expression. He was perhaps more of an impressionist than anything else, with a strong romantic twist. His idiom is individual and distinctive, and remains, in the opinion of Lawrence Gilman, "an apt and expressive vehicle of beauty and eloquence and distinguished musical thought."

Henry Hadley has been one of the most prolific writers of this group. Besides an enormous output in other forms, he produced three tone poems, *Salome, Lucifer,* and *The Ocean,* and five symphonies. The fifth, written for the Connecticut Tercentenary of 1935, conveys in three movements the three centuries of American history. It is lyric, flowing, programmatic, and bland—epitome of all that was Hadley. So lovable a man, so facile a composer, so generous of his talents was he, that as founder, president, and later honorary president of the American Society of Composers and Conductors, he assumed something of the position of Dean of the Society.

Frederick Converse redeemed himself, in the eyes of those who did not care for his operas, with his orchestral writings, of which the fantasy, *The Mystic Trumpeter,* and symphonic poems *Ormazd* and *Ave atque Vale* are representative. He studied with Paine and Chadwick here, with Rheinberger and Jadassohn in Germany, and learned to employ the rules of harmony and counterpoint which enabled him to write freely and with easy fluency in the larger forms. Among his writings are three symphonies and two tone poems, *California* and *American Sketches,* the latter based on Carl Sandburg's *Song-Bag.*

John Powell, the Virginia composer, generally makes use of the orchestra as a background for the solo instrument, although he has written a number of orchestral suites, of which *Natchez-on-the-Hill* is one of the most grateful. In this piece, and in the *Rhapsodie nègre* for piano and orchestra, Mr. Powell has utilized his researches into American folk song to add a racy local tang to his own music. Carefully thought out, following recognized forms, this is an interesting mélange of his own romanticism, the German ideal, and the influences of the South, which have played upon him all his life except for his few years in Germany.

His friends, Daniel Gregory Mason and Rubin Goldmark, both had the advantage of membership in musical families. Daniel's grandfather was Lowell Mason, who probably did more for music education in this country than any other teaching pioneer; his uncle was William Mason, of the Mason-Thomas Quartette. The chamber-music form has been his darling, but he has been unfaithful to her to the extent of a festival overture and several symphonies. His writings about the works of others, and his teachings at Columbia, have influenced many young composers to follow correct, if conservative, rules of creation. Rubin Goldmark was a nephew of the Hungarian Karl, famous composer. Rubin's musical education was a blend of New York and Vienna, with a dash of Bohemian from his last teacher, Dvořák. His tone poem, *Samson;* a *Requiem* suggested by Lincoln's Gettysburg Address; a *Negro Rhapsody;* and *The Call of the Plains* possess, in addition to romantic color, those qualities for which his after-dinner speeches were famous—continuity, spontaneity, and humor.

Ernest Bloch, a Swiss who has paid such long visits here that he probably no longer knows whether he is Swiss or American, is at least partly of this group, since there is a strong romantic quality in his writing, though his idiom is that of a later day. When he came to this country in 1916, at the age of thirty-six, he had been violinist, conductor, and composer in his own country, yet he came without gilt-edged introductions, remaining to reap golden rewards. He elected himself spokesman of his race, explaining, "It is the Jewish soul that interests me, the complex, glowing, agitated soul that

I feel vibrating throughout the Bible." *Schelomo,* a rhapsody on the Song of Solomon for cello and orchestra, the *Israel Symphony,* and the Jewish Sacred Service *Avodath Hakodesh* are some of his racial writings. He wrote the *Concerto Grosso,* and symphony *America* while in this country, the latter bearing as dedication the lines of Walt Whitman, "Oh, America, because you build for mankind, I build for you."

French impressionism, like German romanticism, also left its mark on composers of the symphony in America. Of those who, like Loeffler, took kindly to it, are Edward Burlingame Hill, John Alden Carpenter, to a certain extent Deems Taylor, and Charles Tomlinson Griffes. Griffes, an ardent disciple of Debussy, was a young man gifted with an exquisite imagination, which, in conjunction with his untimely death, caused him to be known as the Keats of American music. Although he died at thirty-six, he left as a legacy, with his slim sheaf of orchestral writings, the general respect of his peers for their unquestionable merit. *The Pleasure Dome of Kubla Khan* for orchestra, after Coleridge's poem, is impressionistic writing of a high order. His *Poem* for flute and orchestra, and his songs and piano pieces, notably *The White Peacock,* which has been arranged for chamber orchestra, are frequently performed. In his three tone pictures, *The Lake at Evening, The Vale of Dreams,* and *The Night-Wind,* he displayed a richness of dissonance, with an absence of tonal root or key center, and a freedom of meter and rhythm not practiced by other composers of his generation.

John Alden Carpenter's *Perambulator Suite* for orchestra, a humorous musical commentary on the fleeting impressions of an infant in a pram, was another piece of impressionistic writing, which has had a place on concert programs since it was first played in 1915 by the Chicago and New York orchestras. Between it and *Sea Drift,* a symphonic poem after the verse of Walt Whitman, there elapsed twenty years of growth for Carpenter. Meanwhile, his jazz ballet, *Skyscrapers,* had appeared on the stage of the Metropolitan Opera House, and his charming song suites from Tagore and other Oriental poets, as well as his jazz *Krazy Kat,* had found their way onto many a program.

Almost all of those thus far mentioned, through adhering to known formulas, have reaped the wheat of public comprehension and approval, along with the tares of criticism of their conservatism. There has been enough of the wheat to furnish flour for plenty of bread. While audiences feed upon it, a new musical generation of men and women has arisen, who speak out with pronounced courage, authority, and belief in the present. They have bathed in the waves of a- and poly-tonalism which have come rolling stormily from Europe to this side of the Atlantic. A few of them have given themselves over wholly to the delights of sporting in the surf of discord, forming strange combinations of sounds which the uninitiated will persist in calling noise. They use many keys at one time, and base their writing on newly constructed scales; they work with new or no forms; they evolve esoteric musical ideas. They are in the sensational minority. The less extreme protagonists of modern expressionism in music are in the vast majority. They have succumbed with reservations, and employ the new techniques as but one of the tools in their equipment. They are in fact the thoughtful students, whose work is the legitimate offspring of Paine and Chadwick and MacDowell, though it has ceased to resemble its forebears.

For lack of a better name, we have chosen to call these the "conservative moderns." Most of the American composers of today belong in this group, some being more, others less restrained.[24]

Roy Harris has steadily elbowed his way to the fore of their ranks. Harris writes with an unmistakable twang, the mark of his pioneer ancestry. In his *Farewell to Pioneers,* a symphonic elegy performed by the Philadelphia Orchestra in March, 1935, he paid direct tribute to "a passing generation of Americans, to which," said he, "my own father and mother belong. I have tried to write an elegy in their memory, reflecting in its structure, harmony, and orchestration a directness and clarity of objectives similar to the quality of their lives." The piece is rugged, substantial, and unsentimentally effective. Two symphonies, an *American Overture on the Theme When Johnny Comes Marching Home* and several single-movement fragments comprise his orchestral output, in addition to his chamber music and choral works. The sinewy body of this blond Oklahoman finds its counterpart in his music, which is sturdy, well knit, and carries little superfluous flesh. His themes swing from medieval plain song and chant, on the one hand, to the Scotch-Irish folk songs he heard in Nebraska in his youth, on the other. It is his theory that American composers do not employ unconventional rhythms with conscious sophistication, but because they cannot avoid them. His own talent being spontaneous, he perhaps attributes to others the type of compulsion which drives him. Paul Rosenfeld says: "Harris's music obviously has the integrity of the thing not made, but created." Harris stated his aims in his notes to *An American Overture:* "The moods which seem particularly American to me are a noisy ribaldry, a sadness, a groping earnestness, which amounts to suppliance towards those deeper spiritual yearnings within ourselves; and finally, a fierce struggle of will for power, sheer power in itself. There is little grace or mellowness in our midst. That will probably come after we have passed the high noon of our growth as a people."

Aaron Copland is frequently compared with Harris. Both studied with Nadia Boulanger in Paris, both won Guggenheim fellowships, and both are about the same age, but there the resemblance ceases. Copland's music is nervous, vital, built up architecturally with deft skill. He has analyzed jazz intelligently, and has employed it daringly and effectively, though careful not to make a fetish of it. His pieces keep moving, they are cumulatively taut and tense. To modern harmonies he adds rhythms and polyrhythms of an interestingly complex nature, which, piled one on the other, make the hearing of his pieces a most exciting experience. He mercifully retains melody, and with it the sense of unity. Copland was born in Brooklyn, and lives and works in New York, while his music is known both in this country and abroad, appearing on every program of importance where contemporary Americans are represented. He has to his credit works in all forms. It is his belief that an American idiom cannot be had for the asking, but will appear in the natural course of events, like a good golf shot, if composers do not press. There are definite foreshadowings of that idiom in his own works, which make up for a certain lack of passion and depth by their power, color, and intensity. The *Symphony for Organ and Orchestra, Dance Symphony, Symphonic Ode,* and First and Second symphonies, as well as the *Music for the Theatre* for chamber orchestra, are characteristically Copland. Regarded a few years ago as a radical, he has taken his place today among the thoughtful moderns of the older younger generation.

Copland fits into both the group of serious composers who employ jazz and the conservative modern group. One of his contemporaries who has thus far kept clear of such entangling alliances with jazz is Roger Sessions. This serious, bespectacled gentleman, who is the very portrait of the college professor, has taken such courageous liberties with form as only one who is thoroughly familiar with it in all its traditional majesty dares to do. A pupil of Bloch, he broke away from that master to attach himself fervently to Stravinsky. He is best known for his orchestral suite, *The Black Maskers,* a highly complicated piece which employs all the resources known to modern composers to contribute to the establishment of a deeply somber mood. He has written a symphony described by Rosenfeld as "the sturdiest, most forceful, and most intricate of his compositions." Sessions, sincerity, and seriousness appear to be synonymous.

More conservative in style is Howard Hanson, Director of the Eastman School of Music in Rochester. In this strategic position, he not only leads the orchestra and forms the student mind, but circulates as guest conductor with major orchestras all over the country. Thus he has had ample opportunity to conduct his own works, and to make them known throughout the length and breadth of the land. The most eloquent of spokesmen for the American composer, he has initiated and directed concerts of American music in Rochester for the past ten years. Many a colleague has been boosted by his efforts to the back of that skittish colt, popular favor, where he himself is firmly seated. To Mr. Hanson,

Americanism in music is "partly rhythmic, partly a sentimental quality of melody and mood, and probably it is
something much less tangible." "Whatever it is," he says,
"it is certainly there, and those who insist on a typically
American idiom can rest content. They are going to get it."
One stage in the evolution of that idiom is illustrated by his
own writing. It is careful, conservative, neither shattering in
its modernity nor syrupy in its romanticism, but somewhere
betwixt and between. His *Nordic Symphony No. 1,* and his
tone poem, *Pan and the Priest,* are familiar to all concertgoers. His Second Symphony, the *Romantic,* was played by
the Boston Symphony under Koussevitzky to celebrate the
fiftieth anniversary of the orchestra's existence. *North and
South, Lux Aeterna, The Lament for Beowulf, The Heroic
Elegy,* and a number of shorter works, attest Mr. Hanson's
skill in writing for the orchestra.

Like the ghosts of the slain on the field of Wagram, crowd-
ing about L'Aiglon, the son of Napoleon, the figures of others
of this group swarm about us, clamoring for at least a word.
There is Douglas Moore, of Columbia University, who has
managed to put into much of his music the infectious laugh
which endears him as a person. William Grant Still of California is perhaps the outstanding negro composer of the moment, with several splendid orchestral works. One of them,
the *Afro-American Symphony,* culminates in a magnificent
finale on the theme, "Be proud, my race, in mind and soul."
Frederick Jacobi, who lived and worked in San Francisco for
many years, and now teaches at the Juilliard School in New
York and Smith College in Northampton, reflects in his music
his cordial emotional reaction to the world. His orchestral
writings are a blend of flowing lyricism with the stac-

cato of today's idiom. Eric Delamarter and Felix Borowski, who have written and conducted in Chicago, and the veteran Frederick Stock, have sent their works to be played outside of that windy city.[25] The list stretches on and on, and must be halted arbitrarily.

The ultramodern group represent the farthest swing to the left which the musical pendulum has taken in this generation. Turned loose upon the rich resources of the modern orchestra, they became veritable bulls in a china shop, smashing crockery with the most ear-splitting disturbance of sound waves. Polytonality and atonality vie for their favor; odd instrumental combinations, such as groups of percussion instruments alone, or half a dozen muted trumpets, or a collection of broken bottles, are used at the composer's whim; and in the orchestral works, strange sounds are added to the familiar instrumental noises. Melody, harmony, and form, as most people conceive them, are out of the ultramodern picture. Each man writeth as he listeth, and at times he listeth passing strangely.

Leo Ornstein came from Russia to lead the assault on the ears of America, and having provoked columns of irate newspaper discussion, retired to a peaceful life playing and teaching others to play the piano, far from the clash of modern theories and practices. His *Lysistrata Suite* for orchestra, and symphonic poem *The Fog,* were storm centers about which eddied much excited comment. Ornstein made the statement that the two most acute experiences of his youth were the pogrom in Russia, from whose horrors he found asylum here, and his colorful and adventurous youth in the poverty of New York's lower East Side. From them, he doubtless drew the hardihood to speak out when the spirit moved him in terms which caused one critic to call his music a "volcanic eruption."

A naturalized Frenchman, Edgar Varese, has made even mightier efforts toward elevating to the level of music sounds ordinarily classed as noise. Varese finds it anachronistic to write of purling brooks, the beat of horses' hooves, and the sighing of the wind in a twentieth-century world filled with the clank of machinery, and the roar of crowded cities. He resembles the novelist Thomas Wolfe in the ruthless drive with which he forces that world upon our consciousness, though, fortunately, without Wolfe's redundancy. Percussion instruments he finds better adapted to his purpose than strings, which convey to him a somewhat mushy romanticism. So he writes pieces like *Amériques* and *Arcana,* for full orchestra, and for chamber orchestra *Intégrales, Hyperprism,* and *Ionisation,* the last for thirteen percussion players in two groups. He selects those noises in which, to his mind, music is implicit, and if the audience, spoilt child that it is, resents the absence of what it calls melody, Varese is rather pleased than otherwise, taking their hisses and catcalls as a tribute to his originality. A man of great personal charm, and considerable expressiveness in explaining his ideas, Varese has been in the forefront of the radicals who insist upon the introduction into symphony programs of the new and the different.

Another atonalist who, though no Frenchman, fell strongly under French influence, is George Antheil. When his *Ballet mécanique* was performed by an orchestra in New York, in 1927, the police reserves had to be called out to quell what threatened to be a riot against the introduction into Carnegie Hall of alarm clocks, steam sirens, and clacking typewriters, in the name of music. In the two Symphonies, *Piano Concerto, Zingaresca,* and *Capriccio,* which he has written for full orchestra, he has been daring and deafening. He has been Peck's Bad Boy in American music, but there are signs, in his writing for the screen, that he is ready to do away with the more sensational aspects of his youthful writings, and employ a less extreme idiom.

A composer who, to a number of watchful contemporaries, has given evidence of an original talent sufficient to class him as a genius, is Carl Ruggles. Though born in Marion, Massachusetts, in 1883, and educated at Harvard, Ruggles never fell into the New England, nor indeed, into any mold. An epic quality dwells in the sonorous orchestral works of this mystic, with his strange cyclic concept of life. *Men and Angels, Men and Mountains, Portals,* and *Sun-Treader* are his larger compositions. Paul Rosenfeld, distinguished critic, has this to say of him: "Ruggles' harmonic schemes are of the greatest distinction. This quality, neither rich nor magnificent, nevertheless exquisitely refined, and new to harmonic writing, associates itself with early American furniture and Hartley's color, Portsmouth's doorways and Hawthorne's prose. His instrumentation timbre is equally this Cape Cod American's own. The melancholy and smothered passion is as characteristic of the New England countryside as anything by Robinson or Frost. So, too, is the harshness of certain of Ruggles' brazen sonorities." On the other hand, it must be confessed that *Angels,* written for six muted trumpets, appealed more to the risibilities than to the musical sensibilities when performed at a League of Composers' concert in New York. But disciples can be developed from scoffers, and the ranks of Ruggles initiates are growing. They are augmented by those who get from the cryptic paintings he is now producing in his home in Arlington, Vermont, an insight into the complicated mechanism of his thought.

Charles Ives, a Connecticut boy who graduated from the organ loft to a business career, composes as an avocation. His business success may have emboldened him to the point of refusing to cater to any but the select musical trade, for his scores are so puzzling to read, what with his original tonal ideas and extra instruments, that supermusicianship, plus hyperintelligence, are barely adequate to decipher them. His four symphonies and three orchestral suites have supplanted the cross-word puzzle in the repertoire of orchestra conductors with a passion for the conquest of difficulties. Ives was sixty before the world took notice of him, but his original experiments in polyrhythms and polyharmonies preceded those of more freely advertised composers. In his later years, he has played with quarter tones, on which some of his colleagues have also been burning their fingers.

Henry Cowell perhaps burned his fingers so badly that he decided to use elbows instead. His name is most intimately associated with the "tone clusters" which result when the piano is played with the elbows. Furthermore, he has made liberal use of quarter tones and heretical intervals in multiple combinations of sound and rhythm in his symphony, and in the tone poems, *Vestiges, Some Music and Some More Music,* and *Communications.* Whether he chooses the symphonic or chamber music form, his works are bound together by a common tie of discord. Many of them, and those of other members of the modern group, were published in Cowell's quarterly magazine, *New Music.*[26]

There are enough programs on which American works appear today to make it difficult to realize that the first hazardous experiment in presenting an all-American program was conducted only about fifty years ago. On July 3, 1884, for the edification of the annual meeting of the National Association of Music Teachers, a certain Mr. Calixa Lavallée, the then president of the Association, presented a program of piano works, songs, and string quartettes, some by men of mark, some by unknown soldiers. Mr. Lavallée probably felt like the circus performer shot from the mouth of the cannon—he had to pinch himself after the performance to make sure there was any of himself left to pinch. Emboldened by his survival, he planned and held a concert of orchestral works the following year at the Academy of Music in New York. It was his fond hope that this would be the first of its kind. But Theodore Thomas had enlivened the month of August, 1882, in Chicago, with a summer concert of works by Paine, Chadwick, and other favorites, and Frank von der Stucken, an enterprising young composer and conductor, outstripped him in New York by six months. The four Novelty Concerts which Von der Stucken conducted in Steinway Hall, beginning in December of that year, were highly praised by Krehbiel, always on the *qui vive* for native talent. After the last program, on which appeared works by Paine, MacDowell, Dudley Buck, George E. Whiting, Ellsworth C. Phelps, G. Templeton Strong, and Von der Stucken himself, Krehbiel commented approvingly on the vigor, freshness, originality, high ideals, and learning displayed, although a French critic, after a similar performance, found that "American composers oscillate between the French and German schools; they have at times expression, but never originality or color" (*American Musician*, August 3, 1889).

Prohibition was repealed, as far as the American symphony went, and the public thirst has been catching up with the increased supply. Apathy and inertia, and an ever-renewed supply of foreign works retard the appreciation of the latest American products. The West appears to be most willing to permit the American composer to fill some of its wide-open spaces with his compositions. During the decade from 1926 to 1936, the Chicago Orchestra performed two hundred and forty-seven compositions from the pens of seventy-four American composers, a formidable number! This orchestra led all the others in thus extending encouragement to the American symphony.

Hans Kindler, director of the National Symphony Orchestra in Washington, D. C., recently performed an interesting experiment upon his unsuspecting audience. He attempted a slow *gradus ad Parnassum Americanum*. That is, having unobtrusively slid one or two native works on the programs of his first two seasons, he boldly came out with first a half, then a whole program, designed "to afford examples of the different styles of composition today in America, from the semi-classic and romantic idioms of Daniel Gregory Mason and Deems Taylor to the masterful and finely tempered modern treatment by Randall Thompson in his *Symphony,* and the uncompromising, farmer-like harshness and asceticism of the *Chorale and Variations* by Roy Harris." On a ballot taken afterward, the Randall Thompson Symphony was voted most popular, the Harris piece least.

By way of proving that statistics lie, however, there is the contrary evidence of the radio poll held in November, 1935, to determine the favorite composers of those who listened in on the broadcasts of the New York Philharmonic Orchestra for a season. Beethoven having been voted the favorite composer of the past, and the Finnish Sibelius of the present, it then appeared that Harris had more votes than any other Americans for whom ballots were cast, including Gershwin, Sowerby, Hanson, Bloch, Taylor, and Carpenter. This proves not only that the public pulse is fluctuating, but that the musical background of the voters may have much to do with the result. Kindler drew his conclusions from a Washington audience steeped in the traditions of Europe. The radio listeners, in all probability, comprised a much more varied group, educationally as well as geographically. Sufficiently musical to listen regularly to symphonic broadcasts and form their own opinions, they showed themselves sufficiently open-minded to admit an original modern like Sibelius to first place in their favor.

A group still more proletarian than the radio audience—those who attend the free symphony concerts provided by the Federal Government in New York—signified their acceptance of their compatriots' orchestral works by applauding, during two seasons, one hundred and four compositions, representing sixty-seven American composers. Not all are destined to live, nor their composers to the enjoyment of enduring fame. But their success with such audiences is a straw which indicates a rising symphonic wind from the native point of the musical compass.

CHAPTER XI

MUSIC WHOSE PLACE WAS IN THE HOME,
THOUGH IT DID NOT REMAIN THERE

SYMPHONY concerts are very well in their place, but that place is distinctly not the home, unless one dwells in the Hall of the Mountain King. Aside from the obvious drawback of lack of space, the implication of home is intimacy, the warm current uniting the individuals within its walls in a common bond of love and understanding. Wholesale intimacy with an eighty-piece orchestra is a manifest absurdity, hence there always has been, and probably always will be, some form of "room music," vocal or instrumental. It is the same whether it makes its appearance in the small concert hall or the family sitting room.

When Francis Hopkinson, probably the most distinguished amateur of his generation, wrote artless art songs for his own pleasure, and performed them in his own drawing room, he fathered a whole dynasty of art songs which found their way

in course of time to the larger audience. Louis Moreau Gottschalk's piano pieces, designed as salon music for the favored
few, appeared on his concert programs when, as a virtuoso,
he made the first European grand tour undertaken by an
American pianist. Other composers interested in exploiting
the possibilities of single instruments followed his example.
Works for small combinations, solos, sonatas, trios, quartettes, and even chamber orchestras seem to have been always with us in some form. Since the turn of the century
and the chamber-music contributions of George W. Chadwick, the number of such compositions to be presented in
this country has enormously increased. It is as if the urge
for bigger and better everything had been tempered by a
return to home life and all that goes with it, including intimate music.

Away back before the Revolution, amateurs lit and fed
the home fires around which clustered an active musical life.
For information about these early days, we are indebted to
Mr. O. G. Sonneck, who hunted it down with the zest of a
child pursuing the rolling Easter egg on the White House
lawn. Mr. Sonneck's conclusion was that sacred and secular
music developed about equally, despite the strong pull of
psalmody in New England. With Boston given over to sacred
song, Charleston frankly secular, and New York and Philadelphia serving both masters, he finds plenty of singing and
playing going on, though much of it was in whispers, behind
closed doors. Richardson Wright, too, in his interesting volume, *Hawkers and Walkers in Early America*, writes: "Again
and again in the local histories of towns and in the records
left by early travelers, we find accounts of family singing,
of singing in the church, and of singing schools and singing

masters." And he goes on to tell of the work of the itinerant teacher, who would come to town, announce in the church and the school that he was opening a singing class, and secure a number of pupils. All the equipment he needed to teach people their notes was a piece of chalk, a blackboard, and a pitch pipe. He would stay as long as attendance was satisfactory, then pull up stakes and move on to another town. But the girls he left behind him, and the boys, too, kept on singing around the old harmonium in the church or home.

That old harmonium, or melodeon, which preceded the piano as the heart of the home, may often have wheezed or played out of tune. Nevertheless, its importance cannot be overestimated. It was as essential as the framed mottoes over the hearth, and its widespread use gave all America a focus in the home for singing and playing. It created a demand eventually gratified to everyone's satisfaction by the introduction of the modern piano. By 1840, the piano-manufacturing business was flourishing healthily, and within a few years America had assumed the leadership in this field, a leadership which she has held right down to the present day.

Long before the piano started showing its teeth in a smile, however, other instruments and teachers were much in demand, judging from advertisements culled from the early chronicles of Boston, Philadelphia, Charleston, and New York. The first music teacher on record in Philadelphia was a Miss Ball, presented to her public in 1730 by her amiable brother, who advertised that "Singing, playing on the Spinet, Dancing, and all sorts of Needle Work are taught by his sister, lately arrived from London." The lady's versatility was not unusual. Had she confined herself to the spinet alone, she would probably have suffered from a marked dearth of pupils. Another advertisement of a considerably later date in the Newport *Mercury* (1766) lumps violins for sale with dress goods, jewelry, sewing materials, window glass, short-handled frying pans, et cetera. Still another in the same journal announces that "any person who plays well on a violin, on application to the printer hereof may be inform'd where he will meet with proper Encouragement." These are among the quaintly worded notices of bona fide sales of "harpsichords, cellos, violins, good German flutes, and all kinds of music." Also, although the correspondence method of learning in ten easy lessons had not been introduced, there seems to have been at least one enterprising spirit who believed in winning neophytes by minimizing difficulties. Mr. Robert Coe advertised his offer to "teach the German flute by an easy method with a new Mouth-Piece which does not in the least alter the tone of the Flute but does the same as if blown by the nicest lip." Most of his competitors were apparently dancing masters first, and music teachers afterward, according to the wording of the inducements which they extended to potential pupils.

Indeed, the early musical history of our country indicates that it was foot-minded long before jazz reared its black head. Music and the dance were sweetly married on every occasion, whether it called itself a "consort" or not. Here again the hand of the amateur may be discerned. The exact place and time of the first concert is debatable. Charleston, according to Mr. Sonneck, has the honor of the first of which there is record, held in 1731, beating Boston by a few months. Since Charleston undisputedly entertained the first ballad-opera, however, many historians, perhaps on the ground of fair distribution, perhaps because he was dancing master as well as impresario, accord to Mr. Peter Pelham, of Boston, the prior claim. He issued his invitation to the public to attend a "Concert of Music on sundry instruments," in 1731. Four months later, Charleston had a similar affair, then New York, and Philadelphia. These so-called Concerts of Music were nice, homelike affairs, part amateur and part professional. The musical part of the program was offset by the ball which followed, for which the concert artists obligingly provided the dance music. It all had a formal informality, beruffled and brocaded and aristocratic in spirit, and social within its group. The stronger the English influence, the more high-toned the affair. The admixture of French in the South intensified the luxurious aspects there, adding the opulence of the French court, jealously cherished by the émigrés before their own Revolution made democrats of them. There were doubtless many more of such concerts than historians have recorded, and they continued to be given after the Revolution with some of the more snobbish features toned down, as befitted a democratic country.

At this time, too, there were individual musicians working away in their own four walls, just for the love of it. In 1744, William Black of Philadelphia wrote in his *Journal:* "I rose from my bed and passed two hours in writing; the rest of the time till Breakfast I spent with my Fiddle and Flute." William was probably the delight of the drawing rooms of Philadelphia, which, from Governor Penn's down, seem to have been graced with a great deal of such music.

There is mention of nothing much more intimate in home performance than that of Benjamin Franklin, practicing his harmonica at night while his wife slumbered beside him.

When she was awakened by the sounds, she vowed that she thought herself dead, and surrounded by angels singing heavenly strains, evidence not only of her husband's excellent execution, but of her own amiability. Franklin's harmonica was not the mouth organ known to us by that name, but an instrument he himself devised. It was a variant of Gluck's "musical glasses," played like a xylophone, and probably resembling it in quality of sound. When his friends wearied of his harmonica, Franklin could always oblige them with variety in the shape of a tune on guitar, harp, or violin. His blue-walled living room, "with musical figures tacked on the ceiling," was a meeting place for the music lovers of the city.

The Father of His Country, although himself not a performer, missed no opportunity to hear music, at the play or in private. When, in 1788, Francis Hopkinson sent him *Seven Songs for Harpsichord or Forte Piano,* containing the famous *My Days Have Been So Wondrous Free,* the dedication modestly stated: "With respect to the little work, which I have now the honor to present to your notice, I can only say that it is such as a Lover, not a Master, of the Arts can furnish. I am neither a profess'd Poet, nor a profess'd Musician; and yet I venture to appear in those characters united, for which, I confess, the censure of Temerity may justly be brought against me. . . . However small the Reputation that I shall derive from this Work, I cannot, I believe, be refused the Credit of being the first Native of the United States who has produced a Musical Composition. If this attempt should not be too severely treated, others may be encouraged to venture on a path, yet untrodden in America, and the Arts in succession will take root and flourish amongst us." To which Washington replied regretfully, "I can neither sing one of the songs, nor raise a single note on any instrument, to convince the unbelieving." But he looked to it that his ward, Nelly Custis, had harpsichord lessons from Alexander Reinagle so that she might sing and play for him his favorite song *The Way-Worn Traveler,* from *The Mountaineers.* Many marches and songs were dedicated to him, but the only one hardy enough to have survived with honor is *Hail Columbia.*

Another President, Thomas Jefferson, might really have become a great musician had he not been so busy as a statesman. He dreamed of importing musical artisans, who would constitute an amateur orchestra when not laying bricks or mixing mortar. He would have had them play for him in his home at Monticello, which would thus have become a court of music. But the dream came to nothing, and he was obliged to console himself by playing the violin, on which he was an excellent performer. He owned one of the first Cremonas known in this country, and kept up his daily practice even when beset with the many duties of the presidency. He might have been a modern parent paying for music lessons, so frequently and earnestly did he adjure his children: "Do not neglect your music. It will be a companion which will sweeten many hours of your life." They appear to have taken his advice, and in their turn to have become excellent amateurs.

That there is a reverse side to the joys of music at home, nobody can deny. Seldom has it been more ably set forth than in a misanthropic anonymous article in the *Massachusetts Magazine* of June, 1796, entitled, "Reflections on the Absurdity, Folly, and Inconsistency of certain Fashionable Customs and Ceremonies Practiced in Public and Private Companies," to wit: "There is another custom which of all others tries the senses and stupefies the fancy. This is the absurd parade of asking some pouting miss to sing, who will bear teasing for a full hour before she complies; and then in a most wretched squall she disturbs your ears for an hour:— for when once set off she rattles away like the clack of a mill, while all the company are under the necessity of praising the screaming demon for the very torture she has given them."

Years have elapsed since the "screaming demon" of 1796. Meanwhile, families have learned the fun of singing together. Dudley Buck and Homer Bartlett, who wrote in 1855, were prolific song composers. They continued Hopkinson's art-song dynasty and ushered in an enormous number of song writers. The instrumentalist also came into his own. One of the most interesting cycles was that which led from the home to the symphony orchestra, back again to the home, and so out to the concert platform. Many chamber-music groups developed in that way. When the symphony orchestra was only a gleam in its father's eye, everybody who could scratch, blow, or beat an instrument was pressed into its service. After the large groups were established, however, some of the members began to hanker for the string quartettes they had played in the Fatherland. Little pieces broke off from the big orchestra body, and drifted back to the parlor. Small combinations were formed. One of the first of these, which established itself securely in the home before extending its activities to the world outside, was the Mendelssohn Quintette Club, whose members gravitated to one another in Boston in 1849. They practiced the Mendelssohn two-viola quintette, Opus 18, with such assiduity at their meetings that their organization adopted the name without question.

The Mendelssohn Quintette Club burst into public notice

with a kid-gloved soirée in Jonas Chickering's piano rooms, to which two hundred select music lovers received cards of invitation. So many more wanted to come than could be accommodated that a subscription series of four concerts was provided for the overflow. Thereafter the Quintette Club led a belle's life, described with gusto by their second violin, Mr. Ryan, in his genial memoir, *Reflections of an Old Musician.* They were in demand for soirées "for a hundred miles around Boston," and later in their career made extended tours. A charming note on their activities appears in a letter written some twenty years after their debut by the Reverend Thomas Wentworth Higginson: "The only entertainment will be light as air musical airs from the Mendelssohn Quintette Club, dispensed in Mrs. Dame's back parlor, while 'all the world' sit on sixty chairs in front. We wish to do something for the public service, and finding this the *cheapest* form of entertainment, do this. Don't you think well of it? Among the guests not sitting in chairs, we are to have Beethoven, Weber, Haydn, and Mendelssohn."

Since the Mendelssohn Quintette Club, there have been any number of combinations, drawn together by accident at a musicale, but remaining together by design because of personal and musical congeniality. The Mason-Thomas group in New York, for example, met one evening to try the Brahms Trio No. 8, which William Mason, one of the first and finest American piano virtuosi, had brought back with him from Berlin. At the same time, they read through a new piano quintette by a young German composer named Robert Schumann. Both pieces pleased them; they decided to meet regularly and work out the difficulties, and soon thereafter they took the step from the drawing rooms of New York's social set to the concert platform.

Hans Balatka in Chicago and Gustav Dannreuther in New York similarly established their groups. Much pioneering work was done by the Kneisel Quartette, founded by Franz Kneisel, and consisting of members of the Boston Symphony Orchestra. German works, new and old, received reverent performance at their hands, while the names of American composers, raising timid voices in chamber music, also appeared on their programs. Many of these pieces were dedicated to Kneisel. Still another group which made chamber-music history was the Flonzaley Quartette, four Belgian musicians headed by Adolfo Betti. They played in the New York drawing room of their patron, Edouard de Coppet, until they had reached a high point of perfection, when he generously released them to give public concerts. For twenty-five years they rejoiced the ears of music lovers with an ensemble which has hardly ever been equaled, never surpassed. Today, groups come and go. They form, dissolve, and shuffle their combinations, vying with one another and with the excellent European organizations who come to tour this country. They have educated a large public to listen with pleasure to what has always been considered a form of music for the limited few. A recent study of music in schools and colleges made by the National Music League of New York demonstrated the growing vogue of chamber music, vocal ensembles, and other small combinations.[27] Vocal and instrumental soloists flourish exceedingly, the local numbers being swelled yearly by foreign visitors, doubly so at present owing to political unrest abroad.

The American composer has accepted the challenge to supply these performers with material. There is no dearth, but rather a glut, for composers of opera and symphony have entered the field, and there are, besides, many others who have found themselves greatly at ease in writing songs and small instrumental works. The days of few composers and stark simplicity are past.

A few engaging figures rise up from the mist of those days. Louis Moreau Gottschalk, one of the most picturesque, personifies a whole romantic era. He was a sardonically handsome, dark-skinned virtuoso, who seems to have been born in a flowing cape, with a broad-brimmed hat on his head, a gardenia in his buttonhole, and white kid gloves on his slim hands. He always appeared on the platform gloved, if not hatted, and dramatically stripped his hands for action before starting to play. When he toured, ladies followed him about, swooning and sighing at his combination of romantic mystery and pianistic pyrotechnics. He was a well-trained musician, and a sound composer, albeit he tossed off sweet little piano pieces for his sentimental admirers to play in their boudoirs. *The Last Hope* and *The Dying Poet* had a great vogue with them. *Bamboula, Ojos Creollos, Le Bananier, Danse ossianique,* and others, containing as themes some of the songs Gottschalk had heard the Creoles sing during his early life in New Orleans, are of stronger caliber. Replete with color and passion, they boast complicated rhythmical devices, with enough syncopations to make them sound extremely modern, though their composer died in 1869.

A program of American piano works was presented by John Kirkpatrick in New York in 1936, containing pieces by Charles Griffes, Roy Harris, Aaron Copland, and Henry Ives, all living except Griffes. Three Gottschalk pieces concluded the program in a blaze of glory—*Souvenir de Porto Rico,*

Danza, and *El Cocoye.* They held their own even in comparison with the others. In rhythm and harmony they were surprisingly jazzy, with combinations of sound that were certainly unorthodox in their own day. Mr. Dwight wrote in his magazine in 1853: "We seriously doubt if Gottschalk's forte is composition. They have wronged him who have assured him that his trivial, though graceful fantasies were enough to place him in the ranks of finely original pianoforte composers. . . . He has most brilliant execution, and a clear, crisp, beautiful touch; but what is great execution without some thought and meaning in the combinations to be executed?" Nevertheless, there is a distinct revival of interest in this New Orleans composer-virtuoso, whose musical patois smacks so strongly of "swing." Whether because of his pioneering as a virtuoso, his solitary and mysterious death in South America, or his compositions, it is most important that he be remembered, for he is a figure of note.

A less picturesque "sweet singer" was Ethelbert Nevin, who was born seven years before Gottschalk's death. Nevin's photographs present a smooth, sensitive, eternally youthful physiognomy, with hardly a line to mar its surface. The many songs and piano pieces he produced have the same innocuous smoothness. They flowed painlessly from his pen, to attain instant favor. *My Rosary,* which has been paid the ultimate tribute of being parodied within an inch of its life, is still one of the best-loved American art songs. Divested of the sentimental claptrap which many singers feel bound to impose upon it, it carries an appeal all its own. The manner of its composition calls to mind Stephen Foster's airy tossing off of some of his best tunes. Nevin was improvising at the piano one evening after dinner, and liked the result enough

to seize a sheet of paper and pencil the notes on it. He handed
the paper to his friend Francis Rogers, who had been dining
with him, saying, "Here is a song I wish you would sing at
our concert next week." As a result, the beads of *My Rosary*
were counted o'er and o'er thereafter in innumerable concert
halls and homes.

The other fruits of Nevin's talent vindicated his claim that
the life of a composer was the only life for him. When his
father, himself a musical amateur, pointed out that a true
Nevin selected law, medicine, or the ministry as a career,
adding that a composer was a poor thing in several senses,
Bertie replied that he would rather be poor and a composer
than wealthy and anything else. The result of this pertinacity
was a series of tuneful, well-written lyrics, such as *O That
We Two Were Maying, Little Boy Blue, Mighty Lak' a Rose,*
and *Wynken, Blynken and Nod.* No graduation exercises of
the nineties were complete without a pianist playing Nevin's
Narcissus, a march which formed part of a suite called *Water
Scenes.* Much of his success lay in his ability to produce
piano works and songs with a special appeal for those whose
test of music is, "Can I sing it?"

The same question with reference to the writings of Edward MacDowell frequently met with an enthusiastic affirmative, although MacDowell had not the simple, unsophisticated approach of Nevin. He did have, in common with
both Nevin and Gottschalk, a passion for poetry, but surpassed them and others of his generation in versatility and
originality. He was the only one of the three who composed
for the orchestra.

It is impossible to discuss the music without first having
an idea of the man, for he was identified to an unusual degree

with his compositions and their performance. Mr. P. T. Currier, writing of *MacDowell as I Knew Him,* says that his playing of his music was as original as the pieces themselves, a species of impressionistic tone painting in the process of which "pieces clearly written and splendid for practice became streams of murmuring or rushing tone." . . . "His personality," says Mr. Currier, "always seemed to me a part of his music. . . . Originality and fertility of invention, love of color, exquisite taste, underlying hints of melancholy, deep-felt and never sentimental, warmth and depth of imagination,—these were the expression alike of the musical genius and of the magnetic personality." Even discounting for the enthusiasm of a friend in this eulogy, we are left with the picture of an unusual individuality, a picture confirmed by the recollection of those who studied with him at Columbia University. A tender glow of retrospective affection suffuses their countenances at the bare mention of MacDowell's name. They have, in fact, become a cult which, from idolizing, has come to idealizing him. His tragic end, in 1908, after a period of insanity caused, in the opinion of many, by worry, opposition, and overwork, only served to heighten the intensity of their devotion to his memory. His summer home at Peterboro, New Hampshire, has become a haven for creative artists, who are given an opportunity to work there surrounded by the peace and beauty which were his inspiration.

Both William Upton and Henry Finck, in their studies of art song in this country, rate MacDowell very high as a song writer. Much of his love of nature is found in his forty-two songs, for a number of which, in the absence of suitable lines, he was driven to writing poetry himself. *The Robin Sings in the Apple Tree* was his own, so were *The West Wind Croons in the Cedar Tree,* his *Slumber Song, Opus 2,* and some choruses. Such others as *Through the Meadows* and *Is It the Shrewd October Wind* have a gentle charm, while *Menie,* despite its sadness, has always been a favorite. *Thy Beaming Eyes* was one of the set of six *Love Songs* which were his first venture into voice writing in this country.

The deeper side of his nature, however, found expression in his piano pieces. After all, the piano was his own, his native land. He made his debut in America playing a piano quintette with the Kneisel Quartette in Boston. The two concertos composed early in his career present in embryo qualities which grew to notable maturity in his four big sonatas, the *Eroica, Tragica, Norse,* and *Keltic.*

These represent the cream of his output. As James Huneker said: "The real MacDowell is in the piano sonatas." The *Woodland Sketches,* "little pieces" for the parlor, include *To a Wild Rose.* This popular melody was retrieved by Mrs. MacDowell from the scrapbasket into which her Edward had thrown it, an instance of excellent judgment on her part. In a collection which included *Will-o'-the-Wisp, From an Indian Lodge,* and the ethereal *To a Water Lily,* it still held its own. The *Virtuosen Étuden,* of which he wrote two sets for his students, emphasized technique, but stressed the development of style at the same time. The *Sea Pieces,* surging and rolling, were compared with Schubert's *Am Meer,* while the *Fireside Tales* and *New England Idylls* are vivid, sincerely felt evocations of mood.

MacDowell lived and died before the upheavals of the World War. He excluded from his workshop all that was ungentle or ungentlemanly, with the result that when he deserted it for academic pursuits, he could not endure even that mild transition. Those who came after him had to be made of sterner stuff in order to meet the sorry world in which they found themselves, as well as the strenuous competition with one another.

MacDowell represents an isle of safety in the midst of a traffic-laden highway. All around him there is confusion. Even when the heavy trucks are diverted to a lane of their own, the family roadsters and coupés come from all directions in a welter of sound and motion. Their drivers observe no traffic regulations, so that the policeman assigned to the task of bringing order out of their chaos has a terrific job on his hands. The conservatives *will* get out of line when they see a new color or hear a different purr in the engine of the modern car alongside. A group of hit-and-run drivers persist in disregarding his uplifted hand and peremptory whistle. The small cars collide with one another and with the trucks, and there are recriminations and reproaches. Yet they are all going in the same direction, toward a distinctive musical idiom which is representative of the best in American life. They are merely taking different roads to attain their objective.

In the Appendix [28] will be found a list of serious composers not previously mentioned for symphony or opera, who are distinguished for songs and instrumental writing in smaller forms. Gleaned from Clare Reis' Catalogue of 1932, from the programs of sundry American music festivals, and from the records of the W.P.A. Composers' Forum concerts in New York, it does not pretend to be complete. Nor has there been any attempt to do other than present the list alphabetically. While these writers can be roughly classified in the same way as the symphony composers, they are even less prone to con-

fine themselves to one way of writing, and would very justi-
fiably resent being limited to one style in any description of
their work.

At a recent festival of American music, someone asked
Roger Sessions, whose string quartette had just been played,
"In what group of composers should you say that you belong, Mr. Sessions?" The composer blinked and swallowed.
"I'm sure I don't know," he replied, "I've never thought
about it. If I knew, I'd be happy to tell you. I write as I feel,
that's all."

It is not nearly so important that Mr. Sessions or any of
the others be placed in a group, as that the public should
recognize how valuable they are to American music. They
are creating continuously and prolifically. Their music is for
the home as well as the hall, and they have the advantage of
hearing their works frequently, thanks to the ease with which
they can be performed. They can profit by that experience to
perfect their product. By that token, the great American
composer may yet emerge from their ranks.

CHAPTER XII

THE WANDERING MINSTRELS AND THE
GREAT BLACK WAY

THE curtain rises on a semicircle of grinning black faces, with huge, painted red lips, gleaming white teeth, and woolly wigs atop high celluloid collars several sizes too large. The sartorial ensemble consists of white trousers, striped calico shirts, colored swallowtail coats, and white cotton gloves with ludicrously long fingers. In the center of the crescent is Mr. Interlocutor. He stands out from the rest, for he alone is white-face. He is clad with sober dignity, and is as imperturbably grave as the rest are hilarious. At one end, fat Mr. Tambo holds his tambourine poised for a jingle, while at the other, skinny Mr. Bones, equipped with

221

bones or castanets, awaits his cue. Red plush and gilt chairs are ranged around the platform behind them. "Gentlemen, be seated," booms the Interlocutor. With a tantalizing premonitory rustle, they lapse into their chairs. The minstrel show is on.

"How dear to our hearts are these scenes of our childhood" —a song, by the way, immortalized by these very minstrels. Memories crowd fast. The timeworn jokes:

Qu. What has a cat that nothing else has? Ans. Kittens.

Qu. Who was the lady I saw you with last night? Ans. That was no lady, that was my wife.

Qu. Why are good resolutions like fainting ladies? Ans. Because they want carrying out.

The parade that preceded the show. That never-to-be-forgotten thrill when the booming of the big drum and blare of brasses apprised the townsfolk that the minstrels had come to town, and were even then parading down the main street. The rush to catch a glimpse of the imposing drum major twirling his gold-headed cane, followed by his troupe in a very special costume of white silk top hats, gray Prince Albert coats, and patent-leather shoes. The free concert in front of the local grand-opera house and the rush for seats for the show afterward. And then the show. The rapturous settling down for an evening of laughter and balladry, of mingled "kidding" and sentimentality, and above all, of song and dance.

These white men behind burnt cork who carried America's music from hamlet to hamlet were as truly minstrels as the medieval bards and minnesingers. Under the guise of tomfoolery, they performed a real service to national song. They linked the early outpourings of slavery days with the ragtime, blues, and jazz which were the negro's later expression, and white men though they were, they managed to catch the spirit of the plantation negro. Even while they laughed at him, there was little mockery in their laughter—in the beginning, at least. The representations of a chicken-stealing, slow-witted, Malaprop coon using long words in wrong places came when they feared the public was growing tired of their more sympathetic impersonation. The minstrel show deteriorated in proportion to their exaggeration of these foibles, and their neglect of true negro song in favor of doubtful negro comedy.

From the first small venture of "Daddy" Rice, who worked alone, to the days of Haverley's Mastodon Minstrels, with its slogan "Forty, count 'em, Forty," the minstrel show occupied a place in the affections of all sorts of persons, old and young, intellectuals and morons. In 1849, when it was approaching the beginning of its heyday, Joseph Gungl, the German orchestra leader who had already disparaged the musical taste in this barbarous land, wrote to his Fatherland: "The so-called minstrels have the best business here. Companies are composed commonly of six or seven individuals of the masculine gender. They paint their faces black, sing negro songs, dance and jump about as if possessed, change their costumes three or four times each evening, beat each other to the great delight of the art-appreciating public, and thus earn not only well-deserved fame, but enormous sums of money." Oddly enough, considering he was a musician, Mr. Gungl was apparently not impressed with the negro songs he mentioned. Yet upon one of them was reared the whole structure of minstrelsy.

A chance encounter, somewhere about the year 1830, between Thomas Rice, a pleasant though undistinguished young actor, and a ragged negro slave released minstrelsy to the world. Rice was playing an engagement in some town—either New Orleans, Louisville, or Cincinnati. He went strolling through the streets to kill time between performances. An old negro attracted his attention, first by his astonishingly tattered clothes, which fluttered in the breeze, scarecrow-fashion, then by his limp, and the hop, skip, and jump he gave at intervals. Following him idly, the white man heard him singing, under his breath, the words of a song which he repeated over and over, often enough for Rice to store them away in his memory. The hop, skip, and jump marked the end of the chorus, which was repeated after every four-line stanza.

Jim Crow

First on de heel-tap, den on de toe,
Ebery time I wheel about I jump Jim Crow.
Wheel about and turn about and do jis so,
And ebery time I wheel about I jump Jim Crow.

Rice "lifted" the entire act—song, clothing, limp, and dance—and went on the stage as Jim Crow the next time he appeared alone. At this performance, he borrowed his tatters from old Cuff, a stevedore whose clothes just managed to hang together. He agreed to return the clothes immediately the act was ended; Cuff meanwhile, in such undies as he possessed, waited in the wings. Neither of them counted on the repeated encores, which prolonged the act far beyond its allotted time. From the wings, Cuff whistled, hissed, and danced up and down to attract the actor's attention, but Rice, intoxicated by his success, heard nothing. Suddenly, the tooting of a steam-

boat whistle floated into the theater. Cuff realized agoniz-
ingly that he had just time to go to the dock and assist in un-
loading if he left at once. His necessity recognized no law.
With a howl, he rushed upon the stage, demanding his
clothes. The curtain was rung down.

Our own Charlie Chaplin made no more of a hit with the
first stage presentation of his oddly pathetic, flat-footed walk
than did "Daddy" Rice when he "jumped *Jim Crow*." Audiences were frenzied in their applause. Like Chaplin, Rice
was enough of a showman to sense the possibilities of his
theme, and to build around it a whole series of variations.
He improvised a set of stanzas on local people, retaining the
chorus in its original form. He made use of Joseph Jefferson,
the Rip Van Winkle of later years, then a child actor of four.
Rice carried him on the stage in a sack slung over his back,
from which he emerged in a costume the replica of Rice's, to
"jump *Jim Crow*" side by side with him. Having worked this
country thoroughly, Rice took himself, as "Jim Crow," to
England and the Continent, where his portrayals of plantation hand and darky dandy were acclaimed as brand-new
and wholly American.

"American actors are now all the rage in England," says
Philip Hone, famous New York diarist, in his entry of August 4, 1837. "Rice, the celebrated Jim Crow, has eclipsed the
fame of Kean, Kemble, and Macready. He entertains the
nobility at their parties; the ladies pronounce his black face
'the fairest of the fair,' and his bowlegs and crooked shins
'the perfect line of beauty,' and the wits of London have established the Crow Club in honor of the Yankee buffoon."
Apparently, Hone was a little put out at what he considered
misplaced commendation, but later, when he met the actor

at dinner and heard his performance, he made amends by pronouncing him a most witty and entertaining companion.

When Rice returned, he cashed in on his European experiences by putting on a series of Jim Crow sketches—"Jim Crow in London" and "Jim Crow in the Foreign Service"— which somewhat resembled those later given by minstrel troupes. He alternated these impersonations with that of a darky dandy, the first of its kind. As Dandy Jim of Caroline and Spruce Pink, he made popular the songs of that name. *A Long Time Ago* and *Such a Gittin' Upstairs* were introduced by him in his impersonation of Gumbo Chaff, a negro hand on a Mississippi flatboat. *Such a Knockin'* was another of his favorites. Daddy Rice belonged to no troupe, although a number sprang up before he retired. He was an individualist, who deliberately underlined his eccentricities with an eye to publicity. He clung to his custom of buttoning coat and vest with five- and ten-dollar gold pieces, even when, old, paralyzed, poor, and alone, his glory a thing of the past, he waited for death.

Rice was not the first negro impersonator, although the first to cut any kind of a swath. The dignified Gottlieb Graupner, father of the Boston Symphony Orchestra, is said to have appeared in black face in 1799, and again ten years later as a dark entertainer for light moments. On the first occasion, he sang *The Gay Negro Boy* in Act II of *Oronooko,* accompanying himself on the banjo. Another gentleman known as Pot-Pie Herbert followed his example. Black clowns were an accepted part of circuses of the early nineteenth century, while between-the-acts diversions of negro song and dance were used to save ponderous dramas from failure. Several songs introduced in this informal fashion were later taken up by the minstrels, and became well known to their audiences. One by Micah Hawkins, composer of the early ballad-opera, *The Sawmill,* was sung by a certain Andrew Jackson Allen, and printed in *The Columbia Harmonist* in 1815.

> "Back side Albany stan' Lake Champlain,
> One little pond, half full o' water,
> Platte-bug dare too, close 'pon de main,
> Town small, he grow bigger, do, hereafter.
> On Lake Champlain
> Uncle Sam set he boat"

et cetera.

Crude as this sounds, it was taken up by the minstrels of later days, and was sung repeatedly. So was *Opossum up a Gum-Tree,* which in the early version, reads:

> "Opossum up a gum-tree
> On de branch him lie,
> Opossum up a gum-tree,
> Him t'ink no-one is by."

But for the more material-minded minstrels it became:

> "Possum up the gum-tree,
> Cooney in the hollow,
> Show me to the man who stole
> My half a dollah."

Another one which was extremely popular from the start was *Coal-Black Rose,* set to the tune of an old ballad. The ever-watchful "Jim Crow," a little jealous of his blooming rival, penned a stanza to the effect that

> "Oh, de coal black Rose
> Once was all de go,
> But now she find a ribal
> In Mistah Jim Crow."

Despite the rivalry, George Washington Dixon, a famous old-timer, planted a *Coal-Black Rose* in many a minstrel performance. He also popularized *The Long-Tailed Blue,* a nonsensical favorite. He claimed the authorship of *Old Zip Coon,* now known as *Turkey in the Straw.* His claim to that honor is questionable, for like other folk songs, it cannot be chalked up to the glory of any individual. *The Arkansas Traveler,* another minstrel favorite, has also become almost a folk song in its general appeal.

After the *Jim Crow* furore, a dozen years elapsed. Then the minstrel show took form as a group entertainment, and again blind chance brought it about. Daniel Decatur Emmett, a vaudeville actor, and another Thespian, Billy Whitlock, were playing fiddle and banjo together after dinner one evening, just for fun. Their friend Frank Brower dropped in, improvised a pair of bones, and started to clack the rhythm as he had heard negroes do. Dick Pell, another actor, seized a tambourine and joined in. The four had such fun that they kept it up all evening, and for several succeeding evenings. Fortunately, they were in a professional boardinghouse with no antinoise clause in the lease, so they were not evicted for disturbing the peace. On the contrary, they adjourned voluntarily to Bartlett's billiard room near by, to try out their act on an audience. The catcalls with which their first audience greeted them speedily changed to loud hurrahs of appreciation, mingled with roars of laughter, and shouts of "more." In burnt cork and exaggerated costumes, they made appearances here and there, calling themselves the Virginia Serenaders. So many imitators at once sprang up that they took boat for England, hoping to duplicate Daddy Rice's triumphs there. Their hopes were dashed. They did the *Lucy*

Long Walk-Around and *Essence of old Virginny,* two of their best numbers, to indifferent audiences. They plunked the banjo, twirled the tambourine, sang and clogged themselves hoarse and footsore, to no purpose. Finally they disbanded, and drifted back separately to this country, where all became members of other companies.

They were the spark which exploded the mine of minstrelsy. Edwin P. Christy, banjoist, actor, and manager, was on the spot to pick up the largest nuggets. He had hung out his shingle in Buffalo, advertising "Christy's Far-Famed and Original Band of Ethiopian Minstrels, whose unique and chaste performances have been patronized by the élite and fashion in all the principal cities of the Union." Christy spoke the truth when he said his performances were unique. In emphasizing the musical part of the program, and offering an abundance of really good negro tunes, which were well sung even if he had to sing them himself, his show *was* unique. Along with all the fooling and wise-cracking, there was a constant supply of new song material to supplement old favorites. Some he wrote himself; some were written by members of his company. But the greatest number, the most appealing in spirit and highest in quality, came from the pen of Stephen Foster.

Christy and Foster call to mind the old riddle about the chicken and the egg—which did come first? For probably neither would have functioned half so well without the other. Christy caught Foster's songs hot from the griddle. He contracted with him for the sole right to sing them prior to publication, and paid Foster from ten to fifteen dollars apiece for the privilege. Foster had the assurance, so valuable to a composer, of a market waiting for his wares. That assurance never failed him so long as Christy was alive. Walter Pritch-ard Eaton suggests that, had it not been for the minstrels, Foster might have spent his life pen-pushing in his brother's office. That seems a rash statement. Stephen was a born songster, with a surgent talent. It seems that his melodious cries must have reached the public somehow. But there might not have been so many, and the folksong quality which is their prime distinction might have been less pronounced had they been written for the concert hall instead of the jolly uninhibited minstrels.

Stephen dashed off *Old Folks at Home* overnight in re-sponse to a letter from Christy begging for a new song. When it appeared in print, after being enthusiastically received in the show, Christy's name appeared on the title page as its composer. This created a misunderstanding which took some time to clear up, and many people are still hazy about it. The substitution seems to have been made at Foster's request. In a letter, he stated that he did not wish his name too closely associated with Ethiopian melodies, to a number of which he had already affixed it. Of course, he had no idea how popular the song would become. Had he realized that it was destined to be one of the most widely known and best loved of Amer-ican folk songs, he would not have parted so easily with his title of author. Translated into every European, and many Asiatic and African tongues, it has been sung prac-tically all over the world. Certainly, it was worth many of the "gentle Annies" and "dear Mabels," whose vaporings he con-sidered more worthy of his signature. There were dissenting voices, even as to the merits of Foster's songs. The Boston City fathers, planning summer "pops" on Boston Common, stipulated, "Only let it be *music,* and not the *Oh Susanna* sort of jingle. Let it refine and educate the millions, and not merely tickle up the idle old whistling, drumming, foot-lifting habit, which is a mere chronic irritation of the rhythmic nerves." While Dwight's *Journal* reports that "Anna Zerr, at a concert in Castle Garden, New York, had, shame to say, stooped to sing *Old Folks at Home* for the boys; one would as soon think of picking up an apple core in the street." Her offense was palliated by the fact that she sang it only as an encore. Still, she had assailed the decorum of the concert hall by her selection.

Decorum was one virtue which concerned the Christy minstrels not at all. They made use of every device, dignified and otherwise, to popularize Foster's melodies, and his productive years coincided with their heyday. The Civil War put a period to both, for while it did not end the shows, the character of the performances changed. Their enormous popularity was not lessened; the emphasis was merely shifted from the music to the dramatic entertainment.

Christy's was the first company to settle down for a good long stay in one spot. He hung out the grandiloquent blurb he had coined in Buffalo on the billboards of the Mechanics' Hall on lower Broadway, New York, in 1846. In a few years, he had evolved the idea of the semicircular arrangement of the chorus. The band, consisting of two banjos, violin, bones, and tambourine, and either accordion or triangle, were seated in the rear. The Interlocutor and end-men were "planted" where they could bandy dialogue to the best advantage. In their wordy arguments, Mr. Interlocutor was usually the loser, and had to yield, with feigned chagrin, to the superior dialectics of his satellites. Thus worsted, he would urge one of them to sing something while he smoothed his ruffled plumage, and in that way many songs were inter-polated between the gags.

Christy did more, however, than set this pattern. He also made a full evening's entertainment of what had been an in-cidental hour. He gave a show in three parts. The first con-sisted of the quips and cranks of Mr. Interlocutor, end-men, and chorus, interspersed with song and band selections. The second, or olio, was a vaudeville show, made up mostly of song and dance specialties. There might be a banjo con-tortionist, an imitator, a slapstick comedian, or a snappy clog dancer. Songs and ballads by guest artists were not out of place here, nor was this part of the entertainment necessarily negro. The third and last part was a "walk-around" or grand review of the entire talent, for which the company's musical advisors were kept busy providing march songs like *There'll Be a Hot Time in the Old Town Tonight* and *Dixie*.

There are many tributes to the quality of Christy's musical offering. Lyman Abbott found a number of entries in his father's diary saying that he often attended the (Christy) minstrels in Buffalo of an evening, because, though he found their fooling silly, he enjoyed their music so much. When the troupe went to England, no less hardened a cynic than Wil-liam Thackeray expressed himself, in an oft-quoted para-graph, as deeply touched by their performance. "I heard a humorous balladist not long since, a minstrel with wool on his head and an ultra-Ethiopian complexion, who performed a negro ballad that I confess moistened these spectacles in a most unexpected manner. I have gazed at thousands of trag-edy queens dying on the stage, and expiring in appropriate blank verse, and I never wanted to wipe them. They have looked up, be it said, at many scores of clergymen without being dimmed, and behold! A vagabond with a corked face and a banjo sings a little song, and strikes a wild note which sets the heart thrilling with happy pity." The black-face boys were so well liked across the water that the English took to calling all minstrels Christys, somewhat as all musicians were known as Bachs in the German village where the illustrious Johann Sebastian and his numerous forebears practiced their art.

The end of the Christy Minstrels came with the retirement of Edwin P. Christy in 1854, the death of his successor, George, fourteen years later, and—final catastrophe—the destruction of Mechanics' Hall by fire. Their dark light had not been hidden under a bushel, however, and other companies carried on. An inky trail of troupers had wound its way across the continent. Those were the days of gas-light and melodeons, buggies and horsecars, Barnum's Museum in New York, and the Handel and Haydn Society in Boston. Women wore hoop skirts and laughed at selected jokes only. Gentility and stuffy respectability were rampant. Yet the stuffiest and most genteel of the music lovers mingled freely with their rowdier brothers and sisters at the minstrel show, which proved as true a leveler of rank as the French Revolution itself.

Another company prominent among the early fun makers was the Bryant Minstrels, led by Dan Bryant, a shrewd manager as well as a good actor. Bryant had the horse sense to sign up Dan Emmett when the latter returned, broke, from his English trip with the Virginia Minstrels. One of Bryant's rewards was *Dixie*, written by Emmett as a walk-around. There are several stories of how he came to write this famous song, one of which sounds so natural that it is probably true.

Mrs. Emmett, it appears, was partly responsible. She was doing the family washing one blue Monday, and giving Emmett a wifely hauling over the coals at the same time. As she soused the suds up and down, her chiding voice went on and on, until Emmett muttered impatiently, "Oh, I wish I was in Dixie." He might as well have said Kalamazoo, but fortunately he didn't. Mrs. Emmett's scolding stopped dead. "That's a good title for the walk-around you have to write," she commented approvingly. And Dan, relieved at the diversion of her attention from him, took the hint, and wrote words and music overnight. It is to be hoped that the hit made by *Dixie* in the show appeased Mrs. Emmett's wrath. From washtub to battlefield is a long distance, but *Dixie* made the transition comfortably via minstrel shows and, as the Confederate anthem, became more popular than *The Star-Spangled Banner* itself during the Civil War. Emmett also wrote *Old Dan Tucker,* a nonsense hit:

> "Old Dan Tucker was a fine old man,
> Washed his face in a frying pan,
> Combed his hair with a wagon wheel,
> Died with the tooth-ache in his heel."

Every company that came along added a new touch to the Christy-established minstrel show. The Congo Melodists introduced part-singing. They may have uttered the first barbershop chord of minstrelsy, but certainly not the last. Buckley's New Orleans Serenaders exploited the humorous possibilities of burlesquing grand opera, and other companies did not hesitate to copy them. Sarah Bernhardt, the great French actress, was convulsed with mirth at a parody of herself in her famous role, Camille, wherein the consumptive heroine was played by a robust black-face man yclept, for the nonce,

Sarah Heartburn. Colored Toreadors warbling *Carmen* with exaggerated action were a common sight. The Ordway Minstrels went another step, and introduced the street parade, which became a regular part of the fun. The gold rush of 1852 sent black-face companies swarming to the coast, to give three shows a day, with seats selling at three dollars apiece, a fabulous price for a minstrel show. Charley White's Company, in the Melodeon on lower Broadway, never collected more than twelve and a half cents for a parquet, six and a half for a gallery seat, in the preceding decade in prosperous New York.

But the days of plenty passed. The Civil War exercised a sobering effect and, for a short while, even the impersonation of negroes was frowned upon. The jokesters had to beware lest they affront sensibilities already rubbed to the raw. But the relief they afforded from thoughts of bitter strife was much needed, and they did not have to soft-pedal their activities for long. They added to their repertoire such songs as Henry C. Work's *Wake, Nicodemus,* and *Babylon Is Fallen,* which suffused the minstrel show with what one commentator, Foster Damon, calls "apocalyptic splendor." The vogue of the Jubilee Singers, and the popularity of the spirituals they introduced, gave the minstrels a new line which they were quick to follow. Spirituals, harmonized to suit minstrel voices, became a part of the show. *Noah's Ark* ("There's one wide river to cross") was one of the most popular. All the sentimental songs popular during and after the Civil War were presented, many for the first time, by the minstrels. In the *Harvest of Minstrel Song,* published in 1879 by White Smith, the majority of the seventy-two songs included are negro. In the *Minstrel Folio,* published by Saalfield eight years later, sentiment is almost entirely in the ascendant, though many of the laudable lyrics are today forgotten, along with their composers. *Silver Threads among the Gold, The Spanish Cavalier,* and *In the Hazel Dell My Nelly's Sleeping* are among the exceptions.

Strife, sentiment, and spirituals notwithstanding, the torrent of black-face jollity roared on. Nothing could stem it. There was Billy Emerson, who sang, *con espressione, Love among the Roses, The Yaller Gal That Looked at Me,* and *Mary Kelly's Beau.* He had audiences rocking and singing with him when, a huge sunflower in his buttonhole, he sang the song which gave him his name of Sunflower Billy Emerson.

> "Oh, I feel just as happy as a big sunflower
> That nods and bends in the breezes,
> For my heart is as light as the wind that blows
> The leaves from off the treeses."

Topical songs reflected significant situations as they came along, for example *Oil on the Brain* during the boom of 1868, and *Casey Jones* in the early days of the railroad. Dave Reed not only urged in song that *Sally Come Up, Oh Sally Go Down!* but had everybody singing with him *Shoo Fly, Don't Bother Me.* This song was written by Captain Bishop, leader of a colored regiment, himself a white man, who overheard a colloquy one morning which suggested it to him. One trooper remarked to another, "I'se feelin' like a mo'nin' star." To which his comrade, in minor mood, replied, "Well, I'se feelin' like a frog that's lost his ma." Whereupon a third broke in, without being asked, perhaps a little bored with the other two, "Go 'way, coon. Shoo fly, don't bother me," which constituted the refrain of Bishop's very simple song:

"Shoo fly, don't bother me
Shoo fly, don't bother me
Shoo fly, don't bother me
For I belong to the Company G." [29]

Most of the well-known minstrels had their own shows at one time or another, and many of them played with Haverley's Mastodon Minstrels as that organization grew. From forty to sixty in the chorus, seated three tiers deep; six or eight end-men; glittering tinsel and red velvet everywhere; much enlarged orchestras; vaudeville stunts of every description; these elaborations struck the knell of the minstrel show. One of the pet gags of the old-timers had been: "What am de biggest room in de world?" To which came the reply, after much circumlocution, "Room for improvement." The successors to the Mastodon Minstrels took this literally, and tried so many "improvements" that the initial purpose of the minstrels was wholly obscured. By this time, there remained no trace of the original negro song. Sentimental ballads and clog dances were offered, and ragtime was available. In 1915, there were more than thirty good minstrel companies in the country; a decade later only a bare half dozen, and today they are the prerogative of the amateur dramatic club or an occasional revival.

It is interesting, in the light of later events, to read an article which appeared in the *New York Music Review and Choral Advocate* of 1854, entitled "Negro Minstrelsy Is Dead." As Mark Twain said when he read in a newspaper of his own death, "The report was grossly exaggerated," and certainly premature. The writer of this article was some sixty years ahead of time. After bewailing that "the minstrel show has exerted so widespread and deleterious an influence upon the musical tastes of this country," he went on to rejoice that "characteristic Ethiopian melodies have ceased to sell, and though troops of singers continue to blacken their faces, they no longer rely upon African platitudes as an attraction. The songs *Jim Crow* and *Jim Along Josey* . . . spawned in the very lowest puddles of society . . . found their way into places of admitted respectability" to his distinct annoyance. "But," he added, reassuringly, "People are now tired of its burlesques upon a degraded race, of its vulgarity, its silliness, and its insipidity. . . . It diverted attention and patronage from worthy and elevating concerts, and made musicians feel that their only road to success was through buffoonery and badinage." And so, gleeful over its downfall, he begged in conclusion that the unsold copies of Foster's *Uncle Ned* be the minstrel's winding-sheet, and that the banjo and bones be buried with him.

Yet, inconsistently enough, in the course of the same year, the *Choral Advocate* sang a wholly different tune. "Before bidding adieu to Jullien and his masterly associates . . . we must say that we regret that none of the celebrated soloists can properly play an American air. . . . [They] do not seem to enter into the spirit of American airs, nor to understand the oleaginousness of Ethiopian melodies. Perhaps they think such things beneath their notice; if so, we simply wish to inform them that few European composers have written better or more artistic melodies than the *Old Folks at Home*, Ethiopian, or 'nigger' though it be called."

Under the rough and ready, catch-as-catch-can technique of the minstrel show, American song assumed a special character. Wholly apart though it was from the field of art song, and remote as the minstrel band was from the symphony orchestra, there was, nevertheless, an interaction between the two. The same audiences listened to both. The wise composer took heed of both. And many of the true negro songs were poured through the funnel of the minstrel show into that dilute, composite fluid known as American music, bringing to it sentiment, humor, and the beginnings of ragtime and jazz.

CHAPTER XIII

BLACKS AND BLUES AND RAGTIME, THE MISSING LINK

"Come on and hear,
Come on and hear,
Alexander's Rag-time band!"

HOW could a rhythm-minded public resist an invitation couched in such terms, especially when sung to a tune of rollicking syncopated simplicity? As irresistibly as the brass rail of a bar attracts the drinker's foot, this tune drew the great public of 1912. They sang and danced; they clapped and stamped to its regular meter, and seemingly never wearied of it.

This was not because it was the first ragtime tune—for it wasn't. Probably nobody knows when the syncopated melodies, with the steadily vamped one-two-three-four bass, were accorded dubious promotion from the darkies' quarters and churches to the white folks' places of amusement. Long before Irving Berlin was inspired to write this particular song, the minstrels had shuffled and clogged to what they called "coon songs." They had borrowed spirituals and work songs, changing them *ad libitum* for purposes of entertainment, adding gay embellishments to words and music. They called their synocopations "ragging." The minstrels laid the groundwork of ragtime, and made a thorough job of it. Their public helped them by buying millions of copies of minstrel songs in sheet music, and obeying with pertinacity the injunction printed thereon to "try this on your piano." In a little while ragtime flooded the country.

The first piece of sheet music to have the tag of "ragtime" actually printed on its cover seems to have been Bert Williams' *O, I Don't Know, You're Not So Warm*, but even this was not the first, nor the most popular. Kerry Mills' *Georgia Camp-Meeting*, written in 1897, was one of the true classics of ragtime, even if nobody then thought of it as any kind of a classic. To hear but a few measures of it is to conjure up a picture. In those days, the summer hotels held periodic cakewalks for their colored bellhops, waiters, and maids. Dressed in Sunday best, all on the broad grin, the participants strutted up and down the ballroom to this tune, improvising the most elaborate and amazing steps, as why should they not when the couple with the most engaging variety took the cake? Not a guest in the hotel would have missed the spectacle, and not a foot in the place, black or white, missed a beat, no matter who carried off the prize.

Another song which never failed to bring out the high-steppers of the day was *My Gal's a High Born Lady*, which went on thus to enumerate her charms:

> "She's dark, but not so shady,
> Feathers like a peacock, just as gay,
> She's not colored, she was born that way."

And the faithful swain further proclaimed passionately:

> "I'm proud of my black Venus,
> No coon can come between us."

In this respect he differed from the disillusioned lady in another song, who lamented:

> "All coons look alike to me
> I've got another beau, you see,
> And he's just as good to me,
> As you, nigger, ever tried to be."

The writer of the latter was a negro named Ernest Hogan. On his deathbed, he is said to have had a bad attack of conscience, with this song to prevent his leaving the world as peacefully as he should have. For he felt that the opus he had thoughtlessly tossed off belittled and ridiculed his race, and set others a pernicious example to do likewise. If he could have withdrawn it, he would have. But it was too late. Everybody was singing it; its sales went into the millions. He need not have felt so badly, for it had its counterpart, so far as disillusion goes, in the pre-Civil War slave song, *Ol' Massa's Got a Yaller Gal*, wherein the fact that all yaller gals looked alike to Ol' Massa was similarly featured. The titles *Whose Baby Are You-oo*, *Won't You Come Home, Bill Bailey?* and *Waiting for the Robert E. Lee* must strike a responsive note in the memory of those who lived through the merry ragtime days.

There was unquestionably a certain monotony in the undeviatingly regular four-four measure of the ragtime accom-

paniment, with the weak beat steadily accented. John Tasker
Howard, Aaron Copland, and other commentators dwell upon
this point. They probably do find it monotonous in comparison with the great variety of effects in present-day jazz. But
in its heyday, it represented hilarity, abandon, and escape
from the humdrum, in more sedate but no less popular fashion
than the jazz of today.

When John Philip Sousa and his band went touring in
Europe, they tried ragtime on the crowned heads and found
them no different than mere commoners in their response.
Both the Emperor William of Germany and the Czar of Russia took to it without ado. "King Edward VII liked it so
well," Sousa reported, "that he asked us to play more of it,
and we gave him *Smoky Mokes* and *Georgia Camp-Meeting.*"
The dignified courtiers at Buckingham Palace must have had
to exercise all their well-known self-control to listen sedately
when Sousa's band, one of the finest of its kind ever known,
invited them with seductive blatancies to shed their dignity.
Sousa made no apologies for playing ragtime, for he honestly
felt, and said, that that which had started as a craze had become an established feature of American music. As such it
was as much entitled to consideration, in his opinion, as *Faust*
or any of the great popular operas—not that he compared
the two, save in the matter of popularity. But he pointed out
that ragtime had a legitimate family tree. It was found in the
songs of the Bohemian gypsies, and in the Scotch cradle songs,
long before America took it up. It became the plaything of
the negroes, who twisted and juggled it to suit themselves
because it was such a congenial utterance. As the white song
writers took it from the negroes, they also changed it. Still,
its family history is no more chequered than that of other

American folk song, a category in which some historians are proud to include it. Ragtime cannot be sung on the green or danced to around the Maypole—in that sense it does not meet a certain popular conception of folk song—but it can be cakewalked, two-stepped, marched, and sung to, all of them activities which are characteristic, individual, and highly esteemed by the American folk.

The battle between the Guelphs of classic and the Ghibellines of jazz music was waged over the very cradle of syncopated song. In an article in *Seven Arts Magazine,* in 1917, Hiram Moderwell wrote: "I like to think that rag-time is the perfect expression of the American city, with its bustle and motion, its multitude of unrelated details, and its underlying rhythmic progress toward a vague somewhere. As you walk up and down the streets of an American city, you feel in its jerk and rattle, a personality different from that of any European capital. This is American. Rag-time, I believe, expresses it. It is today the one true American music."

Daniel Gregory Mason brandished the cudgels on the opposite side with a vigor which in a less gentle man might have been termed violence. For him, ragtime put the sin in syncopation. He called it, among other things, "the musical expression of an attitude toward life only too familiar to us all, an attitude shallow, restless, avid of excitement, incapable of sustained attention, skimming the surface of everything, finding nowhere satisfaction, realization or repose. It is a meaningless stirabout, a commotion without purpose, an epilepsy simulating controlled muscular action. It is the musical counterpart of the sterile cleverness we find in so much of our contemporary conversation. . . . The question is whether it is really representative of the American temper as a whole, or is prominent only as the froth is prominent on a glass of beer." And he adds, angrily, that the "jerk and rattle" so beloved of Moderwell are miles removed from the philosophic serenity of Lincoln and Emerson, who, he points out, are also Americans; that Broadway no more represents America than the Paris boulevards France, or the London music halls England, and so on.

It seems a pity to become acrimonious or overjudicial in arguing this question. Only when taken lightly, with good humor and easy acceptance as a small part of the whole, and one step in its development, can ragtime be accepted. Its object was entertainment. There was no need to cultivate the taste for it by careful lectures on music appreciation, or by study of its form and dissection of its organs. There it was, one could take it or leave it. If one could enjoy a hamburger in a lunch wagon as much as a filet in a French restaurant; or bump along in a Ford without wishing it were a Rolls-Royce—if, in fact, one had that God-given quality, a sense of humor, ragtime was a source of amusement and entertainment. It never was the Big Bad Wolf, trying to devour the three little pigs of classical, romantic, and modern serious music, as its enemies would have it.

"The dance is over, but the melody lingers on," said a popular waltz song some years ago. Ragtime is a thing of the past. Most of the men who wrote the songs that were all the rage are forgotten. Their melodies linger on, in a sense, in present-day jazz. There are a few, however, whose pieces have been tin-panaceas for many woes. Irving Berlin, composer of *Alexander's Rag-Time Band,* is one of them. He is still the darling of the popular-music-loving public, because he is not only an inexhaustible fount of melodiously appealing tunes, but one of those poor boys who became famous who are idolized in this land of opportunity.

A little dark man with big dark eyes, quiet and unostentatious, with a strongly appealing quality in his speaking and singing voice, such is Irving Berlin today. He is the same Izzy Baline who was born in Russia in 1888, came to New York as a baby, and grew up in the Bowery and lower East Side of New York. His life was like that of hundreds of others who came from Russia in the steerage, fleeing religious persecution. Hard knocks and poverty were his first and most persistent instructors. His elementary musical training he received as a singing waiter in the Bowery saloons, with an advanced course at Nigger Mike's in Chinatown. Here he wrote the words of his first song, *Marie from Sunny Italy,* to which the pianist at Nigger Mike's wrote a tune, since Irving could play the piano with one finger only. When his boss decided to dispense with his services, he managed to convince some of the uptown song publishers that he could write songs, if they would only let him try. By some miracle, they did. His formula was to pour sentiment into syncopation, stressing the melody rather than the syncope. "One need not snap one's fingers and sway when syncopated music is played," he maintained. "That is the thing which cheapens it. The syncopated music abounds in melody,—that is why it is so popular."

That is why his own was popular, in any event. And not alone on that account, but because he wrote his own words, and they dealt with the sort of incident which came into everyone's life. He met a friend on Broadway. "My wife's gone to the country," was the gentleman's greeting, with a beaming smile. "Hurray," responded Irving sympathetically.

He continued on his way, making a song as he went which was presently to sweep the country. His grief at the loss of his first wife, Dorothy Goetz, he translated into a song, *When I Lost You*, which uttered the plaint of every bereaved husband. *When I'm Alone, I'm Lonesome, All by Myself, All Alone, What'll I Do* are additional songs of sadness. Like the best of comedians, Berlin, who could be uproariously funny, was equally at ease when indulging in pathos.

He was drafted into the army as a private in the World War when he had hoped to go overseas as an entertainer. While in training at Camp Upton, he took part in a show given by the enlisted men, which gave him an opportunity to air his grievances in music—and how he took advantage of it! Those who were there will not soon forget the pathetic little figure of Berlin peeling imaginary potatoes beside an equally imaginary fire, singing, "Poor little me, I'm on K.P." Nor the inspired, *Oh, How I Hate to Get Up in the Morning*. Nor the exultant postwar cry, *I've Got My Captain Working for Me Now*.

When he wrote *Alexander's Rag-Time Band*, he put no words to it, contrary to his usual custom. He wrote out the tune one day when it came into his mind, thought it not much good, and laid it away on a shelf, where he practically forgot its existence. There came the day when he was asked to write in a hurry something for the Friars' Frolic in New York. The manuscript of *Alexander's Rag-Time Band* happened to come to hand, he put the words to it, and presto! he had his song. After the Friars had set their seal of approval on it, the Columbia Burlesquers took it, and later, it became, as Alexander Woollcott put it, the national curse— as well as a ragtime landmark.

Irving Berlin is in line with Stephen Foster as a writer of American folk song. Ragtime was the form he chose, because it happened to be popular, illustrating the contention of Isaac Goldberg, who said: "Perhaps our world is too old for folk-songs of the ancient type. In any case, not the intention of the composer and the poet determines the category; that alone is folk-song which the folk ratifies." Although, according to his friend Alexander Woollcott, Berlin came into the world "a creative ignoramus, with an unrivaled capacity for inventing themes . . . but little of the art, the patience, the interest in form, and the musicianly knowledge which could elaborate them," the folk have ratified him.

Jerome Kern, one of the best-loved composers of light music in America, is some degrees higher in the musical social scale than Berlin, because, while he wrote good ragtime, he wrote better operetta. He had the advantage of a sound training with Paolo Gallico and Alexander Lambert in New York, and a supplementary course in Germany. So the tools of his trade were sharp and bright, while he possessed, in addition, an innate talent of great refinement and originality. Everybody knows his *Ol' Man River* from the operetta *Show Boat*. If it were a generation or two older, it would be classed as a folk song of negro origin. Other songs from the same operetta, such as *Can't Help Lovin' Dat Man o' Mine* and *Ol' Bill* are almost equally popular. Kern is one writer who succeeds in utilizing ragtime, jazz, or any popular idiom, as it seems to be called for by the work in hand, without cheapening or vulgarizing the composition.

To return to straight ragtime, one or two instrumental pieces are worthy of mention. A negro named Scott Joplin produced the clever *Maple Leaf Rag,* which was something new in piano ragtime. A white man, Zez Confrey, wrote *Kitten on the Keys,* a brilliant original study in chasing a melody up and down the keyboard. Although it takes a fine technique to be able to play it, it became enormously popular, and is one of the outstanding examples of good piano ragtime. Mr. Confrey is a quiet young man who knows his music, and has divulged some of his knowledge in his instruction book on *Novelty Piano Playing.* He has graduated from ragtime to jazz, but has never duplicated the sensational success of *Kitten on the Keys.*

Ragtime and blues merge much like gulf stream and ocean when the twain meet. A change of color and temperature occurs, but salt water remains salt water, by whatever name it is called. *The Memphis Blues,* the first of the indigo plaints to become known, was as the ocean to *Alexander's Rag-Time Band.* Written between the composition and the publication of that immortal piece, it dovetailed in time as well as general character. Moreover, it was produced by a negro, William C. Handy, as true blues should be. For negro blues are different from any other kind. Zora Hurston wrote in *Mules and Men:* "The brother in black puts a laugh in every vacant place in his mind. His laugh has a hundred meanings. It may mean amusement, anger, grief, bewilderment, chagrin, curiosity, simple pleasure, or any other of the known or undefined emotions"—including blues, presumably. Other races weep and wail and agonize, or, when they are feeling desperately sorry for themselves, retreat into silence. The black man, on the other hand, seeks solace in syncope. Grief-stricken though he may be, he spontaneously combusts into a song in which he has flatted all possible thirds, and inserted breaks galore in order to express melancholy. Not his the abysmal depths of despair, the grief beyond words. The blues he sings are no more superficial than the emotions which inspire them, and in this lies their value as entertainment. They have sincerity without seriousness, the light touch is always there, and hence their syncopated sadness can be danced to. The man who put negro blues songs on the American music map recognizes to the full their value as entertainment, at the same time as he insists upon their significance as a form of racial expression. That man is William C. Handy.

A gentle-voiced, chocolate-colored negro, he sits today in a swivel chair behind the desk of his own music-publishing house in New York. He looks every inch the son of a Methodist minister, as in fact he is, as well as the father of the blues. To arrive at the latter distinction, he gave himself a special kind of education which had nothing in common with the Methodist ministry. He was born in Florence, Alabama, in 1873. None of his family being musical, little Bill was always slipping away. He wandered down to the Mississippi docks to hear the laborers sing, around the town barbershops and saloons, and other places his mother would have shuddered at the thought of, had she known. The day came when he acquired a two-and-a-half-dollar cornet, and discovered that he had a not unpleasing tenor voice. With both of these qualifications to hand, he hung around the barbershop, picking up the barbershop chords dropped by the customers, and an occasional cornet lesson from a peripatetic pedagogue. During his years as a teacher in the public schools, and later, when he took a depression job as a factory hand in the pipe works at Bessemer, his ears were always open to pick up scraps of song. The songs of his own people he particularly loved. This was fortunate, for when the panic of 1893 closed the factory, Handy organized a vocal quartette, and started in earnest to earn his living in music. He turned to account everything he had learned. Later he was band leader and soloist with Mahara's Minstrels, and, after some years there, organized his own band and moved to Memphis.

A political candidate by the unmusical name of Crump released the bolt not from, but of the blue. Handy decided to write a campaign song that would elect Crump mayor, and selected a tune he had heard in Alabama in his childhood to turn the trick. Perhaps because of the many stanzas of the song, which went on and on at sufficient length to wear down the most stubborn resistance, perhaps because of its infectious melody, the campaign song achieved its purpose, and Mr. Crump was elected. Handy's Band, which had been plugging the tune all over Memphis for weeks before the election, became more popular than ever. The song was such a success that Handy wrote out the music just as the band had played it, and sent it around to various publishing houses under the title, *Memphis Blues*. They rejected it with brisk decisiveness. Determinedly, he had a thousand copies printed at his own expense, but they went so slowly that he sold the whole lot to a Mr. T. C. Bennett for one hundred dollars. Apparently, listening was one thing, buying another, for the Memphis public. Bennett took the song North, had a new set of words written, marketed it all over again, and did very well with it, while Handy never made another cent on it. This might conceivably have given him the blues so badly as to cure him of writing them, but it didn't. For he had conceived a fondness for the modern improvements he was adding to the simple ragtime form.

The blues which roamed the streets before Handy put salt

on their tails and domesticated them were ultrasimple melodies, sung over and over again in three-line stanzas, or rather, the same line sung three times. The song

> "Gwine take morphine an' die,
> Gwine take morphine an' die,
> Gwine take morphine an' die"

was typical. No Memphis negro could object, "Dat ain't no blues," for it fitted his simple definition of "blues song." Neither did they reject songs which were not unalloyedly doleful, since they did not take their blues any more seriously than they took themselves. When a Memphis boy sang, "Got de blues, but too damn mean to cry," he did so with a full appreciation of the drollery of thrift in the matter of tears; when he bewailed his fate it was with a chuckle breaking throatily through the sobs of self-pity.

Blues à la Handy were like these traditional ones—plus. He interpolated a minor third into a song in the major key, calling it a "blue" note. The oftener it was introduced, the "meaner" the blues, for this was the translation of the supposedly untranslatable quaver in the negro's voice. For a long time, white men had set down all negro songs as being in the minor key, since the singers slurred that third so protractedly that it sounded like but a half step above its neighboring note. Now they have learned that the half step, or "blue" note, was Handy's own idea, and did not just happen. So, too, was his filling in of the "breaks" between lines with instrumental and vocal embroidery, instead of the simple "Oh, Lawdy," "Yes, indeedy," and "Ain't it the truth" of the past. His own energetic foot-tapping when the band played *Mr. Crump* and he felt obliged to do something to fill

in the breaks may have given him the notion of saving wear
and tear on his feet by working up quasi-improvised passages
for those spots. Or possibly he thought of it while listening
to some humble friend take one line and a five-string guitar,
and improvise on a simple tune for hours with only occasional
variations in the words. This was the way he gathered the
material for many of his blues, and it is his boast that he can
still outsit the most persistent player if there seems to be a
good tune around.

The *Memphis* was the first of the blues, but the *St. Louis*,
also Handy's, was probably the most famous. It bobs up in
symphonic suites, concerti, and compositions of serious character, as a sort of theme song of America, a musical symbol
to represent the essence of our country. Since it was a street
song when Handy met it, it has every claim to the honor of
representing a democracy. It was known as *East St. Louis*, in
those days, and was not a very good tune. Handy liked the
spirit of it, however, and wrote his melody with just enough
of the original in it so that, in all honesty, he felt called upon
to acknowledge that it was not wholly his own. However,
when a tune goes unnoticed for years and years and comes
to life only when it has been completely remodeled and repaired, the credit is certainly due to the architect who has
made the alterations. As Handy himself said, speaking of the
St. Louis Blues, "I took the humor of the coon-song, the syncopation of ragtime, and the spirit of negro folk-song, and
called it blues." In writing the throbbing melody to the words,
"I hate to see the evening sun go down," working into it one
variation after another, he created the classic example of
blues at their best. White men imitated, but could not improve on it. He himself wrote many others, the *Joe Turner*,

John Henry, Friendless, Hesitatin', a whole book full of them, but never one which rivaled the *St. Louis*. With the *Beale Street* and *Memphis Blues*, it constitutes a trilogy comparable, in the story of jazz development, to the Wagnerian trilogy in the story of opera.

The imitations of Handy blues, like the imitations of Wagner opera, are not invariably worthy of their model—nor is this a reflection on the latter. Some of them were amusingly described by Hollister Noble. The "weary," "worried," and "Blue Monday" blues stuck pretty close to the original spirit, until suddenly it became the style for everyone north of the Mason-Dixon line to feign a terrific yearning for things Southern. The result was a burst of pseudo-nostalgic wails for everything from batter cake and gin rickeys to Dixie and Mammy. When these began to pall, came a somewhat sententiously affirmative group, led by Gershwin's *I've Got the You-Don't-Know-the-Half-of-It-Dearie*, and Kern's *Left-All-Alone-Again* Blues. After a *Doncha-Remember* interlude, there was an anatomical flood, dwelling on *Red Hot Mamma, Hot Lips, Flat Feet, Ice-Cold Sweeties*, and *Blue-Gummed* Blues. Then followed a cheerful collection: *Blue Mamma's Suicide Wail, Mamma's Prisonyard Blues, Mamma's Death-Bed Shout*, et cetera.

The styles continue to change. The original simplicity is gone, and the more the white men write, the farther they depart from it. In jazz, there is no more than a family resemblance to the original blues and ragtime.

CHAPTER XIV

NOBODY sent out cards anouncing "unto us a son is born" when jazz hilariously capered into the ragtime ranks. So the date and hour cannot be set with any certainty. Nor were birthday greeting cards issued when it passed through the successive phases of hot, symphonic, sweet and swing. It is not even known how the little darling came to be christened by the name of jazz. There are a great many stories, which sound suspiciously as though they had been made up out of whole cloth. The most generally accepted tale seems to be that a band leader named Chas (known in his dignified moments as Charles) roused his hearers to such enthusiasm that they kept calling, "More, Chas, more." And Chas was softened to jazz. Another story has it that the performer's nickname was Jazbo, and that when he put a derby hat on the end of a saxophone to tone down his lay, the effect was so irresistible that the audience clamored for "More, Jazbo."

The name is not important. One certainty about its early history is that it originated in New Orleans, and that the first group of interpreters of which history takes cognizance was known as the Dixieland Jazz Band. Henry Osgood, in *So This Is Jazz*, tells of a blind negro named Stale Bread, who roamed the streets of New Orleans playing syncopated tunes on a fiddle donated by a minstrel in a passing show. By annexing recruits here and there, he gradually acquired Stale Bread's Spasm Band, and took them into all the gin shops up and down the water front for the edification of the patrons. Others followed his example. One group of four—clarinet, cornet, trombone, and drum—playing at a prize fight, so enthralled a certain Joseph Gorham that he decided to gamble on their effect on others. He dressed them up, and took them to Chicago to play for dancing. After the first shock, the dance floor of the hotel where they played was crowded every night to the bursting point. They were engaged at Reisenweber's Restaurant in New York in 1916, and by 1918 had taken the nation by storm. This was probably the original Dixieland Jazz Band, or at least some of its members. And they played the original "hot jazz." White people learned what feet were really intended for. Many of them discovered, too—especially those of New England ancestry—that they had a side to their nature which, be they ever so shamefaced about it, gloried in the forthright vulgarity of the blaring brasses.

The hot jazz bands were small, so that while each member could improvise as riotously as he pleased, it still sounded as though they were all playing together. Cacophonous it was. One of the earliest and best of the hot jazz-ists was Ted Lewis. When he cocked his battered silk hat over one ear and lifted his clarinet high in air, like a dog baying at the moon, the arabesques he shrilled on his instrument bore no apparent relation to any tune. His pianist took care of what melody there was, with some help from the cornetist. The piercing wail of Lewis' clarinet above, and the growl of the trombone below, in completely free elaborations, imparted a wildness which was distinctly "hot." Lewis was one of a very few white men to catch that quality. It took a negro really to "get hot"—incidentally, most of the players could not read a note of music. But when they let go, it was in a savage, exultant outpouring, noisy and unashamed. The simple brasses were supplemented with calliopes, steam whistles, cowbells, and auto horns, not to mention catcalls and other vocal embellishments. To the accompaniment of endless horseplay, the performers muted their instruments at will, with battered derby hats, tin cans, plugs inserted into the ends, and similar grotesqueries.

The American afflicted with the double disease of war and prohibition during the years 1918 to 1921, found there was nothing like hot jazz to relax and release him. Like the bootleg liquor with which he washed it down it was fiery, took action at once, and made him feel free, gay, and utterly irresponsible. "Eat, drink, and be jazzy, for tomorrow ye die," was the motto of many a doughboy. Syncopation followed the army across the seas, into the very trenches. When the men went on leave they demanded their jazz, and London and Paris supplied the demand, for they too had become jazz-conscious. Like the parent who condescends to kneel on the floor to help Johnny with his electric train, only to succumb to its fascination and start playing train on his own, the Europeans took the American toy to their hearts, sensing new possibilities for the European composer in its unorthodox mechanism. Furthermore, they were not hampered by any notions as to the unfitness of the musical strumpet for re-fined, classical society. Having no Puritan ancestry, they did not leap to the conclusion that because they liked jazz, it must be wicked.

The French especially were as free from prejudice against the black man's recreational manifestations as they have always been in the matter of the black man himself. They listened eagerly, enjoyed without reservations, used what they pleased, and asked no one's approval. Darius Milhaud became a great exponent of jazz, wrote it and wrote about it in enthusiastic and voluminous articles. The Six, the group of up-and-coming French composers to which he belonged, fol-lowed suit. Stravinsky, who was living in France, not only wrote out-and-out jazz pieces, but used it as a technical de-vice in several of his serious works. The hotter the jazz, the more plentiful were the ideas it gave to composers, the more responsive the audience, and the better the opportunities for members of the band to show what they could do. So, what with one thing and another, it reached an exceedingly high temperature before someone called a halt.

That someone was Paul Whiteman, and his answer to the

critics of hot jazz was symphonic jazz, the opposite extreme. It followed, though it never supplanted, its boisterous predecessor. Symphonic jazz owes its existence to Paul Whiteman, and he owes his existence in that field, possibly, to the ignoble circumstance of having been kicked out of a jazz band. The son of a supervisor of music in the public schools of Denver, he had been a respectable viola player in the symphony orchestras of San Francisco and Denver. Not a breath of jazz scandal had sullied his reputation, up to the moment he tried to "play hot" in Tait's orchestra. His failure there after one short night's engagement set him to thinking, and to working out some of his thoughts with six or seven others who "couldn't play jazz" either. The World War came, and he saw service there as a band leader, with a chance to try out an idea for effects here and there. Later, he formed a dance band of his own, with tentative and highly successful experiments in soft warm instead of loud hot dance music.

Finally, Whiteman exploded his bomb, a concert of symphonic jazz. On February 12, 1924, he hoisted his three hundred pounds to the stage in Aeolian Hall, New York, before an audience of skeptical elite. Not only the musicians on the platform, but the music, appeared in attire correct to the ultimate shirt stud. At this concert, Whiteman did two things surpassingly well—he orchestrated jazz tunes so beautifully that they sounded classical, and he jazzed classical pieces to the scandalized delight of his hearers. That the delight outweighed the criticism was evidenced by the applause which shook the substantial walls of Aeolian Hall after each number. The program, entitled, "An Experiment in Modern Music," began with the *Livery Stable Blues,* and *Mamma Loves Papa,* worked up to a historic first performance of

George Gershwin's *Rhapsody in Blue,* and concluded with Whiteman's own version of Elgar's march, *Pomp and Circumstance.* Gertrude Lawrence, the English actress who sang the *Limehouse Blues* here, was in despairing tears after the concert at the cleverness of Whiteman's orchestration of her song. As for the Gershwin piece, it brought down the house. In this connection, it is told that Gershwin held jealously to his manuscript, changing, correcting, and improving, up to a week before the concert. Finally, Whiteman came and camped on his doorstep, until Gershwin unwillingly relinquished it, begging for "just a few more days." At the rehearsal that evening, Whiteman, overcome with joy as the last measures were played, exclaimed in irate amusement, "Damn the fool! Did he actually believe he could improve on it?"

After this concert, the newspapers unanimously bestowed upon Whiteman the title King of Jazz, to which he has held ever since, through fat and thin. He took his band, or rather orchestra, abroad to visit other crowned heads, and his success was largely instrumental in instilling into Europeans the idea that American jazz *is* American music. A deputation from the conservative Paris Conservatoire called on the "King" to ask that copies of his scores be placed in their library. Whiteman has turned over to Williams College in Massachusetts his enormous library of records and scores, which constitute a fair cross section of American popular music. And yet, despite all these honors and justifications, Whiteman wrote in 1927, in an article in *The New York Times Magazine,* "What is jazz? Is it an art, a disease, a manner, or a dance? Has it any musical value? After twelve years of jazz, I don't know." Today, after many years of ardent devotion to jazz, Mr. Whiteman holds a unique position. In one moment, he appears in a circus show, riding a white horse as the crowned King of Jazz; in the next, he is conducting the august Philadelphia Orchestra in a concert of "American music." He is perhaps the only man living who has fallen gracefully between two stools and made an abiding place for himself in that most precarious of locations.

Panassié, author of *Le Jazz Hot,* finds Whiteman's arrangements of the classics "ridiculous," as they probably are, by "hot" standards. But he admits their refining influence on subsequent composers and conductors. Not all of the latter followed Whiteman's smooth and polished example. They lacked his Henry Fordian talent for picking men, for one thing. The man who for many years made all Whiteman's orchestral arrangements, Ferde Grofé, attained considerable eminence when he branched out in his own right as a composer. His *Grand Canyon* and *Hollywood* suites he himself described as music designed for the great middle class, neither for high- nor low-brows. If it had not been for Grofé's orchestration of the *Rhapsody in Blue,* that piece might not have leaped to such instant favor, original though it was. The performers Whiteman selected, too, were outstanding in their field. Ross Gorman and Henry Busse shone even in a superlative group. Whiteman himself, past master of the jazz-classical technique which he introduced, was constantly revising, editing, and correcting.

Vincent Lopez and Isham Jones are two conductors who found the Whiteman ways to their liking. Lopez was so impressed that he gave a concert of symphonic jazz in no less a hall than the Metropolitan shortly after Whiteman's Aeolian and Carnegie Hall performances. A symphonic pot-

pourri called *The Evolution of the Blues,* by Lopez' star ar-
ranger, Joseph Nussbaum, was one of the hits of the Metropolitan concert. Lopez himself played the piano parts of *Nola*
and *The Maple Leaf Rag,* just as Gershwin did of the *Rhapsody in Blue.*

Gershwin had been a plugger of songs at Remick's, publishers of popular sheet music. He had written musical shows
containing song hits. As a boy, he was roller-skating champion of his block in Brooklyn. As a very young man, he became champion writer of light, tuneful lyrics. And in his late
twenties, with the *Rhapsody in Blue,* he stepped into a new
class, one which he created. For he was the first American
composer to classicize jazz, instead of vice versa. He was so
firmly convinced that it had its place in the concert hall, if
it were given the right kind of dress to wear, that he went
into the sartorial business to prove it. Probably no one was
more surprised than George Gershwin himself at the speed
with which he proved his point. The fame which eludes the
grasp of him who too zealously pursues it, was his for the
asking, almost without the asking. After the public and the
critics had exhausted their adjectives about the *Rhapsody,*
Dr. Walter Damrosch commissioned him to write a concerto. Gershwin was not daunted by the fact that in order to
fulfill the commission he had to go out and buy a text book
to ascertain what a concerto consisted of. He accepted the
assignment first, and went after the required information
later.

It was headline news in the world of music when the
Dean of American conductors thus bestowed the cachet of
his approval upon a jazz composer, particularly inasmuch
as that Dean was known for his sturdy maintenance of the

highest musical standards. Gershwin then and there decided to drive a musical tandem. He used his natural talent for popular melody in writing musical comedies which provided him with hand-tooled leather bindings and similar expensive hobbies. Meanwhile, he was seriously studying and practicing the technique of writing in classical forms. Few men can serve two masters successfully, but he was young, ambitious, intelligent, and gifted. Had he never written another note, nobody would be able to take away from him the distinction he achieved in writing, in classical form, an entire jazz piece which commanded the respectful attention and admiration of public and critics. Symphonic jazz, in Gershwin creations and Whiteman arrangements, came to spend a week end in the musical world, bringing only a suitcase, but settled down for a long stay, thanks to the warm welcome it received, and has been with us ever since. And if there were some who, listening to the elaborate harp concerto based on the *St. Louis Blues,* presented by Paul Whiteman at a Hippodrome concert in New York in December, 1936, yearned for the straight simplicity of a hot jazz band, there were just as many who applauded passionately every fresh bit of symphonic trimming tacked onto the original, finding in it the glorification, not the decadence of jazz.

Symphonic jazz is a sort of stepson in the royal line. The true descendant of hot jazz, and next in the line of succession, is that which is known as sweet. Between the sweet and the hot, there is, however, little of a family resemblance. Sweet jazz is the acme of simplification. It is perhaps more like ragtime played with a mute and with greatly exaggerated effects. Rudy Vallee is, as much as anybody, responsible for the introduction of crooning, while Guy Lombardo went in for muted instruments, shaded lights, and general pianissimo in the orchestra. Rudy Vallee's lack of vocal equipment was the deciding factor in making a crooner of him. He was engaged at Don Dickerman's night club in New York, with his band of college mates called the Connecticut Yankees, and with the proprietor's consent, he had decided on a gingerly experiment with sweet modifications of the hot jazz then popular. But at the last minute, the singer he had provided proved unsingworthy, and he made a frantic appeal for another. Nobody volunteered, and he had to have a singer. So Vallee himself stepped into the breach. Seizing a megaphone which happened to be sticking out invitingly from a spare saxophone, he sang in a still, small tenor voice, the choruses of a couple of songs he had learned at Yale. No one was more surprised than he at what followed. The crowd went wild. They demanded more and more. Thus a crooner was born, and the public set the seal of approval on him and his sweet jazz.

Radio engagements followed. Other band leaders started to serve jazz à la mode, with plenty of ice cream on the jazz pie. The players had to be prepared to lay aside their instruments from time to time, to croon alone or in harmony. The melody again came into the foreground, and free improvisation fell back. Orchestrations were very carefully figured out, written, and rehearsed. Nothing was left to chance. Gone was the fine wild freedom of the past. Red corpuscles had to be bleached to a decorous pallor within jazz purlieus. There was something in sweet jazz which appealed to the same instincts in Mr. Babbitt as sentimental song. There still were hot bands for dancing—they were indispensable, especially when those jiggly dances, the Charleston and Black Bottom, clacked their way into popularity. But sweet jazz had the advantage of being in place both in the dance hall and as straight entertainment. Restaurants, hotels, and especially radio, thanked their lucky stars for its introduction. It solved the problem of amusement where dancing space was inadequate. It sounded well over the air, at a time when the mechanics of radio had not yet been perfected to their present point. This was only a very few years ago. Modified sweet jazz is still extremely popular. Fred Waring, Guy Lombardo, Wayne King, Ben Bernie, Vincent Lopez, George Olsen, to name but a few, have a coast-to-coast radio audience whose heart at their sweet voice unfolds. Fred Waring's summary of his own popularity is plain and unvarnished. "People like us," he says, "because we give them entertainment that appeals to the average taste. We don't try to educate or elevate, or in any way change their taste. If I've been able to sense in advance what the public wants, it's because my own taste is average." [30]

Sweetening was merely a device, hardly a discovery. It added something to the quality of jazz composition by its stress on correct orchestral procedure, but at the same time it robbed it of the "Let's go" of its red-hot mamma. What one observer describes as the "unbuttoned," might better be put down as the "zipper" characteristic, for it was with the flourish of one releasing motion that the negroes of the Dixieland Jazz Band and their successors plunged into performance. Buttons were rather the afterthought of the more inhibited whites.

It was only natural, then, that a clamor for stronger fare was shortly heard. Alarmed, the pundits put their heads together. Jazz was a paying business, and they had no intention of seeing it slump without taking some action in the matter. Swing music was their answer to the public demand. Swing is strikingly like hot jazz, yet it has points of difference. The usual reply to the query, "How does swing differ from ordinary jazz?" is "Oh, I don't know, it has swing." As a definition, this leaves much to be desired, and on further inquiry one or two points can be added. Improvisation, or the appearance of improvisation, is a *sine qua non*. For this reason, the swing band is kept small, and its brasses are the prima donnas. Drums beating out complicated and imaginative rhythms are the unrelenting bass above which strident brasses and an impertinent violin or clarinet do things to a tune, in comparison with which coloratura singing is simplicity itself. The composition might be called a theme with variations, but the variations are so untamed that the original theme is lost in their shuffle. There are vocal swing ensembles, also. Primarily, swing is to be listened to, not danced, though there are dance bands which go in for it. Shrugging shoulders, twitching muscles, tapping feet, and a tendency to uncontrolled amorousness are the manifestations which take the place of dancing. To be heard at its best, swing should be heard on records, where virtuosi have worked out its complicated excellencies to the ultimate point of musical disturbance.

In swing, as in most other jazz, it is the performer, not the composer, who carries the burden of proof of its right to exist. And why not, since the horn player blows as he wishes, whatever the tune the composer provides? Thus, Louis Armstrong and his acrobatic soprano trumpet are known on both sides of the Atlantic. In his autobiography, *Swing the Music,* the jovial negro gives the following composite definition. "When you listen to a swing band, you will begin to recognize that all through the playing of the piece, individual instruments will be heard to stand out and then retreat and you can catch new notes and broken-up rhythms you are not at all familiar with. . . . The boys are 'swinging' around and away from the regular beat and melody you are used to, following the scoring very loosely and improvising as they go, by ear and free musical feeling." According to "Stuff" Smith, another negro artist renowned in the field, "Swing is what happens to you along about the fifth chorus when you start to get in the groove. The music takes you, you don't take the music." Gilbert Seldes bewailed the fact that the written descriptions of swing are such as no layman can hope to penetrate. In his opinion, the rules were discovered after the event—the men played swing first and then defined it later. He rejoiced wholeheartedly, however, that it came in the nick of time to rescue jazz bands from the "splendid nullity" of their respectable brothers in symphony halls throughout the country.

The Goodman-Wilson-Krupa-Hampton group are to swing quartette as the Flonzaley was to string quartette. They "play in and out together"—quoting Louis Armstrong again —"like one man." Tommy Dorsey's Clambake Seven put forth their best even without the inducement of a "jam session." At that unrehearsed midnight get-together, "gut-bucket," "whackey," "barrel-house," and other special swing effects are released in their might for professionals only.

Duke Ellington is a gifted negro who has applied his ten long fingers and excellent musicianship to the problems of swing. A brilliant pianist, who could have done anything he pleased with his talents, he has elected to devote them to jazz, and at present, to swing. Ellington comes from New York's Harlem, where he has played in night clubs for many years. At three A. M., when the crowds have gone and the lights are turned low, he sits down again at the piano, letting his black fingers flash over the white keys in one improvisation after another. His band master takes them down, and Ellington later fills in the instrumental parts. That is the way he composes. R. D. Darrell says: "He is one of the most striking and original orchestrators of today, and possessor of the most spontaneous, individual, and fertile melodic inspiration of any living composer." And he continues: "The contemporary student who passes over Ellington's best work as 'mere dance music' or 'jazzical curiosity' is incapable of distinguishing the hall marks of an extraordinary and purely American musical genius,—a man who will have a far more important place in music history than the hundreds of orthodox and very minor talents who are given serious attention today." Constant Lambert speaks no less highly of him, while Panassié, in *Le Jazz Hot,* becomes positively elegiac. Ellington is one example of a composer in whom innate racial musical feeling has blended with acquired rules of musicianship to produce works as creative in the jazz field as those of others in so-called serious music.

The hotbed of swing music in New York in 1936—and hotbed is the word!—is found in the night clubs where, to the boisterous delight of a smoking, drinking crowd of addicts, negro bands hold forth nightly, presenting swing music at its swingiest. *The Music Goes Round and Round* was born at one of these. *Mugging It* and *Knock, Knock* had their day. To quote Mr. Seldes again, speaking of a band led by "Stuff" Smith at the Onyx Club, "I have heard a swing band rise step by step in speed and tone, repeating some thirty or forty bars of music until it seemed impossible to listen to it any longer. Yet that was only the beginning, and it was after the music had reached apparently its extreme limits that the really expert work began and the effects were multiplied by geometric progression; in this sort of thing the idea of a climax followed by a lower pitch and a quiet ending simply could not exist. When the leader was exhausted he said 'close,' and abruptly a shattering silence followed."

Swing is the preferred jazz of 1936–37. In its apparent lack of organization and direction, its raucous and discordantly loose frenzy, it is the perfect reflection of a world with the jitters. There is tension in the air, what with unemployment, insecurity, and the dark threat of war in the offing. And there is tension, at times unbearable, in swing. It is not the sort of music to relax that tension, save in so far as it brings it into the open. There is, supposedly, a certain relief in expression. There is, too, according to the psychoanalysts' first principles, an assuagement in merging one's individual tension with that of a group. Swing makes this possible. As the individual gives himself over to the music in a steadily mounting excitement, his identity is lost, and he remains merely one of the group, listening, not to hear, but to feel. It is a group which, having absorbed sound at every pore, staggers home in the small hours intoxicated, not alone with alcohol and tobacco, but with rhythmic orgies which have shattered the eardrums. The hangover after swing is characterized by the complete letdown which follows excessive tension. It ought to be a sure cure for insomnia.

Gramophone records, of which there are a great many, have carried swing to the far confines of the earth. In Europe,

it is taken seriously as a valuable addition to musical literature, although in America, outside of its own amusement
realm, it has not yet attained any such recognition. Rhythm
clubs in London and Paris listen seriously to the disks of
Benny Goodman's band, of Red Norvo, Wingy Mannone,
Red McKenzie, Adrian Rollins, Louis Armstrong, Tommy
Dorsey, Cab Calloway, and Duke Ellington. Critical books
and essays have appeared, analyzing its contribution, treat-
ing it as a permanent, if modern improvement of the musical
landscape.

Recently it was decided to offer a course in jazz in the
newly opened New York High School of Music and Art. On
the theory that "we cannot stop a child from doing what it
wants to do," the Director of Music in Public Schools, Dr.
George Gartlan, made this concession to the trend of the
times. New York University, an institution of still higher
learning, at about the same time instituted a series of illustrated lectures by Vincent Lopez on the origins, history, and
appreciation of jazz.

Isolated as such instances are, their very existence marks
a certain recognition on the part of educators of the importance of jazz in American musical life. They cannot,
ostrichlike, stick their heads in the sand of disapproval at her
shrill approach. She is an enemy in a sense, according to
their standards, but one whom they must face and reckon
with.

Jazz is, taken by and large, a moody jade. She dyes her
hair and fingernails a different color every few months, thinking thus perhaps to alter her "personality." But down under-
neath, she is always the same boisterous, somewhat vulgar
child of nature. She cannot fool her lord and master, the

American public, for whose benefit she makes all that effort. It is flattering to their vanity to have her do so. They applaud each new color scheme, tongue in cheek, saying, "We knew you all the time." They love her, whatever she does, and hold her to be a pleasant and important element in their lives. She stands to many music lovers in the role of the mistress to whom they flee when the wife of their bosom, serious music, becomes a bit tiresome or exacting, or complains of being misunderstood. They are shy of having wife and mistress meet, and do not talk to the one about the other. However, the two are wholly aware of each other's existence and rival claims, and, with the general broadening of ideas, the wife does not disdain the use of some of the technique of the mistress, and vice versa.

CHAPTER XV

PROPHECY—A HEAVEN WITHOUT HARPS

THE man who writes music in this country today may count himself wealthy. While his annual income from royalties on his published works does not invariably extend to yachts and Rolls-Royces, he at least does have an income from that source. Thanks to the copyright laws, his published works belong to him, and cannot be pirated. Thanks to the American Society of Composers, Authors and Publishers, fondly known as the "Ascap," he receives a fee for every performance in concert, radio, and place of amusement. Ascap,[31] founded by Victor Herbert in 1914, exists "to protect the members in their lawful rights and collect for them their infinitesimal portion of the enormous profit made by commercial users of their products in enterprises which, but for the availability of music, could not be successfully operated." The society has a large membership here, and affiliations with similar groups in Europe. Not the least of its virtues is the fact that within its leveling ranks, jazz and serious composers meet to enjoy the benefits of protection without partiality. Another large organization, the National Association for American Composers and Conductors,[32] confines its attention to serious composers, with the ultimate object of discovering their best creative work and making it available for public performance on a national scale. The serious composer complains, as he always has, that he is obliged to teach, write, and lecture to eke out his income from compositions, and that these exertions leave him too tired for creative activity. He is still much better off than he used to be.

Does he possess the competitive instinct? If so, all the better for him, for there are numerous competitions upon which he may exercise it. Columbia University, for instance, encourages the incipient composer by offering a substantial prize every year to undergraduates still in their musical swaddling clothes. Various conservatories—the Juilliard School of New York, the Eastman of Rochester, and New England of Boston—dangle prizes for songs, symphonies, and chamber music before their students and graduates and the general composer with gratifying liberality. The New York Philharmonic, Boston Symphony, and other orchestras have run competitions for symphonic works, so too has Paderewski, leading Polish pianist, who offers two prizes periodically for symphonic and smaller works. The Philadelphia Musical Fund Association, the Victor Talking Machine Company and the magazine *Musical America* are some of the organizations which adopt this means of stimulating native composition.

Paul Whiteman recently inaugurated an annual competition for contestants under thirty-five years of age who could offer new compositions in the modern American idiom.

The David Bispham medal for opera has been won by practically every American opera of distinction to date. The radio broadcasting companies have adopted an increasingly expansive attitude, with less of condescension and more of indulgent understanding dominating their policy of prize awards.

Is the composer daunted by the thought of competition, but the sort of person who writes his best when a work has been commissioned for a definite purpose? There are commissions galore. The Litchfield County Choral Union, of Litchfield, Connecticut, one of the oldest singing groups in the country, has made a practice of ordering one or more pieces for each of its large annual festivals from an American composer.[33] The National Federation of Music Clubs, composed of thousands of feminine music lovers, has commissioned a work a year practically ever since the club has been in existence. Up to 1936, it had presented commissions and awards to forty-three American composers, and generous cash awards to young performers in state and national events. At every World's Fair—and there have been a number—the musical director has followed the example set by Theodore Thomas at the Centennial. Certain composers have been asked to write works for performance at the fair, for which they were well paid. The plans for the New York World's Fair of 1939 are not yet public, but it is to be hoped that there, too, this tradition will be observed.

Other festivals create further opportunities. The Saratoga Spa Music Festival, held in September, 1937, the first state-

sponsored music festival, presented in eight concerts fourteen especially commissioned works, the majority by Americans. The festivals of Mrs. Elizabeth Sprague Coolidge, for
which pieces are commissioned a year in advance by this
large-hearted patroness, are held in Pittsfield, Massachusetts,
and in Washington, D. C., and recently went as far afield as
Mexico City. They have been of tremendous value in ac-
quainting the American composer with new foreign works,
and also encouraging him to write chamber music. The Metropolitan Opera gives opportunities to American singers as
well as composers, particularly in its recently inaugurated
spring season of popular-priced opera. Radio and gramophone companies supplement prize competitions with specially commissioned works, with first performances of
American works, with all kinds of paternal and fraternal encouragement. Only recently, experiments in the writing of
streamlined operas specifically for the radio have resulted in
Cadman's *Willow Tree* and Jean Paurel's *Ballade of the
Bayou*. The League of Composers of New York devotes a
large part of its proceeds to paying for the works it commissions; has them played in concerts and on the air; dis-
cusses them in its magazine, *Modern Music,* and gives them
every opportunity to win public recognition. Musical scores
for motion pictures are much in demand, both in serious and
popular vein, and such commissions are multiplying fast. The
day is past when a newspaper critic dare say, "I never go
near a concert of native works." In 1894, according to Rupert
Hughes, one did so express himself, to the rejoinder, "I don't
blame you." Today, he would lose his job for that remark;
if he is a wise critic, he comes, he hears, he concurs.

Does the American composer seek a publisher? That need,

too, is gratified. The Society for the Publication of American Music, founded by Corwen Tuthill, which for a while published both orchestral and smaller works, now limits itself to chamber music only; but the New Music Society, the Cos Cob Press, and up to a short time ago the Wa-Wan Press of Arthur Farwell, all have specialized in native works. Most of the pieces which take prizes in competitions are published by the organization sponsoring the competition, while publishers in general are increasingly receptive to native offerings. Publishers of jazz and popular music still outnumber the others, in obedience to the economic law of supply and demand.

Is it a hearing which the composer craves? He may carry his works to festivals of American music in many places. Yaddo in Saratoga Springs, the MacDowell Colony in Peterboro, the Eastman School in Rochester, the Westminster Choir in Princeton, and the Chamber Music Society of America in New York are some of those which have put on all-native series within the past twelvemonth. Leon Barzin, director of the National Orchestral Association, spends his summer in Lake George hearing new works by Americans which are played under his baton during the ensuing winter. Other conductors have heard so much about the poor downtrodden native that they are constantly on the lookout for new material.[34] The Composers' Forum Concerts sponsored by the W.P.A. Federal Music Project in various cities were inspired by Ashley Pettis, who directed them in New York. They gave the new-fledged as well as the established composer an opportunity to hear his works played, expound his intentions in writing them, and meet his audience in friendly discussion. Composer-teachers in universities are awakening their classes to the merits of American music, and arranging as well for its frequent performance.[35] In fact, if virtuosi, conductors, and publishers are not exactly waiting for sugar-plums of native origin to fall into their mouths, it may still be said that, when they do fall, they are consumed with good grace.

Does the composer long for better-informed audiences? The radio is doing its best to purvey music education whole-sale. Ever since putting forth its first programs in 1920, it has been a powerful means of breaking down the barrier be-tween serious and jazz music by conditioning the public to both. The American gramophone offers an equally tolerant assortment of native works on disks, where they can be studied admirably. More music teachers and conservatories, settlement schools, and free instruction in W.P.A. schools; more music courses in schools and colleges; more school bands, orchestras, and glee clubs; more students taking music les-sons, are preparing the audiences of tomorrow.[36] The finest virtuosi play American works on concert tours, and broad-cast them as well. The movies have progressed from the days of the orchestra through the movietone to the sound film, with music made in America.

Is it written comment for which our composer longs? Since the days of Dwight's *Journal*, with its monopoly of the field, others have become articulate, not to say vociferous, and every newspaper or magazine worthy of the name now allots considerable space to accounts of musical events. Certain magazines devote themselves wholly to discussions of what's what and who's who in music. They exist and can continue to do so only so long as the humming activity in the beehive of American music provides them with the honey on which they feed.[37]

That activity is further stimulated by Foundations. Some endow creative artists for a year or more, supporting them while they work. The Guggenheim Foundation and the Frank Huntington Beebe Fund are of this nature, while the American Academy in Rome, and the Pulitzer Prize offered by the editor of the now defunct *New York World* reward accomplishment with the wherewithal for further efforts. The Sonneck Memorial Fund promotes research in the field of early American music, and the Carnegie Corporation Fund sets aside a substantial amount for "support, development, experiment, endowment, equipment, research and study" of music, as well as other cultural subjects.

The American composer is additionally blest with a form of wealth which cannot be corrupted by rust nor consumed by moths. He has in his own back yard a huge mound of native material, into which he need burrow but a short distance to find rich stores. Religion, love, patriotism, and humor, with folk song, are the foundations of music in general. America has an abundance of them all. The dramatic struggle for freedom in religious music paralleled the revolutionary assertion of political integrity. Patriotism has been generously nourished on five wars in three centuries. As for love, despite the reserve inherited from English ancestors, the expression of the tender passion is free enough, due perhaps to the melting-pot nature of this civilization. The humor, too, is of a different character from that described in an English song collection of 1719 as "Wit and Mirth, or Pills to Purge Melancholy." Its most popular form is the horselaugh, rough and tumble of the Marx Brothers. In that form it finds its way with a joyous whoop into jazzland, whence it is gradually penetrating, in slightly more decorous form, the regions dedicated to serious music. When composers turn to folk song, they need not leave humor behind. The utterances of aboriginal Indians do not require a heavily serious handling in order to make their wild purity a credible element in composition; Negro spirituals have their humor, and the same is true of the utterances of pioneers and mountaineers, cowboys and lumbermen.

In addition to these, the native composer of foreign descent has a store of ancestral folk songs, learned at his mother's knee, which dance into his consciousness when he sits with his manuscript paper before him. They deepen and enrich, like good topsoil, the sometimes scrubby garden of his thought, doing more good than harm to the produce germinating there. Frankie and Johnny are as American a couple of song lovers as Hans and Liesel are German, yet the man who is familiar with both has a better chance than his all-American colleague of combining the best elements of both. John Bunyan, Paul Revere, Bill Cody, Nathan Hale, Miles Standish, and Daniel Boone—to name a few—are folk heroes about whom a composer may weave, if he can, the same kind of magic that Beethoven spun for Napoleon in the *Eroica,* or Schumann for his distinguished friends in the *Carnaval.*

The unplumbed world of new sounds invites the American composer to become a plumber, for the nonce. An instrument, for example, like the ptolemy, invented a few years ago by Harry Partsch of California, is a pianolike affair with many keys representing infinitesimal intervals. Mr. Partsch also devised a viola with a special finger board for which he composed and arranged pieces with more gradations of sound than are to be found in existent literature. Such inventions constitute a challenge to the bolder spirits, since they call for a literature all their own.

Both Hans Barth and the enterprising young pianist David Barnett have done interesting things with the quarter-tone pianos they devised to take care of the ultramodern harmonies in their own works and those of their confrères. Leopold Stokowski, one of the most constructive minds in the music of America, has conducted a series of experiments in electrical transmission, with the cooperation of the Bell Telephone Company of Philadelphia and the National Broadcasting Company. He hopes not only to improve in transmission sounds already known, but to titivate the jaded ears of the musical public with tones of hitherto unknown pitch and quality. The sounds added by George Antheil, who used typewriters, doorbells, and aeroplane propellers, by Gershwin, with Klaxon horns blaring brightly in the overture to *An American in Paris,* and by others, show that our composers are alive to the possibilities of enlivening their writings by departing from the beaten sound-track.

The challenge, however, continues to be more intellectual than emotional. American music proceeded from the preponderantly religious to the pseudo-romantic, with the New England school making restrained use of both. The succeeding generation strove to put aside borrowed romanticism and be themselves, but became such musical highbrows in that conscious process that the amount of emotional spontaneity in their music was negligible. Roger Sessions compared them, many of them his own colleagues, to the alchemists of yore.

Calculating and computing, delicately lifting one note at a time with their pincers, weighing it carefully before putting it in its exact spot on the paper, they give evidence of feeling nothing beyond the delight of solving a mathematical problem. It is well that the composers themselves recognize the dangers of this emotional sterility, and the need for reform if they are to hold their audiences.

They are studying the methods of those who purvey jazz, who are not nearly so concerned with the necessity for creating listeners, since there is always a ready-made audience for pure amusement, especially if it be not pure in every sense. While jazz may cater to the baser emotions, base emotions are better than none at all. Some serious composers have accepted this truism and decided to conform to the popular trend. They have admitted jazz into their compositions for one reason or another, either as an emotional device, for purposes of humor, or for its entertainment value.[38]

Aaron Copland and George Gershwin have set out from opposite poles of the musical universe, to meet for a comfortable visit, if not a permanent sojourn, in the realm of jazz. Gershwin's natural instinct for the feeling of negro music, which caused one of the actors in his opera, *Porgy,* to ask him in all seriousness whether he did not have negro blood in his veins, helped him to write with a certain inevitability in an idiom which is far from being as simple as it appears. Gershwin maintained that there was no such thing as mechanized composition without emotion, and compared the "intellectual" works of today with American skyscrapers, at once a mechanical triumph and a breath-taking achievement productive of emotional thrills. In his own works the thrill is always present, which is probably the reason why thousands of people were turned away when the New York Philharmonic put on a program of them at a Stadium concert, and why many laymen, asked to express an opinion about American composers in general, reply, "I don't know if he is great or not, and I don't care much, but give me George Gershwin, every time."

Young as he was at the time of his death in July, 1937 (only thirty-eight), he had definitely established himself in a role to which it seems likely that more and more composers will aspire. He glorified the light touch, combining his talent for jazz with a genuine feeling for the finest, to produce work which was the first of its kind and which is distinctively American. Olin Downes said of him: "Gershwin was far enough from the bottom and near enough to the top to foreshadow an art that will spring from the people and will sublimate their expression, but in a way that reflects the individuality of the thinker and artist. . . . He talked, musically speaking, the language that his countrymen and generation knew. . . . When the tumult and shouting are over —and already they are subsiding—he will have a secure place in the American tonal art."

It is a question whether it is more difficult to make a jazz composer into a serious one, or vice versa. Aaron Copland, who at one time delved into the whole jazz question, found out to his own satisfaction what it is that makes the jazz wheels go round. He was attending to his business of writing serious music at the time, and began using the rhythms freely in his own work. The *Piano Concerto* written in 1926 presents a series of brilliant and exciting variations on the *St. Louis Blues*. His *Music for the Theatre*, produced the preceding year, is in a sort of staccato-jazz with surprising variety of rhythmic and harmonic resource. Jazz has been compared to measles. Copland has had his measles, and has drawn certain conclusions from the attack. Jazz, he says, being a matter of rhythm and technique, not of material, is a fine instrument for interpreting some moods, but too limited for universal application. To put it differently, it is spirited, not spiritual. J. A. Rogers, writing in *The New Negro*, calls it a "tonic for the strong, a poison for the weak."

These composers belong for the most part to what might be called the contemporary intellectuals who, ten years ago, were the young composers. The future is in the hands of a still younger group, many of them mere fledglings. It is for them to say whether the angels that people their heaven are to discourse heavenly strains upon the harp, or to plunk the ukulele and blare the saxophone, or, after all, to take the safe middle way and utilize all the instruments of the orchestra including jazz whistles and "hot" clarinets in effective fashion. Not alone the presence or absence of jazz as such in their music will determine whether a halo with its accompanying sanctity is to be affixed to the brow of American music. But the spirit of jazz, its humor and freedom, its looseness and abandon may be present in the conventionally correct guise of serious music. What are the indications that it will be?

It is hazardous to prophesy too specifically about the young composers of the moment. They have not as yet expressed themselves sufficiently to make it possible to form an opinion, and there is always the probability that, at their time of life, they are going through some phase which, in their later years, they will have thankfully sloughed off and will resent being reminded of.[39] Still, one or two attributes seem fairly general. In their writing, as in that of their predecessors, there is a great deal of competence, an easy command of technical resources, and complete intellectual control. They become acquainted at a tender age with all the known devices for expression, employ them with taste and judgment, even essay to add to their number. They are vividly and sensitively alive not alone to the rich background behind them, but also to the tempo of living of today, the possibilities of the civilization of tomorrow. The fever of present-day existence in America is a stimulant to creation; they seek no aspirin of detachment or aloofness to bring down its temperature. Like the school children of Europe who learn in the classroom to adjust their gas masks in the event of attack, these young men are schooled to adjust their artistic sensibilities to invasions from the world about them which, to the contemplative scholarly men of the past, would have been insupportable. The class struggle is as valuable a subject in their eyes as any war with a foreign nation. The international political situation presents elements which stimulate them creatively, so too do the political unrest, the financial depression, and so on. They are keenly responsive to, without necessarily imitating, the currents of thought in musical and artistic circles abroad. Practically all of them have had some study in France or Germany. They are hampered by very little of the snobbery of the older generation. Many of them have written for theater or cinema, have composed pieces which were either wholly jazz or jazz in spirit, associate with jazz composers as colleagues, admit them and their music to terms of close friendship.

These young composers find awaiting them a public in a state of mind closely akin to the war period. The psychology of depression is practically the psychology of war. People

crave distraction. Educated beyond the point of fleeing ex-
clusively to the jazz band they must have distraction nevertheless. And so, when they seek it in music, they look for
something which is not too heavy, which has humor and
warmth and a certain amount of emotion and perhaps inspiration, which is no strain to listen to and yet has sufficient
body to permit them, as it were, to get their teeth into it.
Their idea of heaven is not the smoke-beclouded haunts of
the night club, with its ear-shattering, if intriguing swing
band. Nor is it the ethereal realm above, draped with silken
silver clouds in Joseph Urban fashion. It is a region which
combines the best elements of both, and resounds to a type of
music which is a composite of both styles. According to one
writer, the trouble with the music of the decade 1920–30 was
that there wasn't a laugh in a carload. In the American music
of the future, we predict, humor will paradoxically lighten
carloads with many a good laugh.

· Accepting the broad definition of humor as that which
causes laughter, there are a few recognized instances in classical foreign literature. Saint-Saëns *Carneval des Animaux,*
Haydn's *Surprise Symphony* and *Toy Symphony* are deliberate mirth provokers. Wagner's use in woodwinds of the
mastersingers' theme to create a gay theme for the appren-
tices in *Die Meistersinger* is a delightful example. Bach's
Coffee Cantata is well known, and the *Golliwog's Cakewalk*
of Debussy always brings a laugh. There are smiles galore in
many Haydn, Mozart, and Beethoven rondos and scherzos.

This humor is produced in various ways—by the use of
certain instruments, or by an amusing context or theme suggestion, or by unexpected twists of musical idea or rhythmic
pattern. It is a tool absolutely God-given for American com-

posers, a few of whom have already availed themselves of it. If in the past, the bassoon has been the clown of the orchestra, why, in the future, should not saxophone or clarinet, traps or bones, join it and make a clown troupe? If jazz is an acknowledgedly American invention, why may not the humorous possibilities of its unexpected rhythms and musical ideas be exploited to the utmost? And if Americans have an unique ability, both to create and enjoy laughter, what is there to prevent their reaping to the full the benefit of that gift? The world about them teems with incitements to mirth in spite of the dark lining to every silver cloud. They have only to stop, look, and listen.

We have not the temerity to suggest that the serious artist feel obliged to compromise with his own sense of beauty in order to win an audience. We know that each composer has, locked in his soul, his particular ideal, with which he cannot and should not come to terms other than those of absolute truth and sincerity. Some of the music of the young men now writing has been produced in an agony of spirit, a depth of conviction, a nobility of conception which consort not at all with humor.

Let those who see in those terms continue so to interpret. But let those who can do so, with all due regard to the serious aspects of life, think in terms of relief from its tension. Let them utilize the entire musical experience of the past three centuries, plus their own magnificent twentieth-century equipment, their alertness and aliveness, to make a new heaven of American music. Let it be a meeting place for grave and gay, for symphony orchestra and dance band, for black, red, and white races. Let there be no snobbery of any kind, but a mingling on common ground of all the elements, foreign and native, which constitute this unique civilization. Let there be flocks of "angels," to promote composition and performance, so that never again can an artist or a writer complain that he lacks the means to proceed with his work. And let the people who look to that heaven for their musical sustenance be prepared to receive it with open minds and hearts.

APPENDIX

CHAPTER II

1. *Tammany,* an opera by Mrs. Hatton produced in Philadelphia in 1794, was popular for *Alkmonook, the Death-Song of a Cherokee.* Anthony Philip Heinrich (1781–1801), a transplanted German, turned out many pages of symphonic writing based on the lore of the redskin. He wrote *The Indian Carnival,* or *The Indian's Festival of Drama,* sixty-four pages' worth of orchestral score. His *Mastodon, a Grand Symphony,* comprised *Black Thunder, a Patriarch of the Fox Tribe, The Elkhorn Pyramid,* or *The Indians' Offering to the Spirit of the Prairies,* and *Shenandoah, a Celebrated Indian Chief,* in three volumes. *Manitou Mysteries,* or *The Voice of the Great Spirit,* and *Pushmataha, a Venerable Chief of a Western Tribe of Indians* are equally prolix and orchestral. *Indian Fanfares* on a somewhat less impressive scale, could be played by a military band, or on the piano. After Edward MacDowell's *Indian Suite,* in 1896, a lengthening line of composers walked, Indian file, in his footprints. Frederick R. Burton wrote a cantata, *Hiawatha,* in 1898; Carlos Troyer published *Songs of the Zuñi Tribe,* after living for years among the Zuñis in California with his violin. Homer Grunn's *Zuñi Impressions* for piano deal with the same tribe. Carl Busch wrote a symphonic poem, *Minnehaha's Vision;* a cantata, *The Four Winds;* an *Indian Legend,* for violin; and a group of *Indian Songs.* Rubin Goldmark's *Hiawatha Overture* appeared in 1900. Charles Skilton wrote *Indian Dances* for orchestra, *Three Indian Sketches* for piano, and *Three Indian Scenes* for string quartette, as well as the operas *Kalopen* and *The Sun Bride;* Henry F. Gilbert wrote *Indian Sketches* for piano. Charles W. Cadman transposed more than six hundred Indian songs to the diatonic scale, and wrote two Indian operas,

Daoma, the Land of Misty Water and *Shanewis*. He also has a
Thunder-Bird Suite for orchestra, a suite for strings, *To a
Vanishing Race;* song cycles, *From Wigwam and Tepee, The
Sunset Trail, The Father of Waters;* and so on.

Arthur Farwell composed for orchestra *The Dawn* and *The
Domain of Hurakan*. Others are *A Navajo War Dance, American Indian Melodies, Pawnee Horses,* and *Impressions of the
Wa-Wan [Omaha] Ceremony.* Frederick Converse's *Peace
Pipe Cantata* and *Flight of the Eagle* are among his most pop-
ular works. In *Lyrics of the Red Man,* for piano, Harvey
Worthington Loomis created effective Indian music without
the use of actual Indian themes. Frederick Jacobi, on the contrary, frankly utilized melodies collected during a sojourn in
New Mexico to produce a *String Quartette on Indian Themes,*
and *Indian Dances* for orchestra. Thurlow Lieurance's song,
By the Waters of Minnetonka, is one of nine Indian songs he
arranged and published. *The Indian Love Call* from Friml's
Rose Marie is noteworthy. Victor Herbert's Indian opera *Natoma* had a Metropolitan production; so did Alberto Bim-
boni's *Winona* and Cadman's *Shanewis,* while Arthur Nevin's
Poia, slated for production, missed by a fluke.

CHAPTER III

2. The following spiritual was one of those sung for me by
Lydia Banks, John Powell's negro maid. The words are traditional, and the tunes she sang were Dorian, Aeolian, etc., although Lydia doesn't know that. Mrs. Powell kindly transcribed and sent these words to me.

> "Saviour, visit thy plantation,
> Grant us, Lord, a gracious rain.
> All we come to disobtain thee,
> Unless thou return again.
>
> "Keep no longer at obstention,
> Shine upon us from on high,

Less the want of thine assistance
Every plant must droop and die.

Refrain

"Lord revive us, Lord revive us,
All our help must come from thee,
Lord revive us, Lord revive us,
All our help must come from thee."

3. Henry F. Gilbert wrote a number of pieces, particularly the popular *Comedy Overture on Negro Themes* and *Dance in the Place Congo,* which demonstrated the value of negro material. The pieces of Henry Schoenfeld and E. R. Kroeger were popular in the nineties. A composer like John Powell, of Virginia, who has grown up with negro song in his ears, brings it convincingly into his music. His *Rhapsodie nègre* for piano and orchestra, Overture *In Old Virginia, Banjo-Picker,* and other works have the ring of authenticity. Mr. Powell has interesting theories, not generally accepted, as to the origin of many of the negro tunes. Daniel Gregory Mason and Rubin Goldmark, Harold Morris and Louis Gruenberg, David Guion, Robert Russell Bennett, Leo Sowerby, Lamar Stringfield, Lucius Hosmer, Cecil Burleigh, Douglas Moore—one after another occurs to us as having made liberal use of negro song. Among those who have arranged or used in large compositions the songs of their own people are Harry Burleigh, Clarence Cameron White, Robert Nathaniel Dett, William Dawson, William Grant Still, James Weldon Johnson and his brother Rosamond, and others.

CHAPTER IV

4. *Lord Lovel, The Two Sisters, The Golden Willow Tree, Fair Margaret and Sweet William, The Cherry Tree, The Greenwood Side, Earl Brand, The Brown Girl,* and *Lady Isabel and the Elf Knight* are other beloved traditional English ballads which have found their way into the mountains.

5.   SOURWOOD MOUNTAIN

Chickens a-crowin' on Sourwood Mountain,
Ho-dee-ing-dong-doodle allay day,
So many pretty girls I can't count 'em,
Ho-dee-ing-dong-doodle-allay-day.

My true love, she's a blue-eyed dandy,
Ho-dee-in-dong-doodle allay day,
A kiss from her is sweeter than candy,
Ho-dee-ing-dong-doodle allay day.

My true love lives over the river,
Ho-dee-ing-dong-doodle allay day,
A hop and a skip and I'll be with her,
Ho-dee-ing-dong-doodle allay day.

My true love is a blue-eyed daisy,
Ho-dee-ing-dong-doodle allay day,
If she don't marry me I'll go crazy,
Ho-dee-ing-dong-doodle allay day.

Back my jenny up the Sourwood Mountain,
Ho-dee-ing-dong-doodle allay day,
So many pretty girls I can't count 'em,
Ho-dee-ing-dong-doodle allay day.

My true love is a sunburnt daisy,
Ho-dee-ing-dong-doodle allay day,
She won't work and I'm too lazy,
Ho-dee-ing-dong-doodle allay day.

6.   THE LONE PRAIRIE

(Selected stanzas)

O bury me not on the lone prairie,
These words came low and mournfully,

From the pallid lips of a youth who lay
On his dying bed at the close of day.

O bury me not on the lone prairie,
Where the wild coyotes will howl o'er me
Where the buzzard beats and the wind goes free,
O bury me not on the lone prairie.

Yes, we buried him there on the lone prairie,
Where the owl all night hoots mournfully,
And the blizzard beats and the winds blow free
O'er his lonely grave on the wild prairie.

7. The Shantyboy sang of untrue love in *Flat River Girl*, and in the next breath borrowed one with a racy French flavor, *On the Lac San Pierre*.

"Come all you jolly raftsmen,
I tell you von good plan,
You marry von good French woman
And live on von good farm.
For the vind she may blow from the nor', sout', eas',
Bimeby she blow some more;
But you never git drown' in the Lac San Pierre,
So long 's you stay on the shore."

CHAPTER VI

8. In the *Song and Chorus Collection*, published by Ditson in 1878, is one called *Put My Little Shoes Away*.

"Mother dear, come bathe my forehead,
For I'm growing very weak,
Mother, let one drop of water
Fall upon my burning cheek.
Tell my loving little school-mates
That I nevermore will play,
Give them all my toys, but Mother,
Put my little shoes away."

Bringing Pretty Blossoms to Strew on Mother's Grave, Why Did the Angels Take Mamma Away, and *I'm Going to Write to Papa* gave the little ones a further chance to weep and be wept over.

9. Charles K. Harris also had a juvenile department, *Always in the Way,* and *Hello, Central, Give Me Heaven.* He called on Cupid in *Give Back My Sweetheart to Me* and *I Want to Buy a Little Bit of Love.*

CHAPTER VII

10. A few representative titles are *La Dame blanche, Le petit chaperon rouge, La Clochette, La Fille du régiment, Don Quichotte,* and *Zampa* on the lighter side; *Lucia di Lammermoor, Le Prophète, Les Huguenots, La Juive,* and *Salammbo* for tragedy. *Faust, Carmen, La Reine de Saba, Le Cid,* and others composed later, also found their way into the repertoire.

11. *The Castle of Andalusia, Love in a Village, Guy Mannering, The Slave, The Miller and his Men, Inickle and Yarico, No Song, No Supper,* are a few of the works of Englishmen which were presented in the New Chestnut Street Theatre in Philadelphia.

12. The Italians Rossini, Donizetti, Verdi, Bellini, Puccini, Montemezzi, Wolf-Ferrari, Mascagni, Leoncavallo; the Frenchmen Gounod, Bizet, Halévy, Massenet, Charpentier, Delibes, Debussy; the Russians Borodin, Tschaikowsky, Moussorgsky; the Austrians and Germans Gluck (who wrote French music), Beethoven, Weber, Mozart, Meyerbeer, Strauss, Wagner; and others as earnest, if less distinguished, were made welcome. And with the operas came golden cages of illustrious songbirds, flashing as to plumage and magnificent as to voice. Their very names spell glamour and wonderment— Melba, Nordica, Eames, Fremstad, Sembrich, Ternina, Farrar, Homer, Schumann-Heink, Matzenauer, the De Reszkes, Scotti, Dippel, and many others.

13. Oscar Hammerstein gave, at popular prices, first per-

formances in America of *Thaïs, Pelléas et Mélisande, Louise, Sapho, Le Jongleur de Notre Dame, La Damnation de Faust, Les Contes d'Hoffman, Samson et Dalila, La Princesse d'Auberge, Herodiade,* and *Griselidis.* Many of them have found their way into the standard repertoire. Melba in *La Bohème, Otello,* and *Rigoletto;* Calvé in *Carmen;* star performances of *Salome, Elektra, Don Giovanni*—all were his inspirations. The names of his singers still bring a reminiscent thrill—Mary Garden, Louisa Tetrazzini, Marietta Mazarin, Emma Trentini, Jeanne Gerville-Reache, Alessandro Bonci, Maurice Renaud, Jean Perrin, John McCormack, Hector Dufranne, Charles Dalmores, Maria Sammarco, and others.

CHAPTER VIII

14. Victor Pelissier's *Ariadne Abandoned by Theseus in the Isle of Naxos,* a melodrama with expressive emotional music between the actors' speeches, and *Bourville Castle,* in which Benjamin Carr collaborated, were both given in New York in 1797. Three songs—*I Laugh, I Sing; Hope, Gentle Hope; Ah, Why on Quebec's Bloody Plain*—preserved in Pelissier's own collection of *Columbian Melodies*—are all that remain of his opera *The Vintage,* produced in 1799.

15. On the subject of *The Sacrifice,* a three-act opera to which Frederick Converse supplied both music and text, when it was performed in Boston the following year, criticisms were tepid, Puccini, Liszt, and Wagner being said to have contributed as much as Converse.

16. Deems Taylor, when he wrote *The King's Henchman,* had already written *The Siren Song, The Chambered Nautilus, The Highwayman, The City of Joy,* and *Through the Looking Glass.*

CHAPTER IX

17. The Boston Orchestra has had a royal line of conductors, from Georg Henschel, through Wilhelm Gericke, Arthur

Nikisch, Emil Paur, Karl Muck, Max Fiedler, Henri Rabaud, Pierre Monteux, and now the Russian, Serge Koussevitzky.

18. Of the conductors of the New York Philharmonic, Theodore Eisfeld, Carl Bergmann (a Germania man), Leopold Damrosch, Theodore Thomas, Anton Seidl, Emil Paur, Walter Damrosch, Gustav Mahler were all Germans or of German descent. Josef Stransky, Wassily Safonoff, Willem Mengelberg, Arturo Toscanini, and John Barbirolli departed from that pattern. In 1935, Otto Klemperer, Bruno Walter, and Hans Lange, all German or Austrian, shared the season with Toscanini. The following year, the Rumanian Georges Enesco, the Russians Igor Stravinsky and Artur Rodzinski, and the Mexican Carlos Chavez came as guest conductors during the season of John Barbirolli, Italian-Englishman.

Some of the other distinguished symphony conductors of today are Eugene Goossens, Eugene Ormandy, Fritz Reiner, Alexander Smallens, Ernest Schelling, Artur Bodanzky, José Iturbi, Frederick Stock, Hans Kindler, Nikolai Sokoloff, Willem van Hoogstraten, Vladimir Golschmann, Karl Krueger, Basil Cameron, Issay Dobrowen, Chalmers Clifton, and, until his death in 1937, Ossip Gabrilowitsch.

19. For example, on the first day of his festival, after the opening prayer, Martin Luther's hymn, *Ein fester Burg ist unser Gott,* rose from the chorus. There followed Wagner's *Tannhäuser Overture,* the *Gloria* from Mozart's Twelfth Mass, Gounod's *Ave Maria* sung by Madame Parepa-Rosa to the accompaniment of two hundred violins, and the *Star-Spangled Banner.* This concluded the first half of the program. There was no letdown in the second half, which offered a *Hymn of Peace* with words especially written by Oliver Wendell Holmes, the *William Tell Overture,* and Rossini's *Inflammatus* from *Stabat Mater,* with a thousand instruments, ten thousand voices, an organ of a thousand horsepower, and Madame Parepa-Rosa as soloist. The *Coronation March* from Meyerbeer's *Le Prophète,* the *Anvil Chorus,* and finally *America,* sung by all, wound up the proceedings. Ole Bull played

first fiddle in the gigantic orchestra. And these were but one day's doings. The festival lasted five days.

20. There was not a music-festival pie in which Thomas did not have a finger, or rather, a baton. When he left the New York Philharmonic, a farewell dinner was given, at which George William Curtis paid him this tribute: "It was Thomas with Bergmann, Mosenthal, and Mason in the old Dodworth salon; it was Thomas in Central Park Garden; Thomas in the Philharmonic Society; Thomas in the great festival of 1882. It was always Thomas and his orchestra, always Thomas and his baton, like valiant Henry of Navarre and his white plume waving in the van of victory. . . . He has given to New York a musical distinction without which no great city is a metropolis."

21. A few, selected at random, are so familiar on today's programs, they seem always to have been known. Schubert's *Marche Militaire* and *Unfinished Symphony*, Berlioz' *Romeo et Juliette* and *Benvenuto Cellini*, Weber's *Invitation to the Dance*, Schumann's *Genoveva Overture*, Wagner's *Tannhäuser Overture*, Tchaikowsky's *Nut-Cracker Suite*, Strauss' *Til Eulenspiegel* and *Heldenleben*. There is a list of "firsts" covering several pages in Upton's *Theodore Thomas, an Autobiography*.

CHAPTER X

22. The *Columbus March* and a *Hymn* were given in Chicago, Paine's Second Symphony, entitled *Spring*, and a symphonic poem, *An Island Fantasy* had preceded these; likewise a cantata for the Cincinnati Festival of 1888.

23. David Stanley Smith, Philip Greeley Clapp, Mabel Daniels, Paul Hastings Allen, C. Hugo Grimm, Margaret Ruthven Lang, Rosseter Gleason Cole are some others of the conservative-European school.

24. Some of those whose names appear most frequently on the programs of major orchestras are Roy Harris, Howard

Hanson, Aaron Copland, Leo Sowerby, Frederick Jacobi, Roger Sessions, Randall Thompson, Emerson Whithorne, Deems Taylor, Robert Russell Bennett, Douglas Moore, Walter Piston, Arthur Shepherd, and William Grant Still.

25. Bernard Rogers of Cleveland is known for the clever *Once-upon-a-Time Suite* and symphony; Leo Sowerby calls himself Dr. Jekyll and Mr. Hyde because he writes, first church music, then jazzy symphonic pieces; Abram Chasins' symphonies and piano concerti, played by the Philadelphia Orchestra, have won him praise for the clearness and originality of their writing; Bernard Wagenaar, a naturalized Hollander, finds dissonance useful in his two symphonies, his *Sinfonietta* and *Divertimento;* Werner Josten writes a *Concerto Sacro* and *Jungle* in ecclesiastical, nondissonant style; Carl McKinley's *Masquerade,* descriptive of the New Orleans Mardi Gras, is full of French and Spanish tunes. Others are Philip James, whose radio suite, *Station WZGBX,* won a prize; Harl McDonald, James Philip Dunn, Robert McBride; Albert Stoessel, Edwin J. Stringham; Samuel Barber, Otto Luening, Ernest Schelling, Paul White.

26. Cowell is a determined and eloquent protagonist of atonality. Others who are more or less of his opinion are Wallingford Riegger, who has carried into his own music some of the interesting heresies of Alban Berg, Schoenberg, and other modern Germans; Lazare Saminsky, whose four symphonies and choral works, especially the *Litanies of Women,* have been performed in Berlin, Petrograd, Vienna, Paris, Rome, and Venice, besides New York; the Mexican Carlos Chavez, composer of orchestral music of distinction, notably the symphonies *Antigona* and *India,* and the ballet-symphony *H.P.;* Carlos Salzedo, master of the harp, who writes prolifically in large and small forms; Ruth Crawford; and others.

CHAPTER XI

27. Pierre Key lists fifty-five small ensemble groups. A few which we have heard with the utmost pleasure are such native

string quartettes as the Gordon, Coolidge, Musical Art, Stradivarius, and Perolé, such visitors as the Roth, Pro Arte, Hart House, Budapesth, Kolisch, and London String. The delightful Barrère Woodwind Ensemble, the Salzedo Trio, the Madrigal Singers under Lehman Engel, the English Singers, and the chamber orchestras of Rudolph Ganz, Fabien Sevitzky, Hans Lange, and Quinto Maganini, touring colleges and schools, and cities large and small, sow broadcast the seed of interest in intimate music in the concert hall.

To select a few soloists from the hundreds now appearing is a task for another day, but their influence in educating the public taste for American music cannot be too strongly emphasized.

28. Below are listed some of the contemporary composers in smaller forms who have not previously been mentioned.

Bacon, Ernst	Campbell-Tipton, Louis
Bailey, Parker	Chandler, Theodore
Balogh, Erno	Citkowitz, Israel
Barth, Hans	Clokey, Joseph
Bauer, Marion	Collins, Edward
Beach, John	Creston, Paul
Becker, John	Crist, Bainbridge
Berckman, Evelyn	De Brant, Cyr
Berezowski, Nicolai	Deis, Carl
Bingham, Seth	Delaney, Robert
Blitzstein, Marc	Diamond, David
Bornschein, Franz	Dillon, Fanny
Bowles, Paul F.	Dinsmore, William
Boyle, Frederick	Donovan, Richard
Braine, Robert	Dougherty, Celius
Branscombe, Gena	Dubensky, Arcady
Brant, Henry	Duke, John
Bricken, Carl	Elwell, Herbert
Burleigh, Cecil	Engel, Carl
Busch, Carl	Engel, Lehman

Erb, John Warren
Fine, Vivian
Finney, Ross Lee
Fiorillo, Dante
Freed, Isador
Gallico, Paolo
Gardner, Samuel
Gerschefski, Edwin
Giannini, Vittorio
Giorni, Aurelio
Godowsky, Leopold
Grainger, Percy
Grasse, Edwin
Griffis, Eliot
Hammond, Richard
Harling, W. F.
Harmati, Sandor
Harris, Victor
Haubiel, Charles
Haufrecht, Herbert
Heilner, Irwin
Helfer, Walter
Heniot, Hans Levy
Herrman, Bernard
Hier, Ethel Glenn
Hill, Mabel Wood
Homer, Sidney
Howe, Mary
Huss, Henry H.
Inch, Herbert R.
James, Dorothy
Johnson, Horace
Johnson, Hunter
Kernochan, Marshall
Kerr, Harrison
Koutzen, Boris

Kramer, A. Walter
La Forge, Frank
Lane, Eastwood
La Violette, Wesley
Lockwood, Norman
Luckstone, Isidor
Maganini, Quinto
Mana-Zucca,
Mannes, Leopold
McPhee, Colin
Milligan, Harold Vincent
Naginski, Charles
Nordoff, Paul
Pimsleur, Solomon
Piston, Walter
Porter, Quincy
Read, Gardner
Rubinstein, Beryl
Rudhyar, Dane
Rummel, Walter
Russell, Alexander
Salzedo, Carlos
Saminsky, Lazare
Sanders, Robert L.
Schindler, Kurt
Schuman, William
Siegmeister, Elie
Smith, Charles Sanford
Speaks, Oley
Spelman, Timothy
Steinert, Alexander Lang
Stojowski, Sigismond
Strang, Gerald
Stringfield, Lamar
Tuthill, Burnet
Tweedy, Donald

Watts, Wintter
Weiss, Adolph
Wessel, Mark
Whitmer, T. Carl

Wilson, Mortimer
Wolfe, Jacques
Woodman, R. Huntington

CHAPTER XII

29. Other famous minstrels were Dick José and "Honeyboy" Evans of the monstrous lips, Eddie Leonard, Neil O'Brien, Primrose and West, Williams and Walker, Al Fields, Lew Dockstader, Willis P. Sweatnam, and Harrigan and Hart.

CHAPTER XIV

30. A number of writers of popular lyrics are catering to this average taste in better-than-average fashion. Vincent Youmans is one of the most frequently played composers of light music on the air. Carrie Jacobs Bond has published many successful songs. Ray Henderson, who works in collaboration with Lew Brown and G. B. de Sylva; Vernon Duke, whose other name is Vladimir Dukelsky, with Harold Arlen; Richard Rodgers with Lorenz Hart, have written any number of song hits in their musical shows. Lou Hirsch, Walter Donaldson, Cole Porter, Johnny Green, and Jerome Moross are names worth remembering for really entertaining, well written jazz tunes.

CHAPTER XV

31. Gene Buck, President.

32. Dr. Sigmund Spaeth, President, Henry Hadley, Founder and Honorary President.

33. Horatio Parker, George Chadwick, Henry Hadley, Edgar Stillman Kelley, Henry Gilbert, Charles Loeffler, John Alden Carpenter, David Stanley Smith, Edward Burlingame Hill, and John Powell have been distinguished contributors to this festival.

34. Ernest Schelling recently announced for his first season

of children's concerts in Baltimore a very fair list of the works of his countrymen, including his own *Tarantella*, Rudolph Ganz's *Animal Pictures*, Victor Herbert's *American Fantasy*, Edward MacDowell's *The Saracens*, Roy Harris' *When Johnny Comes Marching Home*, Henry Eichheim's *Siamese Sketches*, and Deems Taylor's *White Knight* from the *Looking Glass Sketches*. Leaders of smaller groups, such as Quinto Maganini, Fabien Sevitzky, Hans Lange, Alfred Wallenstein, Otto Luening, Charles Adler, Georges Barrère, Rudolph Ganz, and Alexander Smallens, all make a definite effort to include American compositions on their programs.

35. Roger Sessions at Yale, Walter Piston and Edward Burlingame Hill at Harvard, Otto Luening at Bennington, Roy Harris at Princeton, Quincy Porter at Vassar, Daniel Gregory Mason and Douglas Moore at Columbia, John Powell at the University of Virginia, Fred Jacobi and Werner Josten at Smith, Arthur Shepherd at Western Reserve, Marion Bauer and Charles Haubiel at New York University are a few of these.

36. Recently, a publisher issued a volume of piano pieces especially written for children by distinguished American composers of today. Edited by Lazare Saminsky, the volume contained pieces by Howard Hanson, Douglas Moore, Henry Cowell, Randall Thompson, Werner Josten, Frederick Jacobi, Deems Taylor, Aaron Copland, Bernard Wagenaar, Isador Freed, Emerson Whithorne, Arthur Shepherd, A. Walter Kramer, Roger Sessions, and Saminsky himself.

One of the most encouraging symptoms of growing tolerance in teachers and appreciation in the public is their acceptance of a contemporary American collection of this sort as legitimate and desirable teaching material.

37. The *Musical Quarterly* is the most scholarly of these; others are *Musical America, The Musical Courier, The Musical Digest, Metronome, Modern Music, New Music, Musical Leader, Music News*, and numerous trade journals.

38. Louis Gruenberg treated it as symphonic material,

writing a *Jazz Suite* which was played by the Boston Symphony Orchestra. His *Jazzettes* for violin and piano, and the *Daniel Jazz* for voice and eight instruments are jazz-with-a-difference, to be compared with the dance-hall species in the matter of rhythmic movement, but stamped with the hand and seal of a talented composer who knows his métier. Werner Janssen's symphonic *New Year's Eve,* as well as Emerson Whithorne's *New York Days and Nights,* and Deems Taylor's *Circus Days,* by their very subjects invite jazz treatment, an invitation to which their composers respond with wholehearted alacrity. Harold Morris confesses that in his youth he wrote a jazz piano sonata "just to be different," but that now he has come to use it as a legitimate tool, finding it most effective when his theme derives, as it frequently does, from negro folk song. Robert Russell Bennett and Thomas Griselle both won Victor Machine prizes for works in the idiom. Bennett's *Sketches from the American Theatre,* in the form of the old Concerto Grosso, employ a dance orchestra with accompaniment of symphony orchestra, a significant juxtaposition. Randall Thompson's *Second Symphony* is jazz plus old American dance forms; his *Americana,* a choral work, is successfully jazzy when the text so decrees. Leo Sowerby swings from jazz to sacred music and back again. William Grant Still, negro composer from California, has a long list of works in which he employs with logic and complete unself-consciousness, the jazz rhythms which seem to come naturally to him. These are only a few of many serious composers who have seen fit to accept jazz as a legitimate means to an end.

39. Some of those still young in years are David Diamond, Lehman Engel, Marc Blitzstein, Dante Fiorillo, Paul Creston, Goddard Lieberson, Hunter Johnson, Arthur Cohn, Harl MacDonald, Henry Brant, Herbert Haufrecht, Gian Carlo Menotti, Edwin Gerschefski, Robert McBride, Evelyn Berckman, Ernst Bacon, Adolph Weiss, Samuel Barber, David Barnett, Herbert Elwell, Norman Lockwood, Beryl Rubinstein, Paul Nordoff, and Otto Luening.